THE COMPLETE SOY COOKBOOK

THE COMPLETE SOY COOKBOOK

Paulette Mitchell

Macmillan USA

Other books by Paulette Mitchell

The 15-Minute Vegetarian Gourmet
The 15-Minute Single Gourmet
The 15-Minute Chicken Gourmet
The Complete Book of Dressings

MACMILLAN
A Simon & Schuster Macmillan Company
1633 Broadway
New York, NY 10019-6785

Macmillan Publishing books may be purchased for business of sales promotional use.
For information please write: Special Markets Department, Macmillan Publishing USA,
1633 Broadway, New York, NY 10019-6785.

Copyright © 1998 by Paulette Mitchell
Photographs copyright © 1997 by Thom Lang

MACMILLAN is a registered trademark of Macmillan, Inc.

Library of Congress Cataloging-in-Publication Data

Mitchell, Paulette.
    The complete soy cookbook / Paulette Mitchell.
      p.   cm.
    Includes index.
    ISBN 0-02-861457-7 (alk. paper)
    1. Cookery (Soybeans)   2. Soyfoods.   I. Title.
TX803.S6M58   1998
641.6'5655—dc21   97-32741
                                      CIP

Book design by Amy Trombat

Manufactured in the United States of America

10 9 8 7 6 5 4 3 2 1

Dedication

To my 14-year-old son, Brett,
whose fondest childhood food memories just may be of tofu!

Acknowledgments

Special thanks to the people who played special roles in this project:

Jane Dystel, my agent, for her guidance and help in making this book possible.

Jennifer Griffin, my editor, for her much-appreciated communication.

Tom McReynolds at Mori-Nu and Dr. Mark Messina for sharing valuable information on soy.

Denise Dobrzenski, my friend and cooking assistant, for all the hours of chopping, cooking, tasting, and chatting.

Fran Lebahn, my friend, for her inspiration.

Carla Waldemar, my friend, for her words of wisdom.

Darryl Trones, my companion, who never tired of soy cuisine and always made me smile.

Contents

ix Preface

xiii Introduction
The Whys, xiii
The Hows, xxi

xlii Soy Success
Stocking Your Refrigerator and Pantry, xlii
Using the Recipes, xliv
Kitchen Equipment, xlix

1 Chapter 1 Appetizers

32 Chapter 2 Soups

58 Chapter 3 Salads

98 Chapter 4 Entrées

220 Chapter 5 Desserts

259 Appendix: Recipes Listed by Soy Food Categories

264 Index

Preface

AN ANCIENT ASIAN SECRET ISN'T A SECRET anymore—almost everyone is discovering soy. The humble soybean has become a national nutritional headliner; newspapers and magazines are filled with convincing evidence that soy is good for us. The favorable news is far too compelling to dismiss, but few accounts offer enticing recipes or explain how to make these powerful mystery foods taste good. Listen up! Here is the only soy book you will need to learn not only the "whys" but also the "hows" of soy cooking.

As a cooking instructor and the author of six cookbooks, I have spent years developing recipes my students and readers have told me are exceptional. Delicious soy recipes? No problem. Here's why.

Since the early 1970s, when I became interested in vegetarian cooking, my recipes have evolved considerably. In the very beginning, my family never objected to the new regime of meatless meals—but often they didn't rave either. At that time most vegetarian cookbooks (and even large bookstores carried only a few) were filled with dreary, unglamorous, meatless recipes that tended to be too heavy, too bland, and too high in fat, with an overwhelming reliance on dutiful, lackluster rice dishes with cheese, eggs, and nuts as protein. Since I had turned to a meatless diet for enhancing good health, tofu and beans eventually became staples of my vegetarian cooking, but in all honesty, those dishes also needed some pizzazz.

Over the years my passion for cooking developed in the pursuit of adding flavor and style to this new style of eating I'd adopted. In the evolution my philosophy also changed. Inspired by my travels and studies of ethnic cuisines, I became determined to take a gourmet approach and turn meatless mealtime into vegetarian dining. Rather than solely approaching no-meat dishes as virtuous food, I looked on vegetarian cuisine as exciting and elegant in its own right. It was really quite simple, since in many cuisines meat has been used sparingly, if at all. And I discovered that traditional meatless or low-meat cuisines are also highly flavored, since an abundant use of spices and herbs and fresh ingredients are called on to provide robust flavors.

As I learned to appreciate true gourmet ethnic cooking with its vibrant personalities, my collection of gourmet vegetarian recipes multiplied. I began to share them with students in my cooking classes and eventually began writing cookbooks. To my students and readers, I have became known for my repertoire of delicious, healthful recipes—but more than that, these are recipes that can be served with style as part of an exciting gourmet cuisine.

Some of the students in my vegetarian cooking classes and users of my cookbooks are strict vegetarians. Others are interested in tasty alternatives to red meat, fish, and chicken for those "vegetarian days." And everyone seems to acknowledge that an ethnic flair adds variety and excitement to ordinary weekly menus.

The evolution continues. I have found that ethnic recipes make it easy for me to use soy in its many forms. "Fusion cooking," as it is now called, gives us permission to blend the elements of diverse cuisines. This philosophy also allows us to use soy products in the dishes of countries where soy may not exist. For example, tofu, traditionally an Asian ingredient, can be used in nearly all cuisines because it absorbs the flavors of their seasonings and sauces. Raghavan, an East Indian friend of mine and fellow cooking instructor, says tofu is unknown in Bombay, where he grew up. But he acknowledges that my Tofu and Vegetable Curry is delicious.

Even though I have been preparing gourmet vegetarian meals for more than twenty-five years, creating 180 soy-based recipes at first seemed to be a formidable challenge. But approaching the recipes with a fresh and artful outlook rather than the mundane rice-and-beans approach of the 1970s turned this project into a pleasure. On my daily trips to the supermarket, nearly every food I saw began to spark ideas for soy recipes; every time I ate in a restaurant, I found myself saying, "Now here's another inspiration to adapt for tofu!"

After eating soy nearly daily for a year, I am still amazed at the possibilities for good taste. This culinary chameleon truly is one of the most versatile foods on earth. Forget about limitations: the variety is nearly endless. In its various forms, soy combines well with almost every herb and vegetable—and even chocolate. I'm hooked!

This is the book to show you, too, how to make soy a part of your healthful lifestyle—simply, flavorfully, and with a gourmet, multiethnic flair. Be assured, you don't have to become a vegetarian to derive many of the benefits. Soy recipes can be used as accompaniments to meat-oriented entrées, or you can go meatless just one or two days a week. If you can't get excited about eating beans (some people have a hard time overcoming childhood memories of those dreaded canned limas), soy can be used in its many other forms. Whether you're a novice or experienced cook, you will find that most of these recipes are quick enough for everyday cooking—yet many are ideal to serve to your most discriminating guests.

As the author of a successful series of *15-Minute* cookbooks, I've become accustomed to efficiency in the kitchen. Following my organized procedures, which often suggest doing two procedures at once, you can make many of these recipes in minutes; those that require more time usually need to bake or simmer, basically unattended. These recipes rely on the imaginative use of fresh ingredients rather than elaborate techniques.

The nutritional evidence is convincing—soy is not just another food fad. It is a food of the future, available today. However, virtuousness can have its drawbacks. Because soy is so nutritious, you may believe that soy foods are only for health food purists and that nothing good for us can taste good too. Whether you are a committed vegetarian, an occasional vegetarian, or even a tofu skeptic, I guarantee that you will enjoy soy foods for their nourishment, sustenance, and healthful properties—but most of all for an exquisite sensory pleasure.

Introduction

THE WHYS

Until recently, soy cuisine has been relatively unknown in the United States—yet roughly one-quarter of the world's people rely on soy foods as their primary source of protein. In fact, it is estimated that the soybean is the most widely eaten plant in the world. As we learn more about the complexities of nutrition and the links between diet and health, it becomes clear that there are many convincing reasons to consider relying upon soybeans.

Legumes, edible seeds enclosed in pods, including soybeans, kidney beans, pinto beans, black-eyed peas, and lentils, are rich sources of vegetable protein. Among the legumes, soybeans—and foods made from soybeans—contain protein that most closely resembles animal protein. In fact, soybeans are the only legume whose protein is complete. About 35 to 38 percent of the calories in soybeans come from protein; other beans contain about 20 to 30 percent protein. One-half cup of cooked soybeans contains about 15 grams of protein—just a little less than 4 ounces of ground beef, but with none of the saturated fat and cholesterol.

Amino acids are the building blocks of protein. After protein is consumed, it is broken down into individual amino acids. These amino acids rearrange to form helpful antibodies and enzymes for our bodies. Our bodies produce 11 of the 20 amino acids we require. The remaining 9 amino acids must come from the foods we eat. Soy protein contains all of the 9 amino acids; however, one of these amino acids is in somewhat short supply. Therefore, consuming a variety of plant foods throughout the day will provide your daily requirement of protein, as well as other nutritional components for optimum health. If you eat several servings of grains, beans, and vegetables throughout the day and get enough calories, it is virtually impossible to be deficient in protein.

If you are considering switching to a partly or completely vegetarian diet, the soybean in its varied forms may persuade you.

Asians have used this high-protein legume as a major protein source for over five thousand years. Since the early 1800s Americans have grown soybeans, mainly to feed cattle, and since the 1930s as a source of vegetable oil. Only since the 1950s has this product been transformed into forms that appeal to Western palates.

In 1971 in *Diet for a Small Planet*, Frances Moore Lappé addressed the issue of consciously choosing a diet that is both good for our bodies and for the earth. As a starting point, she described what she called "protein factories in reverse." In affluent countries we feed as many as 20 pounds of high-protein feed, such as soybeans, to cattle to produce a single pound of beef. Lappé wrote, "Clearly the earth cannot support this level of waste." An acre of land, which will produce about 7 pounds of beef, will yield about 340 pounds of soybeans. While I am not proposing that everyone switch to a meat-free soybean diet, it makes sense to be aware of the huge cost to the environment of our meat-rich diets. Another ecological plus: soybean plants even return nitrogen to the soil rather than deplete this important natural resource.

Health food fads come and go. Remember oat bran? Most recently it is the health benefits of soybeans that have been creating a stir. A flurry of research suggests that soybeans are more than just a rich source of plant protein. In addition to the frequent articles in newspapers and magazines, entire books are addressing the soybean and its ability to protect us against America's leading killers—cancer and heart disease—as well as diabetes and osteoporosis. In fact, as evidence builds, some nutritionists feel so strongly about the benefits of soy that they claim it actually crosses the line from nutritional to medicinal. It isn't really surprising that plant properties could have such potent effects on health. All ancient cultures used plant materials to cure ailments, and today more than half of the world's population continues to use plants as medicine. Also, many of the most commonly used drugs come from plants.

In a simplified manner, here are the facts regarding soybeans as they relate to many of today's primary health concerns:

Cancer

Since 1990, when the National Cancer Institute launched an extensive research program, the research on soy and cancer has escalated; scientists have identified several potential anticancer substances, or anticarcinogens, in soybeans. Some anticarcinogens prevent tumors from developing. Others cause existing tumors to grow more slowly or even halt their growth entirely. Still others counteract the effect of cancer risk factors such as hormones.

Soybeans and the foods made from them are rich in a group of compounds called phytochemicals. These compounds are not nutrients; we are just beginning to understand their unique properties. Evidence indicates they may play important roles in lowering the risk of a wide range of cancers. One group called isoflavones, which are found almost exclusively in soybeans, is especially important because it may fight cancer in a variety of ways. One isoflavone, called genistein, has especially caught the attention of scientists. When genistein is added to many different types of cancer cells (such as breast, colon, lung, prostate, skin, and leukemia) growing in laboratory test tubes, the growth of these cells stops. More than 100 studies have demonstrated the effectiveness of genistein working in ways similar to some of the common drugs used by scientists to treat cancer. Scientists believe that certain enzymes in the body convert normal cells to cancer cells. Often cancer drugs work by inhibiting these enzymes. In cancer cells genistein has been shown to work in a similar fashion: it interferes with the activity of these enzymes. *So far, soy is the only food in which genistein has been found in high concentrations.*

Genistein also may act against many cancers that are "hormone-dependent," such as breast and prostate cancer. Weak estrogens, like the isoflavones in soy foods, may actually act as antiestrogens. It is a fact that high levels of natural estrogen can increase the risk of breast cancer because when estrogen attaches to sites on the breast tissue, it can induce the cancer process. Instead of acting like estrogen in the body, the isoflavones block the activity of naturally produced estrogen; since they look like estrogen, they can attach to the same sites on breast tissue. By occupying these sites, they may keep the more powerful estrogen from exerting its cancer-causing effects. In men phytoestrogens block the activity of testosterone—not enough to affect maleness, but perhaps enough to suppress the growth of prostate tumors.

Added to all these very encouraging findings is another important one: genistein not only may be useful in cancer prevention but also may be beneficial in cancer treatment. Laboratory studies indicate that genistein can interfere with angiogenesis, the process in which new blood vessels grow and nourish malignant tumors with nutrients and oxygen. Genistein may be one of the first of a new class of anticancer drugs; however, you do not have to take a drug to get genistein. All you have to do is eat soybeans. (Note: Whole soybeans, tofu, soy milk, tempeh, miso, soy flour, and texturized vegetable protein [TVP] are excellent sources of isoflavones. A few soy products, such as soy oil, soy sauce, and soy protein concentrate, have little or no isoflavones.)

People in major soy food–consuming countries have markedly lower death rates from breast and prostate cancer than we do in the United States. Breast cancer is the second most common cause of death among American women and is the leading cause of death in women between the ages of thirty-five and forty-four. The American breast cancer rate, for example, is 22.4 per 100,000—almost four times Japan's rate of 6 per 100,000. The American prostate cancer rate is 15.7 per 100,000, also roughly four times the Japanese rate of 3.5 per 100,000. This type of information is considered inconclusive because soy foods represent just one variable in the diets of the Japanese, which include less animal food, generally less fat, and more fiber, as well as other lifestyle differences. But in addition to the work done in laboratories, case-control studies in Japan and China have compared people within the same country. These studies have found that people in Japan who eat soy foods daily are less likely to get cancer than people in Japan who seldom eat soy foods. In these cases other diet and lifestyle factors are similar in the two groups.

The amount of soy protein necessary for optimum health is somewhat speculative, but judging from Asian diets, Dr. Mark Messina, co-author of *The Simple Soybean and Your Health*, says that one serving a day of soy may decrease the risk for a number of cancers by nearly 40 percent. As little as one serving of soy foods (or 25 grams of soy protein) each day should contain enough phytoestrogens to protect against many types of cancer, including lung, colon, rectal, stomach, prostate, and breast cancer. (A serving is equal to $1/2$ cup cooked soybeans, tofu, textured vegetable protein, or tempeh, or 1 cup soy milk.)

Heart Disease

Eating soy foods may help reduce the risk of heart disease, the leading cause of death in the United States. Many foods that are rich in protein are too high in saturated fat and cholesterol. Soy foods are high in protein but low in saturated fat and free of cholesterol. The fat in soy foods is mostly polyunsaturated fat, which doesn't raise blood cholesterol levels. The high fiber in soybeans is another important positive factor.

The link between soy and lower cholesterol rates is easy to prove. Almost thirty years ago researchers showed that protein from soy foods could lower blood cholesterol. Since then, more than 40 studies involving human subjects also have shown this. Soy protein decreases blood cholesterol levels by about 10 to 15 percent in people with elevated cholesterol. It reduces the LDL (bad) cholesterol, while HDL (good) cholesterol levels remain unchanged. Even in people who have already reduced their blood cholesterol by eating a low-fat diet, eating soy produces further drops in cholesterol. Statistics have shown that a 10 percent decrease in cholesterol reduces the chance of having a heart attack by 20 to 30 percent. "For the 50 million Americans with high cholesterol, soy is a safe, inexpensive, effective alternative to drugs, with no negative side effects," says Messina.

About 20 to 25 grams of soy protein per day may be enough to lower cholesterol. This is the amount of soy protein found in just 1 cup of soybeans. Higher amounts of soy protein (25 to 50 grams) are likely to produce even bigger decreases.

In test tubes genistein inhibits the growth of cells developing into plaque, which contributes to artery blockage. Studies on blood clotting are still speculative, but they indicate that genistein may also inhibit the formation of blood clots.

Osteoporosis

Osteoporosis is a worldwide problem, but the United States has one of the world's highest rates of this disease. It develops in older age, especially in women who have gone through menopause, and is characterized by thin, weak, and brittle bones. Increased life expectancies mean that many women will spend almost one-third of their lives at risk for osteoporosis.

Many factors contribute to reducing the risk of osteoporosis. Weight-bearing exercise, for example, can slow down the loss of bone matter and actually lead to an increase in bone density. A healthy diet is also important for strong bones. Some dietary factors like high caffeine consumption and excess protein may speed bone loss. Nutrients like calcium and vitamin D help promote bone health. Adding soybeans and soy foods to your diet may also help reduce your risk of osteoporosis.

Most people think of milk first as a source of calcium, but legumes such as soybeans are also good sources of calcium. Whole soybeans, fortified soy milk, texturized soy protein, and tempeh are especially rich in calcium. Some brands of tofu are made with a calcium salt; these are also high in calcium. Best of all, the calcium in soy foods is very easily absorbed by the body.

Even healthy bones constantly break down and rebuild. Since some calcium is lost from the body every day, more must be supplied by our daily diets. Actually, even more important than calcium *intake* is the factor of reducing the amount of calcium being *lost* from the body. A high intake of animal protein can increase the loss of calcium, and this may increase the risk of osteoporosis. All protein is not handled in the same way by our bodies, and studies show that soy protein does not have the same calcium-wasting effect as animal protein. When people eat soy foods in place of animal proteins, they excrete far less calcium, so soy protein helps to conserve calcium.

Compounds in soybeans may protect the strength of bones. These, again, are the isoflavones. One type of isoflavone called daidzein is very similar to a drug widely used in Asia and Europe to treat osteoporosis. When the drug is metabolized by the body, it produces daidzein, which inhibits the breakdown of bones and the loss of calcium. Soybeans are the only foods that contain isoflavones in significant amounts, so it seems that soy foods, as a natural source of daidzein, could reduce the risk of osteoporosis. In a recent animal study, genistein was also shown to inhibit breakdown of bone.

Menopause

Researchers also have suggested that the weak estrogenic effect of isoflavones may help to relieve the symptoms of menopause. Menopause occurs in women when natural production of estrogen in the ovaries declines; many physiological changes that take place during menopause are related to this decrease in estrogen production. These include difficulty in regulating body temperature, which can result in "night sweats" and "hot flashes."

In a recent study menopausal women who ate soy had almost a 50 percent reduction in such symptoms. Dr. Barry Goldin, a nutritional biochemist at Tufts University School of Medicine, says, "Interestingly, the way you respond to phytoestrogens depends on how much estrogen you already have in your body." In post-menopausal women phytoestrogens partially *replace* the activity of the natural hormone. This could explain why phytoestrogens seem to help relieve menopausal troubles. Increasing the estrogen levels in a woman's body provides a natural alternative for women either unwilling or unable to take hormone replacement therapy.

Diabetes

The best diet for most people with adult-onset diabetes is one that is low in fat, high in complex carbohydrates (both starch and fiber), and moderate in protein. No single food is essential, and no single diet will meet the needs of all people with diabetes, but soy foods may have an interesting role to play in this disease.

Soy foods may slow the absorption of glucose into the bloodstream. The glycemic index is a measure of how much blood glucose rises when a particular food is consumed. Foods with a low glycemic index produce smaller rises in blood glucose, which is beneficial in the control of diabetes. All legumes have a low glycemic index, but soybeans are even lower than others.

Soybeans and some soy foods, including tempeh, texturized soy protein, and soy flour, are also high in soluble fiber; this same soy fiber that helps control cholesterol levels also delays the absorption of nutrients into the bloodstream. By reducing the speed at which glucose levels rise in the bloodstream after eating, diabetics are better able to regulate blood sugar levels in their body, whether they are controlling their disease by diet or by medication.

Soy protein also may help to prevent or control some of the complications of diabetes. Since people with diabetes are at high risk for developing heart disease, they need to make a special effort to keep blood cholesterol levels low; soy has been shown to help. People with diabetes also are at high risk for developing kidney disease; replacing animal protein in the diet with soy protein has been shown, in some cases, to improve kidney function in patients.

Eating more soy foods isn't a guarantee against disease, and many of the findings about soy and health are speculative. But the evidence that soy can positively impact health is growing. Adding soy to the diet is easy and may reduce the risk for a number of diseases. For the vast majority of the population, soy foods are not allergenic and provide good nutrition and health benefits. Obviously, it's time for Americans to start taking the soybean seriously.

The optimal dose of soy products remains elusive. Two or more servings weekly provide a low-fat, high-fiber alternative to meat and should benefit overall health. But increasing consumption of soy should be just one part of a better eating plan. Messina notes, "It is not enough to wash down your Big Mac and fries with a glass of soy milk." But by adding soy foods to an already healthy diet based on a variety of high-fiber, low-fat plant foods, and a healthy lifestyle, you can certainly increase your chances of preventing disease and living a long and happy life.

THE HOWS

Despite all the optimistic research and the proliferation of soy foods, Americans don't seem to have embraced the humble soybean. But if even half of what researchers predict is accurate, soy should be earning some long-overdue respect. It is indisputably worth making an effort to get acquainted with this miracle food in its many forms.

Soybeans and the foods made from them are among the most versatile foods in the world, and they can be a part of almost any meal. Making soy foods a regular part of your diet is easy for vegetarians and nonvegetarians alike. If you are a vegetarian—and that category of diners is growing by leaps and bounds—soy foods probably are not new to you. Government experts now assure us that "vegetarian diets are consistent with the Dietary Guidelines," but it is not necessary to replace all animal products with soy to reap the benefits. Work soy into your diet as much as possible, using it to reduce a total reliance on animal protein, especially on high-fat, high-calorie meats.

For the health-conscious, the good news is that soy foods are cholesterol-free. And for the calorie- and fat-conscious, many soy foods are fat-free or come in reduced-fat forms, so replacing high-fat animal foods with them can save you fat and calories. Best of all, recipes incorporating soy products can add variety, good nutrition, and top-notch flavor to your meals. If you're not fond of beans, soy is available in a wide variety of forms; in fact, sometimes processing actually improves the nutritional value of soy foods. For example, the soy protein isolates in tofu are easily digested and well assimilated by the body, and when the tofu is made with calcium salt, the calcium content becomes higher than whole soybeans.

If your family is not impressed by soy's health benefits, then dazzle them with tasty soybean dishes that incorporate the bean in its many forms. You might want to introduce soy foods in dishes that are familiar, perhaps adding a layer of tofu to your traditional lasagna recipe or tossing soybeans into a bean salad; then try new soy recipes that contain vegetables and seasonings you and your family enjoy. Later, experiment with unfamiliar ethnic flavorings and ingredients. And once you have discovered your favorite recipes from the pages of this book, enjoy them often; using the suggested variations will provide even more possibilities.

SOY FOOD INGREDIENTS

Soybeans

Rural peasants in ancient China planted the seeds of a wild local flower in hopes of creating for themselves an additional source of food. By 1100 B.C. the Chinese had already begun to realize the versatility of their discovery and, in turn, made it an integral part of their diet. They called the soybean *dadou*, which means "greater bean." Early users mashed and strained the beans for tofu, grew bean sprouts, and made soy milk and cooking oil.

Soybeans made their debut in the United States in 1765, when they arrived not as a food source but as ballast for ships. More than a century passed before U.S. farmers started growing soybeans for cattle feed. In 1904, with the release of George Washington Carver's findings on soybeans done at Tuskegee Institute, America began to view the crop as a primary source of protein and oil.

Today the United States is the world's top producer of soybeans, growing half the soybeans in the world. Nearly 2 billion bushels are grown annually by some 440,000 farmers in 29 states. Most of these are fed to animals; some are found in unexpected places in myriad shapes, forms, and practical uses, including adhesives, paints, building materials, pesticides, fuels, and soaps. Soy protein–enriched foods can be found in virtually every supermarket aisle; soy oil is an ingredient in many commercially produced products. Soy ink, another important soybean by-product, is fast becoming the newspaper industry's ink of choice. The rest of the crop is exported, with major markets being Japan, the European Community, Taiwan, Mexico, and South Korea. Japan buys the most; its people consume soybeans in many forms to their great benefit. Because soybean meal is high in protein and fiber, it is the world's choice for feeding livestock. In a relatively new application, soybean meal has become a key ingredient in aquaculture (the farming and harvesting of fish and shellfish) feeds worldwide.

Because of their mild flavor, soybeans have long been thought of as plain and boring. Yet they can be delectable. As soybeans mature in their fuzzy green pods, they ripen into a hard, dry bean. Most are yellow, but there are also brown and black varieties. A common complaint is the advance preparation required before using them in recipes. The hard beans first must be soaked and then cooked; both are lengthy processes because of the beans' high protein content.

In my early vegetarian days, when I had time for growing many of my own vegetables and making yogurt, peanut butter, and mayonnaise from scratch, bean preparation was part of my culinary regime. Somehow those procedures fit only occasionally into today's e-mail world. In developing recipes for this book and in preparing soybean recipes on busy weeknights, canned soybeans proved to be a most acceptable alternative. Thanks to their "just-right" texture and slightly salted flavor, they are a reliable recipe ingredient. Unfortunately, the cost is higher and the cans rarely are found in mainstream supermarkets, but they are likely to be available at your favorite health food store. For this book the recipes calling for soybeans were developed using Westbrae Natural Canned Organic Soy Beans. (For further information, call Westbrae Natural Foods at 1-800-776-1276.)

Nutritionally, canned soybeans are nearly equal to those cooked from scratch; the B vitamin content is slightly reduced, and they do contain added salt. I recommend draining off the liquid and rinsing the beans with cool water before adding them to your recipes; neither presoaking nor cooking is necessary. (If you use soybeans cooked from scratch, you may need to add a little more salt when preparing these recipes.)

Whole soybeans can be purchased in health food stores and some supermarkets in bags or bulk bins. Choose beans with a smooth surface or bright color; if available, choose organically grown beans because they will have a richer flavor. Dried beans will keep for years if stored in an airtight container but are best if used within a year; older beans become drier and take longer to cook. Two cups of dried beans (1 pound) will yield 6 to 7 cups after cooking. When time permits, prepare a large pot of soybeans for use later. Cooked beans can be refrigerated for up to 4 days or frozen for up to 2 months.

Cooking Procedure for Dried Beans

> Rinse the beans in a colander and remove any stones, debris, or shriveled beans.

There are two soaking methods; make your choice depending on how much time you have. Select your container, taking into consideration that dried soybeans expand greatly while soaking; they will approximately double in volume. (The first time I soaked dried beans, they became so tightly packed in the jar that I could not remove them!)

> **For the traditional soaking method,** use 3 cups of water for each cup of dried beans; soak the beans for 8 hours or overnight. To prevent spoilage, I recommend soaking in the refrigerator. (Do not add salt to the soaking water, since this will produce tough beans and skins.)

> **For the quick-soak method,** use hot water. Bring the beans and water to a boil; then reduce the heat, cover, and simmer for 2 to 3 minutes. Remove from the heat and allow to stand for about 1 hour.

> With either method it is important to drain the beans, discard the bean soaking water, and rinse the beans before cooking them in fresh water. This will help in

the reduction of bean sugar, which is believed to be the primary culprit in producing digestive discomfort in some individuals.

➤ Put the beans into a large pot, cover with fresh water, and bring the water to a boil. Don't add salt because it will delay the softening of the beans; you can, however, add seasonings such as onion, garlic, bay leaf, or epazote (see Tip, page xxvii). Tomatoes can be added near the end of the cooking cycle. Cover the pot with the lid tilted slightly so the steam can escape. Gently simmer the beans for 2 to 3 hours; fresher dried soybeans will cook more quickly. Peek occasionally, add more water if necessary, and stir occasionally to keep the beans from sticking. After 2 hours, start tasting them for doneness. When they reach the consistency you like, they're ready.

In general, the beans are done when they are soft enough to be crushed easily between the tongue and the roof of the mouth. In addition to tasting a cooked bean, I usually cut one lengthwise and take a look; the inside should have an even color and consistency, with no white or hard portions. Personally, for salads, I prefer soybeans with a slightly firm, nutty texture; when I plan to purée them to use in a dip or spread, I cook the beans until the texture is softer. Once they are cooked, drain the beans well in a colander; I usually give them a quick rinse before either adding them to a recipe or refrigerating or freezing them for use later.

➤ Using a pressure cooker greatly reduces the cooking time. Follow the manufacturer's instructions for your cooker. Generally, the pot should be no more than half full. Use 2 cups water per cup of dried beans; cook at 15 pounds pressure for 12 to 20 minutes. Adding 1 tablespoon oil per cup of beans will reduce foaming. Pressure-cooked beans will usually be softer than those cooked on the stovetop.

❧ This may be surprising, but when I cook soybeans from scratch, I usually use my twenty-five-year-old Crockpot! Using a slow cooker requires less supervision for effortless preparation. Sometimes I even eliminate presoaking and just cook the beans longer. Put 1 pound of dried beans and 5 cups very hot tap water into a 3^{1}/2-quart slow cooker. Cover and cook on the high heat setting for 3 to 4 hours or on a low setting for 5 to 7 hours.

Sweet Beans

Edamame (pronounced aid-a-MOM-ee) is a special type of large-seeded soybean that is harvested when it is about 80 percent mature. In East Asia, where the beans originated, this sweet-tasting, nutritious vegetable is eaten both as a snack and as a main dish. When green, edamame beans have none of the stronger, "beany" flavor associated with mature soybeans. No other bean has as much protein or fiber; like mature soybeans, they are cholesterol-free.

Edamame beans are found both fresh and frozen in Asian food stores and fresh during the summer months in some specialty farmers' markets. Usually only the beans themselves are eaten, but the pods are edible as well. Although it is a lot of work, the beans can be removed from the pods before cooking, or the whole pods can be simmered in salted water for 10 to 12 minutes to make removing the beans easier.

For simpler and quicker preparation, most supermarkets and natural food stores now stock edamame in shelled frozen form; they are packaged as "sweet beans." Since the beans have been blanched prior to freezing, they can simply be thawed and added to recipes. However, if they are cooked briefly, the texture softens to crisp-tender and the flavor develops. Microwave them on high for about 6 minutes, boil on the stovetop for about 10 minutes, or steam for about 3 minutes. (For further information on frozen sweet beans, contact SunRich Foods at 1-800-297-5997.)

Sweet beans can be served alone as a side dish (with a dash of salt and pepper) or added to rice dishes, casseroles, soups, salads, or stir-fries.

Some people have problems with flatulence when they eat beans. This may be because our diets are traditionally low in fiber and our bodies are not used to the amount present in beans. As a result, certain carbohydrates in beans may remain undigested until they reach the large intestine, where bacteria ferment, resulting in gas and bloating. Here are a few suggestions for prevention:

- Discard the bean soaking water, rinse the beans, and cook them in fresh water.

- Salt beans only at the end of the cooking time.

- Eat more beans and your digestive system will adapt.

- Slow down and chew the beans well.

- Add epazote to the soybean cooking water or flavor bean dishes with this fragrant light green herb that tastes somewhat like fresh cilantro and is traditionally used in Mexican and South American cooking. When used in bean dishes, it reduces gas; it also is used as a medicinal tea to treat digestive disorders.

- A product on the market called Beano contains a natural food enzyme that breaks down the complex sugars in beans, and makes them more digestible; it actually helps stop gas before it starts. (For more information call the Beano hotline at 1-800-257-8650.)

Tofu

Let's face it—tofu has a bad rep. Not surprisingly, the country is full of what I call tofu skeptics. In fact, most of the students who attend my tofu classes admit they enrolled in the class after buying numerous packages of the stuff, which sat in the refrigerator unused, turned pink and slimy, and were discarded.

Since I didn't own a tofu cookbook in my early vegetarian days, I began adding just small amounts of tofu to some of my favorite recipes. I used tofu in place of part of the ricotta cheese in my stuffed pasta shells and added it to my twice-baked potatoes to turn them into a protein-rich entrée. Later tofu was the first protein I fed to my baby—puréed with cooked vegetables and even with prepared baby food, it was an easy-to-digest form of protein. Believe it or not, to this day, as a fast-growing fourteen-year-old boy, many of his favorite dinners and desserts are tofu based.

Tofu simply does not make a statement on its own. Right out of the container, tofu admittedly is exceedingly bland, but that very blandness and its absorbency are its greatest assets. Use this to your advantage. Tofu is the chameleon of food; it has the miraculous ability to absorb the flavors of seasonings and other foods. In its various forms, it can be stir-fried, broiled, grilled, sautéed, and baked. It is splendid in spicy entrées; and it can be puréed to create desserts, soups, dips, and sauces with creamy, smooth textures. Sometimes it is the focus of a recipe; other times it is a hidden healthy ingredient.

Tofu, or "bean curd," is sometimes called the cheese of Asia. It is made by coagulating the protein of soybeans in somewhat the same way as cheese is produced. Years ago, intrigued by this strange, water-bathed food, I visited a tofu factory where I could actually see tofu being made. Massive quantities of beans were cooked in enormous vats and then passed through large strainers to remove the skins, or crude fiber, of the soybeans. The fresh hot soy milk was then curdled with a coagulant. Traditionally, the curdling agent is nigari, a compound found in ocean water, or calcium sulfate, a naturally occurring mineral. The curds then were pressed into a solid block weighing from 8 ounces to 1 pound. Since the bean skins are removed in the process, tofu becomes an easy-to-digest form of soybeans with very little fiber.

It is possible to make your own tofu, but I have known only one person who followed the lengthy—and what I consider unnecessary—process. Once available only in health food stores and Asian markets, thanks to its growing popularity, reasonably priced packaged tofu is easy to find in supermarkets everywhere, usually refrigerated in the dairy case or along with Asian vegetables in the produce department. Beware of the unpackaged tofu that floats loose in water; the water is a breeding ground for potentially harmful bacteria, which, if not cooked thoroughly, may lead to gastrointestinal illness. Tofu is most commonly sold in vacuum packs or in aseptic packages. As with any perishable food, check the expiration date on the package; try to buy tofu that has at least a week left on its date code. Also make sure the package is sealed tightly and is not bloated.

If using tofu is new to you, I suggest that you experiment with several brands; since taste and texture are personal matters, make note of the brands that appeal to you. You will notice that tofus differ widely in texture; some are a bit more grainy and, if blended, require more time to achieve a smooth texture. Tofus also vary in flavor; some brands are more "beany."

Mori-Nu, my favorite tofu, which was used in developing the recipes for this book, has a "silken" texture and mild flavor. It comes in aseptic packaging that has favorable flavor and nutrient retention and ensures against bacterial contamination. Because of the addition of isolated soy protein (ISO), it is especially rich in isoflavones. The tofu actually is pasteurized as it is formed in the package with no preservatives and, surprisingly, can be stored for up to 1 year without (or with) refrigeration. (For more information, call Mori-Nu at 1-800-669-8638.)

Because of the potential for harmful bacteria developing in other types of tofu packaging, I exclusively select tofu in aseptic boxes when I don't plan to cook it, such as in cold-blended or puréed puddings, dressings, and dips. Use only the freshest tofu for recipes that call for no cooking.

Unless it is aseptically packaged, tofu should be kept cold and should be rinsed with cool water before using. Once the package is open, all tofu must be refrigerated. Rather than mashing it, store leftover tofu in block form; put it into a clean container and cover with water; then cover and refrigerate. To keep the tofu fresh, change the water daily and use the tofu within 3 days; fresher-tasting tofu is always better. If mold becomes visible, or the tofu turns a pinkish or greenish color or becomes slimy, throw it away. Like poultry or meat, tofu is susceptible to harmful bacteria; wash work surfaces and your hands when handling tofu.

If you are unable to use the tofu while it is still fresh, it can be frozen. Any tofu can be frozen, but those that freeze the best are regular firm tofu, regular extra-firm tofu, and "lite" silken extra-firm tofu by Mori-Nu. Freezing tofu drastically changes its properties; after thawing it will be spongy, chewy, and more meatlike in texture. It may also darken to a creamy beige color. After freezing, even soft tofu cannot be blended into a smooth texture, but recipes such as Cabbage and Noodles with Tofu (page 144) make the most of the chewy texture.

To freeze tofu, drain it well and cut the block into quarters; place them in a zip-top plastic bag, press out the excess air, and seal. For the best texture, freeze tofu for at least 12 hours or for up to 5 months. I usually thaw the tofu in the refrigerator; then I put it in a colander, rinse under cool water, squeeze dry, and crumble before using. For faster thawing, microwave the frozen tofu for 1 to 2 minutes. Or you can put it in a bowl, cover with boiling water, and let it stand for about 5 minutes, or until thawed. Rinse the tofu with cold water, then use your hands to squeeze out the water. This water loss decreases the volume: 12 ounces of fresh tofu yields $1^1/2$ cups when mashed; the yield is 1 cup after being frozen, thawed, and squeezed.

For some recipes, such as Tofu Teriyaki (page 160), freeze firm or extra-firm tofu slices about $1/4$ to $1/2$ inch thick; layer them with plastic wrap and then wrap in foil. Cover and freeze overnight; additional days in the freezer will result in an even more meatlike consistency. Because of a high protein density, "lite" silken extra-firm tofu slices acquire a particularly pleasing consistency after being frozen. Thaw the tofu in a bowl with boiling water or in the microwave. After pressing to remove the liquid, the slices can be marinated and then sautéed, baked, broiled, or grilled.

Variations in packaging aside, tofu is available in a number of different varieties, which vary in water content and are suited to different types of recipes.

> **Firm (or Chinese) tofu** is dense and solid and holds up well when sliced or cubed for use in stir-fried dishes, soups, or on a grill—anywhere that you want the tofu to maintain its shape. Firm tofu is also denser in nutrient content; it is higher in protein, fat, and calcium than other forms of tofu.

- **Soft tofu** is a good choice for recipes that call for blending tofu, such as blender drinks, dips, dressings, and some sauces and soups. The extra liquid it contains will yield a smooth and creamy texture. For some recipes, rather than blending, soft tofu is left slightly textured by mashing with a fork or potato masher.

- **Silken (or Japanese) tofu,** originally strained through silk during production, is made by a slightly different process using whole beans with less coagulant. The result is a creamier, custardlike product that is less "beany" in flavor. Silken extra-firm tofu will hold its shape if it is stirred gently into recipes. Silken firm tofu purées beautifully because of its high water content. It is ideal for dips, dressings, and puddings, and it can be used in recipes calling for regular soft tofu. For some recipes it can also be mashed. (Silken soft tofu is less commonly available; it also is a natural for puréed recipes.) One nutritional benefit is that the absorption of iron is better from silken tofu than the absorption from firmer textured tofu.

- **"Lite" tofu** is available if you are especially concerned about your consumption of fat. "Lite" silken firm tofu by Mori-Nu, for example, has 75 percent less fat and 50 percent fewer calories than regular tofu. (A 3-ounce serving provides 5 grams of protein and just 1 gram of total fat.)

In Asian markets you can buy many other forms of tofu—dried (ropelike or in squares), canned, powdered, baked (often with teriyaki flavoring added), fried, smoked, fermented, and sweetened; the nutritional value varies among them. These are not used in the recipes in this book.

If you prefer a firmer tofu texture, pressing it will increase the density; even extra-firm tofu can be pressed to remove excess water. This is also a way to substitute soft tofu when your recipe calls for a firm variety. (It is not possible to turn firm tofu into soft tofu, but with added liquid and a little more patience, firm tofu can be puréed into a creamy product. Be warned—some brands will retain a slightly grainy texture.) Thinner slabs work best for pressing, so begin by cutting your block of tofu horizontally into slices about $1/2$ inch thick unless your recipe specifies another size. To maintain the form, wrap the tofu slices in cheesecloth or, if you prefer, in paper toweling. Put them on a small aluminum foil–covered cutting board with its edge over the sink. Use a book to prop up the other end so the board slants into the sink. Put another foil-covered cutting board over the tofu and top with a weight such as a heavy can or book. Let the weighted tofu stand and drain for 20 to 30 minutes. If the slices are not firm enough or are not evenly shaped, replace the top cutting board and weights and press for an additional 15 or 20 minutes.

I usually use the pressed tofu right away; it is ideal for marinating and then sautéing or grilling. If necessary, pressed tofu can be wrapped in plastic wrap and refrigerated for up to 24 hours before using. If you are not in a hurry, the tofu can be pressed for up to 24 hours in the refrigerator: put the tofu slices between 2 plates weighted on top with something heavy.

Another method for making the texture of tofu more firm and meat-like is to freeze tofu slices, as in Sherried Tofu Steaks (page 158). At least 4 hours before it is needed, tofu can be sliced (up to $1/2$ inch thick) and placed in a single layer on a nonstick baking sheet; cover with plastic wrap and freeze. Once frozen, the slices can be layered between pieces of plastic wrap, stacked, and sealed in a plastic freezer bag; they can remain frozen for up to 3 months. (Note: Due to a high protein to fat ratio, slices of "lite" silken firm or "lite" silken extra-firm tofu have an especially meaty texture after being frozen and thawed.)

Marinating is a great way to add flavor to tofu. Firm or extra-firm tofu slices or strips (as well as those that have been frozen, thawed, and pressed or fresh tofu that has simply been pressed) are the best choices. Pour your traditional favorite marinade or the Teriyaki Marinade (page 160) into a flat dish made of glass, stainless steel, or enamel. Since tofu is very absorbent and is already tender, a long marinating time is not necessary, but allow at least 30 minutes for the flavors to soak in. For 1 hour or less, marinate the tofu in a covered dish at room temperature. For longer periods of time (up to 8 hours), to avoid the growth of bacteria, cover and refrigerate. If the tofu is not submerged in the marinade, gently turn the tofu occasionally while marinating. Drain well; then sauté, bake, broil, or grill to bring out the flavors.

Tempeh

Tempeh (pronounced TEM-pay) is considered one of the most nutritious soy foods. This traditional Indonesian food is made from cooked fermented whole soybeans formed into a cake when mixed with a grain such as brown rice, millet, or barley, each of which lends a somewhat different flavor. One variety even contains sea vegetables. Experiment with the different types; they are interchangeable in recipes calling for tempeh.

When you buy tempeh, don't be alarmed when you see the black spots on its surface; they simply indicate that the bacteria are still active. The flavor, sometimes compared with that of mushrooms, is somewhat smoky or nutty. Its dense, chewy, meaty texture is appealing to Western palates, and the fermentation enhances the beans' digestibility and nutritional profile.

As an ingredient, tempeh is remarkably versatile; in strips or cubes, it can be sautéed, baked, grilled, or braised. Marinating tempeh, as in Wild Rice and Apricot Salad with Marinated Tempeh (page 66), softens the texture and adds flavor.

Since tempeh is made from the whole soybean, it is considerably higher in fiber than are tofu, soy milk, or any of the concentrated soy-protein products. It is also lower in fat than are either tofu or soy milk. Soy foods are generally high in iron, but the protein, as well as the phytates, in soybeans inhibit iron absorption. The iron in tempeh, which is fermented, may be better absorbed than the iron in other soy foods. Consuming a source of vitamin C will help to increase this iron absorption. Some studies also have shown that fermented soy products such as tempeh increase the amount of isoflavones usable by the body, compared with those in tofu.

Tempeh usually is sold in natural food stores and in some supermarkets, where it is found in the refrigerator or freezer section. Tempeh can be refrigerated in its package up to the printed expiration date. As with other aged or fermented products, like cheeses, a little mold on the surface is harmless; just cut it off and discard. For longer storage, tempeh can be frozen for up to 6 months; thaw in the refrigerator before using.

Texturized Vegetable Protein (TVP)

Texturized vegetable protein (TVP) is a dry granulated product made from compressed soy flour; it's found in health food stores and some supermarkets. In some markets TVP is also available in chunk-size pieces that take on the consistency of stew meat when rehydrated. Check the labeling; sometimes TVP is beef- or chicken-flavored. TVP is interchangeable with another product, textured soy protein (TSP), which is made using a slightly different process.

Dry TVP can be stored in an airtight container at room temperature for up to 2 months, which makes it a great vegetarian convenience food to keep on hand. To rehydrate before using it in recipes, combine 1 cup dry TVP with 3/4 to 7/8 cup boiling water; allow to stand until the water is absorbed and the TVP is softened, about 5 minutes (the chunks need to be simmered for a few minutes). When moistened, TVP doubles in volume; it can be used right away or refrigerated for a few days.

TVP is low in fat and high in calcium; it provides a meaty texture to vegetarian dishes such as Broccoli Burritos (page 174). For nonvegetarians TVP can be added to meat burgers or meat loaf.

Soy Milk

Soy milk is a creamy liquid made by boiling soybeans and squeezing out the "milk." The liquid then is cooked under special conditions to remove the bean flavor.

Because it is not technically "dairy milk," package labels use the term "soy beverage" or "soy drink." Check the labeling further when selecting soy milk because there are several choices. Most soy milks are made from organically grown soybeans. Sometimes soy milk is fortified with calcium and vitamin D; some varieties have reduced calories. Other soy milk is flavored with vanilla, chocolate, or carob. Like tofu and other soy products, the protein content varies from brand to brand, and so does the flavor. You should conduct your own taste test. You'll also find that some brands are nearly white in color; others are slightly brownish, which is undesirable in certain recipes.

Soy milk is most commonly available in aseptic packaging found on the shelves of health food stores, specialty food shops, and most supermarkets. It is sometimes also sold refrigerated in plastic containers. Unopened, aseptically packaged soy milk can be stored at room temperature for several months; use by the freshness date printed on the packaging. Once opened, it must be stored in the refrigerator, where it will stay fresh for about 5 days. Always shake the container before measuring the soy milk for recipes. Soy milk also is sold as a powder, which must be mixed with water; check the labeling, since some brands contain hydrogenated oil and corn syrup rather than all natural ingredients. The powder should be stored in the refrigerator or freezer.

Soy milk is easy to add to your diet. Most simply, you might begin the day by pouring it over your breakfast cereal; some coffee shops now offer soy milk as an option for your latte. It also can be substituted equally for dairy milk in almost any cooking application. For people who are lactose intolerant or allergic to milk, soy milk provides a nutritious alternative. Children can drink homemade or commercially prepared soy milk after one year of age; infants under one year should be fed commercial soy milk infant formula. In this book soy milk is used in place of milk or cream in Cremini Mushroom Sauce (page 216), Fresh Pea Soup (page 41), and Caramel Custard (page 234), where it provides a touch of sweetness and a creamy, rich texture.

If you need soy milk for a recipe and have none on hand, make a quick-to-prepare substitute following this procedure: Bring 3 cups of water to a boil. Slowly pour 1 cup of full-fat soy flour into the water; stir constantly with a whisk to prevent lumps. Reduce the heat and simmer for 20 minutes, stirring occasionally. Line a colander with cheesecloth or nylon mesh and place it in a large bowl or pot. Strain the soy flour mixture through the lined colander. Refrigerate the soy milk immediately. To use as a beverage, this mixture can be flavored with a sweetener, vanilla, or other flavorings as desired.

Soy Flour

Soy flour is made from roasted soybeans that have been ground into a fine powder. Rich in high-quality soy protein and other nutrients, soy flour adds a pleasant texture and a slightly sweet flavor to a variety of products. In fact, it is used extensively by the food industry both for its flavor and because it helps keep baked goods from becoming stale.

Two types of soy flour are available in health food stores and many supermarkets. Natural or full-fat soy flour contains all of the oils that are naturally found in soybeans. Defatted soy flour has had those oils removed during processing. Both types will add protein to recipes; however, defatted soy flour is even more concentrated in protein than full-fat soy flour. Toasted soy flour, which has a nuttier flavor, is less commonly available. To toast it yourself, put the soy flour into a dry skillet and cook it, stirring occasionally, over moderate heat.

Because soy flour can become rancid, store it in a tightly closed container in the refrigerator for up to 6 months or longer in the freezer. Because it may become packed after setting, always stir soy flour before measuring it. In your favorite baked goods, soy flour can be paired with wheat flour or other flours; it will add fine texture and moistness. Because it contains no gluten, soy flour usually replaces only 15 to 25 percent of wheat flour in yeast-raised products. Just put 2 tablespoons of soy flour in your measuring cup before measuring the all-purpose or other flour called for in the recipe. In baked products that are not yeast raised, such as quick breads, muffins, cookies, and brownies, it can replace one-quarter to one-third of the regular wheat flour. Increasing the leavening agent in the recipe will lighten the baked product. Since soy flour browns quickly, it may be necessary to shorten the baking time and lower the oven temperature by 20 degrees. When full-fatted soy flour is used, often the amount of eggs and oil in the recipe can be reduced. Soy flour can also be used like regular flour to thicken gravies and sauces.

Soy Oil

About 40 percent of the calories in soybeans come from fat, compared to just 2 to 14 percent in other beans. Because of their high fat content and because soybeans are plentiful, soy oil is one of the most commonly used soybean products. Most of the oil labeled vegetable oil is soy oil, which is the natural oil extracted from whole soybeans.

Soy oil is low in saturated fat, which means that it does not raise blood cholesterol levels. In addition, soybean oil contains a type of polyunsaturated fat called omega-3 fatty acid. Soybeans are among the few plant sources with appreciable amounts of this type of fat, which may help to reduce the risk for both cancer and heart disease. In cooking, soy oil has a nearly imperceptible flavor and odor. It also has a high smoke point, 440°F, which means it can be used for sautéing, stir frying, and deep-fat frying. Soy oil also is used commercially by the food industry in a variety of products, including mayonnaise, coffee creamers, sandwich spreads, and salad dressings.

Sometimes soy oil is hydrogenated to make margarine. Hydrogenation is the process by which hydrogen is added to oils to make them more solid at room temperature; in the process the fats change to resemble saturated fats. Take note that many nutritionists believe that hydrogenated oils have the same effect on blood cholesterol as saturated fats like butter.

Soy oil can be used in any of the recipes in this book calling for safflower oil (cold-pressed safflower oil is my choice when a neutral-tasting oil is called for), but taking into account the minimal amount of oil used in low-fat cooking, using soy oil is not considered a way to consume soy for its health benefits.

Soy Sauce

Soy sauce, made with almost equal portions of soybeans and wheat, is a high-sodium soy extract that is fermented and then used as a cooking condiment. It is available in low-sodium varieties, which usually contain about 40 percent less sodium. Tamari, naturally brewed and made without wheat, is a more concentrated type of soy sauce, with a stronger flavor and darker color. China and Japan produce many other types of soy sauce that range in color from light to dark and in texture from thin to very thick.

Once opened, soy sauce should be refrigerated, where it will keep for up to 1 year. As a table condiment and a recipe ingredient, soy sauce is used for its flavor. It is not rich in the phytochemicals prevalent in other soy foods and is not consumed for nutritional attributes.

OTHER SOYBEAN PRODUCTS

Many other soybean products, which are not included in my recipes, are available in supermarkets and Asian markets. Some traditionally Asian soy products, such as salted soya beans and ground bean sauce, seem quite salty for Western palates, but many are definitely are worth trying for their flavors and healthful properties. Here are a few products to add to your soy shopping list.

Soybean Sprouts

Delicious and nutritious soybean sprouts are found in the produce department of many Asian markets. Untreated dried soybeans can also be sprouted in your kitchen. Soak the beans overnight in water—about $1/2$ cup in a quart jar. Drain the water and place the jar in a dark place. Rinse the beans, then drain them 2 to 4 times daily. The sprouts should be 2 to 4 inches long in about 5 days. Blanch them before using in salads, as a vegetable, or in stir-fries.

Okara

Okara is the pulp that remains when soy milk is strained. It has less protein than the whole bean but still is a good source of protein and fiber. Because of its coconut-like texture and almost neutral flavor, it can be added when making granola and cookies. It is also often used in commercially prepared vegetarian burgers.

Okara is sold frozen in Asian markets and some health food stores; keep it frozen. Since it is very perishable, once thawed, refrigerate and use it within a few days.

Miso

If you have eaten soup in a Japanese restaurant, you have probably tasted miso. It is a salty condiment made by fermenting soybeans for several years in cedar kegs with a grain such as rice, barley, or buckwheat. Also called fermented bean paste, miso is available in natural food stores and Asian markets, either fresh in the dairy case or pasteurized in shelf-stable plastic pouches. The addition of different ingredients and variations in the length of the aging process produce different types of miso, which vary greatly in flavor, texture, color, and aroma. Be sure to read the labeling: pasteurized miso contains none of the beneficial cultures.

Once opened, store miso in the refrigerator, where it will keep for several months. The white mold that sometimes forms on miso is harmless; remove it or stir it into the miso.

Miso can be used in place of soy sauce, salt, or anchovy paste. It's often a flavoring for soups, sauces, dressings, and gravies, Because it is high in sodium, use miso sparingly. Used in small quantities, it is not considered a source of soy nutrition.

Roasted Soynuts

Soynuts are roasted split soybeans that can serve as a crunchy snack food; sometimes they are flavored or even dipped in chocolate. They are a rich source of protein, but $1/2$ cup also contains 18.6 grams of fat. You can make your own lower-fat version following the recipe on page 31.

Isolated Soy Protein (ISP)

Isolated soy protein, the most highly refined soy protein, is simply the protein portion of the soybean separated, or isolated, from the rest of the bean. Since most of the carbohydrate and fat has been removed, what remains is at least 90 percent soy protein. ISP maintains all the health benefits of soy, and it serves as a highly digestible source of amino acids.

Soy isolate is found in natural food stores as an ingredient in nutritional protein powders that can be added to beverages. Soy protein isolates have been used in infant formulas as a protein source in the United States since 1960; they are also included as a protein source in special formulas for geriatric patients and for postoperative feeding.

Isolated soy protein allows food processors to incorporate soy protein into many familiar food products. It not only increases the protein content but also lengthens the shelf life of the food. Look for ISO in the ingredient lists on powdered beverages, nondairy products, soups, breakfast cereals, nutritional food bars, athletic and health food supplements, and more. If you find it as one of the first few ingredients in the product and if the product has a large amount of protein, you know the product can contribute to your soy intake. Although these products are highly refined, they contain most of the healthful properties of soy.

Dairy and Meat Analogs

The dairy and freezer cases in natural food stores are filled with soy products imitating dairy foods, a boon to the lactose intolerant. These include soy yogurt, sour cream, and nondairy frozen desserts that taste like ice cream; there are also soy cheeses resembling mozzarella, cheddar, Parmesan, cream cheese, and other cheeses. Like soy milk, the cheeses are cholesterol-free; however, many contain oil. Only those made with casein, a cow's milk derivative, melt well; casein is unacceptable if you follow a vegan diet. (Taking this information into account, soy cheeses can be used as a substitute for dairy cheeses in some of the recipes in this book.)

A wide variety of foods has been made from tofu or other soy products mixed together with other ingredients to resemble foods like burgers, hot dogs, and lunch meats. They can be used in the same ways as the foods they mimic. With so many different meat analogs available to consumers, the nutritional value and the flavor of these foods vary considerably. Generally, they are lower in fat than the foods they replace; however, the meat analogs themselves vary greatly in fat content. With the increasing demand for low-fat products, some low-fat meat analogs are now available. It's a good idea to study the nutritional profile on package labels.

Some people—and I am one of them—choose vegetarian foods because they want a "natural" diet; they object to the additives and processing involved in making meat analogs. For others, the meat imitations remind them of foods they grew up on; they may find them attractive alternatives to meat.

A NOTE ON FOOD ALLERGIES

For the vast majority of the population, soy foods provide excellent nutrition and health benefits and are not allergenic, but many foods, including soybeans, have the potential to cause allergic reactions in some people. Soy foods that are fermented, like tempeh, may be less likely to cause reactions in people who are allergic to soy protein. Also, within a given soy product, methods of processing used by different manufacturers can cause variations in allergic reactions. People with documented soy allergy need to read product labels very carefully, since many commercially prepared foods contain soy products.

On the flip side, one of the most common food intolerances is to dairy products and milk; for many years lactose-intolerant people have turned to soy milk as a milk replacement. If you are allergic to eggs, soy also provides some alternatives, since tofu can be scrambled (see recipe, page 154) and sometimes is used in baked goods as an egg replacement.

Note: Further information on soy products and their health benefits is available from the United Soybean Board. (Call 1-800-TALK SOY or visit their web page at http://www.talksoy.com.)

Soy Success

Here are some tips to guarantee your success in using these recipes.

STOCKING YOUR REFRIGERATOR AND PANTRY

❧ Since these recipes call for many fresh ingredients, begin by planning your trip to the market. Read your recipe and select garnishes and accompaniments; look at the suggested variations in order to make the most of in-season produce.

❧ When shopping, remember that your culinary creations will be only as good as the quality of the ingredients you use. Unless specified otherwise, use fresh vegetables and fruits at their peak of ripeness.

❧ Weekly shopping can be limited mostly to fresh and ethnic ingredients if you keep some staples on hand.

Begin with soy staples; in some communities this may require a trip to a natural foods store.

Aseptically packaged tofu (both firm and extra-firm); also freeze tofu slices for use later (see page xxx)

Aseptically packaged soy milk

Canned and dried soybeans

Texturized vegetable protein (TVP)

Frozen sweet beans

Tempeh—freeze for longer storage

Soy flour—store in the freezer

Nearly all supermarkets stock these staple items. Shopping, storage, and nutritional information are included in the recipe Tips.

Canned tomatoes—whole and diced

Tomato sauce and tomato paste

Frozen corn, peas, and chopped spinach

Frozen cholesterol-free egg substitute

Cooking oils: olive oil, extra-virgin olive oil, cold-pressed safflower oil or vegetable (soy) oil, nonstick cooking spray

Dark sesame oil

Pastas: mostaccioli, penne, rotini, spaghetti, egg noodles, lasagna, jumbo pasta shells

Rice: brown, white, and basmati

Couscous

Dried herbs and spices: basil, oregano, marjoram, tarragon, thyme, chili powder, ground cumin, curry powder, ground cinnamon, ground nutmeg, paprika, red pepper flakes

Salt and pepper, both black and white (preferably freshly ground)

Pure vanilla extract

Cornstarch

All-purpose white or unbleached flour

Baking powder and baking soda

Sugar: white and light brown

Honey

Pure maple syrup

Minced garlic and jalapeño peppers in jars

Hot pepper sauce

Low-sodium soy sauce

Vinegars: white rice, red wine, and balsamic

Dijon mustard

Oil-packed sun-dried tomatoes

Vegetable stock powder or cubes (see page 34)

Recipes that can be made solely with staples are important parts of your repertoire for busy days when there is no time for shopping. Some of these recipes include Creamy Tomato-Basil

Soup (page 48), Sherried Tofu Steaks (page 158), Chili-Rice Skillet (page 132), and even Chocolate-Maple Tofu Pudding (page 223).

USING THE RECIPES

> Read the recipe carefully before you begin. Assemble the equipment and ingredients on your counter before you begin cooking.

> Quantities for soybeans are given in cup measurements. An entire 15-ounce can ($1^1/2$ cups) has been used whenever possible. (Extra beans can be refrigerated or frozen for use later.)

> Tempeh is used in 8-ounce quantities, the most common packaging size.

> Quantities for tofu are provided in both cups and ounces if the recipe calls for a whole package (based on the Mori-Nu standard 12-ounce package size); if less is called for, or if the tofu is mashed or cut into cubes, only a cup measurement is provided. Other than puréed recipes, precise quantities often are not necessary; for example, if a recipe calls for 12 ounces of sliced tofu or 1 cup of cubed tofu, add more if you like.

> If a recipe calls for firm tofu and you have only soft tofu, plan ahead to allow time for pressing (see page xxxii).

> When recipes call for mashed tofu, simply mash it with a fork before measuring.

> If a recipe calls for soft tofu, it is usually okay to use firm. If blended, processing may take longer. It may also be necessary to add more liquid; add a small amount at a time until the mixture is smooth and creamy.

> When blending tofu using a food processor, use a rubber scraper to push down the sides occasionally so the mixture will have an even, smooth texture; if using a

blender, it may be necessary to add the ingredients in several batches.

- Measure flours by dipping your measuring cup (the individual dry-measure type) into the flour rather than pouring it; level the measuring cup with a spatula. Do not shake or press down the flour.

- Some ingredients, such as curry powder, red pepper flakes, and pepper, are followed by the words "or to taste." Before serving, always taste the food and adjust the seasonings to suit your preference.

- Salt also is a matter of personal taste. In my previous books I avoided the addition of salt; however, the blandness of soy products usually requires some salt. Because of its fuller flavor, I use sea salt, preferably in coarse crystals that I grind in a salt mill. Since the recipes were developed using canned beans that already contain some salt, you may want to add a little more salt if using soybeans cooked from scratch. When recipes call for ingredients such as soy sauce, Parmesan cheese, or canned tomato products—or sometimes lemon or lime juice—I include little or no additional salt. Adjust to suit your taste.

- I prefer using fresh herbs, which are now available in most supermarkets year-round. Quantities are provided for herbs in both their dried and fresh forms, where applicable; some fresh herbs lose their flavor if over-cooked and may needed to be added later in the cooking procedure, as specified.

- The amount of oil is based upon the use of nonstick cookware. Olive oil is used when its fruity flavor and distinctive aroma are compatible with the other ingredients; extra-virgin, the most flavorful (and expensive) of olive oils, is the best choice in uncooked recipes like salad dressings (its flavor dissipates somewhat when heated). Recipes with Asian flavors provided by soy sauce, sesame oil, and ginger call for a neutral cooking oil. In these recipes I use cold-pressed safflower oil, but vegetable (soy) oil can be substituted.

❧ Because of the high water content in tofu, in order to achieve browning with a minimum of oil, the slices or chunks of tofu (whether fresh or frozen and thawed) should be patted dry before sautéing. In some recipes, such as Batter-Dipped Tofu with Ginger Sauce (page 24), the tofu squares are dipped into a beaten egg and then into a flour mixture, which also enhances browning. Sometimes the tofu is gently stirred into a sauce without browning, as in Tofu Newburg (page 116).

❧ Cooking and baking times are guidelines and not absolute. The time may vary depending upon the weight and type of your pan, the use of a gas or electric stove, differences in microwaves, and in some cases the freshness or brand of your ingredients. As you become experienced in using my recipes and cooking with soy products, you will be able to judge doneness by appearance, smell, and taste.

Garnishes

When applicable, suggestions for garnishes are provided. Choose one or two when making your shopping list; after cooking, add them to complete the dish. Much of the pleasure of foods is visual; in addition to color, garnishes will also add texture and flavor. Your family and guests will perceive garnishes as a special touch that shows their meal was prepared with care. Let the artist in you emerge!

Advance Preparation

Advance preparation tips have been included whenever applicable. They apply to original recipe ingredient lists and, in some cases, may not apply to variations. When entertaining, it is always helpful to have at least some of the work done before your guests arrive. Refer to this information as a guide for storing leftovers too. Admittedly, I am quite conservative in determining how long food will keep. My suggestions will guide you in how long the dishes will retain their freshness and top-notch flavor; most recipes are safe to eat for far longer. I do not recommend freezing because, personally, I think the quality of nearly all food suffers in terms of both flavor and texture after being frozen and thawed. Prepared dishes containing tofu become watery and change in texture after being frozen and thawed.

Variations

Variations give you permission to use ingredients you have on hand, your favorite vegetables, or in-season produce. They also provide quantities for using cholesterol-free egg substitute in recipes calling for eggs; in a pinch, frozen egg substitute may save you from making a special trip to the store for fresh eggs. After you have worked with soy products, you'll feel comfortable improvising with your own ideas for culinary innovation. (Keep in mind that variations may increase cooking time, and additions and changes will alter the nutritional values.)

Tips

Some of the ingredients may be new to you; in the Tips I have included detailed information on how and where to purchase these items and how to work with them. Be adventuresome!

Nutritional Analysis

Each recipe is accompanied by a nutritional analysis per serving, based on the stated number of servings that the recipe yields. Included are the values for calories, protein, carbohydrates, fat, sodium, and cholesterol. The ingredients have been analyzed in the form as listed—such as low-sodium soy sauce, nonfat ricotta cheese, and nonfat yogurt. Dressings and sauces are included, as are the amounts of marinade that are absorbed. The use of garnishes and variations will alter the figures.

Soy nutrients are based on the nutrition facts for silken firm or extra-firm (not "lite") Mori-Nu tofu, White Wave tempeh (original soy), and Eden Soy soy milk (regular, not "lite"). Variations of products within these brands and the use of other brands will have slightly different nutritional profiles.

Serving Information

All of the recipes provide generous portions. In smaller portions some of the entrées can serve as side dishes, and in larger portions some of the appetizers can serve as entrées. For serving larger groups, all of the recipes can easily be doubled. When doubling recipes, use $1^1/2$ times the amount of herbs, spices, or extracts called for; taste and adjust the amounts.

Icons

A vegetarian is defined as a person who does not eat meat or other animal foods. However, today vegetarianism is viewed in varying degrees. To make this book the most useful, accompanying each recipe you will find an icon representing a category of vegetarianism. I have made an effort to include plenty of recipes to suit each type of vegetarian.

Please note that only the ingredients in the recipe lists were used in determining the icons; garnishes and variations may change the categories. If you are a vegan, many lacto recipes can be adjusted to suit your needs by eliminating the cheese or substituting soy cheese or by substituting soy milk for dairy milk.

The icons represent the following vegetarian categories:

 Vegan.   Vegans, or strict vegetarians, do not eat meat or animal-derivative foods, including dairy products (butter, cheese, eggs, and milk). They may or may not use honey or animal by-products. (Please note that in this book honey may be used in the recipes designated "vegan.")

 Lacto-ovo.   People in this category do not eat meat, but they do eat animal-related foods, including eggs and dairy products.

 Lacto.   Lacto vegetarians do not eat meat or eggs but do eat dairy products.

Ovo.   This type of vegetarian does not eat meat or dairy products but does eat eggs.

KITCHEN EQUIPMENT

Working with soy products requires no out-of-the-ordinary kitchen equipment. My best advice is to buy the best you can afford—quality equipment will last you a lifetime.

In addition to the basics, there are several items that will be especially useful in using this book:

- Nonstick pans with heavy bottoms and tight-fitting lids. They will distribute heat evenly and allow you to use a minimum of oil. (Be sure to use nonabrasive spoons and cleaning equipment.) You'll need a large (10- or 12-inch) skillet, a 12-inch sauté pan (with straight rather than sloping sides), a Dutch oven or large saucepan, and a smaller saucepan.

- Electric rice cooker.   With this appliance you can have perfect rice every time with no fuss or mess. I usually make a large pot of rice at the beginning of the week; I reheat it to use as an accompaniment or recipe ingredient.

- Food processor.   This is *essential!* In seconds you can make puréed soups, sauces, and desserts. (Using a blender often requires doing the task in several small batches.) A food processor also makes short work out of procedures like shredding carrots and chopping onions.

- Knives.   Select a paring knife and a chef's knife in a size that fits your hand comfortably. An entire set is fun to have but really not necessary for these recipes. Learn the proper techniques for the use of your knives and care for them meticulously: sharpen them at home regularly, and have them professionally sharpened once a year. Wash them by hand and do not soak wooden handles in water. Store all knives in a knife rack, not loosely in a drawer.

1

Appetizers

Tofu Spreads and Dips

Mushroom-Almond Spread

Sun-Dried Tomato–Tofu Spread

Tofu-Chèvre Spread

Tofu-Basil Pesto

Tofu Guacamole

Hoisin Peanut Sauce

Parmesan-Peppercorn Dip

Peanut Chili Dip

Roasted Garlic–Tofu Spread

Tofu Baba Ghanoush

Fruit Dip

Tofu Sour Cream

Green Goddess Dip

Soybean Spreads and Dips

Roasted Red Pepper Hummus

Spinach-Bean Dip

Soybean-Salsa Dip

Soybean Hummus

Other Appetizers

Pita Crisps

Baked Tortilla Chips

Sweet Bean–Corn Salsa

Batter-Dipped Tofu with Ginger Sauce

Ginger Sauce

Stuffed Mushrooms

California Rolls

Roasted Soybeans

Remember those popular appetizers of years past? By today's standards, their high fat and other ingredients we now consider undesirable inspire feelings of guilt, not pleasure. Luckily, soy is a natural when it comes to healthful, low-fat appetizers.

Here tofu is puréed to make dips and spreads with the creamy smoothness that is traditionally provided by sour cream or mayonnaise. Assertive ingredients such as sun-dried tomatoes, chèvre cheese, roasted garlic, fresh basil, and hoisin sauce add an array of colorful flavors to tofu's own mild palette. It's even possible to make Tofu Sour Cream (page 15) to serve as a heart-healthy appetizer component or to keep on hand for use in place of dairy sour cream in some of your favorite recipes or as a low-fat topper for baked potatoes.

To achieve the best texture in puréed recipes, I prefer silken firm tofu, but you can substitute regular soft tofu. If necessary, silken extra-firm or regular firm tofu can be used, but you will need to add extra liquid and allow extra time for the texture to become smooth, without a trace of graininess. My recipe procedures achieve this with a food processor; you can use a blender, but you may need to add the ingredients in several batches. Since the tofu is uncooked in these dips and spreads, for both flavor and food safety it is very important to use very fresh tofu. Tofu in aseptic packaging is the best choice.

Several of these recipes call for silken extra-firm tofu. Strips are rolled into vegetarian "sushi," or they can be sautéed and served with a lively sauce.

Cooked whole soybeans are puréed to serve as a foundation for several dips and spreads; use canned soybeans for speedy preparation. Sweet beans (see page xxvi) become a colorful and toothsome salsa ingredient.

Nearly all of my soy appetizers can be made in advance. In fact, most of the dips and spreads will taste best if you plan ahead so they can stand in the refrigerator for several hours to allow the flavors to develop before serving.

The uses for these versatile appetizers are innumerable. Many of the dips and spreads can be served with an array of fresh vegetables, Pita Crisps (page 21), or Baked Tortilla Chips (page 22). Some, such as Roasted Red Pepper Hummus (page 17), can be spread on bread to turn an everyday sandwich into something special. And I often make a bowl of Mushroom-Almond Spread (page 3) to use in place of butter when serving crusty bread with soups and salads. With the addition of a few other ingredients, dips such as Parmesan-Peppercorn Dip (page 10), Tofu-Basil Pesto (page 6), and others can be transformed into salad dressings or pasta toppers. Stuffed Mushrooms (page 27) make an elegant side dish to accompany a number of the entrées in this book. And Batter-Dipped Tofu with Ginger Sauce (pages 24 and 26), when served in larger portions, can double as a light entrée.

Turn to these recipes when preparing a snack to enjoy as you work or relax and when you are planning a dinner for special guests. No one will ever guess that such appealing appetizers are also so healthful. Divulging the truth—or not—is up to you.

Tofu Spreads and Dips

mushroom-almond spread

This spread can be served warm shortly after preparing, but it improves in flavor if it is refrigerated overnight. Bring the spread to room temperature, then serve with thick slices of crusty French bread, water crackers, or Pita Crisps (page 21).

Heat the oil in a large nonstick skillet over medium-high heat. Add the mushrooms, onion, and garlic. Cook, stirring occasionally, until the mushrooms and onion are tender but not browned, about 5 minutes. Stir in the fresh or dried tarragon.

Transfer the mixture to a food processor; add the tofu, almonds, soy sauce, lemon juice, and white pepper. Process until the mixture is smooth. Adjust the seasoning to taste.

Per serving (1/4 cup): Cal 175/Pro 6.6g/Carb 8.4g/Fat 12.8g/Chol 0mg/Sod 153mg

ADVANCE PREPARATION Covered and refrigerated, this spread will keep for up to 4 days. Bring to room temperature before serving.

VARIATIONS

❧ Substitute white mushrooms for the cremini mushrooms.

❧ Substitute fennel for the tarragon, and pecans for the almonds.

tip

There are thousands of varieties of mushrooms. The readily available cultivated white mushroom has a mild, earthy flavor; those labeled "button mushrooms" are immature, smaller white mushrooms. Cremini mushrooms (sometimes labeled "Italian brown mushrooms") are very flavorful, with a denser, less watery texture than white mushrooms; portobello mushrooms are larger, matured creminis.

makes 1 cup

1 tablespoon olive oil

1 1/2 cups sliced cremini
    mushrooms (see Tip)

1/2 cup coarsely chopped onion

2 teaspoons minced garlic

1 teaspoon minced fresh
    tarragon (or 1/4 teaspoon
    dried)

1/2 cup mashed silken firm tofu

1/2 cup blanched whole
    almonds

1 tablespoon low-sodium
    soy sauce

1 teaspoon freshly squeezed
    lemon juice

Dash of white pepper,
    or to taste

garnish *(optional)* strips of red bell pepper or cherry tomatoes, sprigs of fresh flat-leaf parsley

sun-dried tomato-tofu spread

Sun-dried tomatoes seem to dress up anything they touch. For a quick lunch, spread this mixture on toasted sliced bagels, sprinkle with shredded mozzarella cheese, and place the open-faced sandwiches under the broiler until the cheese melts.

makes 1 cup

1/2 cup drained and coarsely chopped oil-packed sun-dried tomatoes

1/2 cup mashed silken firm tofu

2 tablespoons tomato paste (see Tip)

2 tablespoons freshly squeezed lemon juice

1 tablespoon red wine vinegar

1 teaspoon minced garlic

1 teaspoon honey

Dash of freshly ground black pepper, or to taste

Dash of salt, or to taste

2 teaspoons minced fresh basil (or 1/2 teaspoon dried)

Put all the ingredients except the fresh basil, if using, into a food processor (if using dried basil, put it in the processor); process until smooth. Stir in the fresh basil. Adjust the seasonings to taste.

Per tablespoon: Cal 31/Pro 1.4g/Carb 5.9g/Fat 0.2g/Chol 0mg/Sod 25mg

ADVANCE PREPARATION Covered and refrigerated, this spread will keep for up to 3 days. Bring to room temperature before serving.

tip

Tomato paste is available in tubes, ideal for recipes calling for less than a 6-ounce can. Refrigerate the tube after opening.

tofu-chèvre spread

If you like the flavor of chèvre—and who doesn't?—you'll enjoy this elegant spread. Keep it in mind for garnishing pasta dishes, such as Penne with Cremini Mushrooms and Tomato-Tofu Pesto (page 133), or dollop it onto soups, such as Creamy Tomato-Basil Soup (page 48). It's also delectable stuffed into roasted red peppers to create an unusual salad (page 84).

makes 2/3 cup

1/2 cup chèvre (goat cheese) (see Tip)

1/2 cup mashed silken firm tofu

1 tablespoon freshly squeezed lemon juice

garnish *(optional)* freshly ground black pepper, red bell pepper strips

Put all the ingredients into a food processor; process until smooth and creamy.

Per tablespoon: Cal 26/Pro 1.8g/Carb 0.4g/Fat 1.9g/Chol 8mg/Sod 61mg

ADVANCE PREPARATION Covered and refrigerated, this spread will keep for up to 1 week. Bring to room temperature before serving.

tip

Chèvre and Montrachet are tangy, creamy cheeses made from goat's milk. Domestic goat cheese is a fine substitute for the more expensive, imported brands. After opening, wrap tightly in plastic wrap; store in the refrigerator for 1 to 2 weeks. (Do not confuse chèvre and Montrachet with caprini, an Italian goat cheese that is dried, less creamy, and more acidic.)

tofu-basil pesto

makes 1 cup

1 cup mashed silken firm tofu

1 cup loosely packed fresh
basil leaves (fresh is
essential)

1/4 cup freshly grated
Parmesan cheese

2 tablespoons extra-virgin
olive oil

2 tablespoons freshly squeezed
lemon juice

1 teaspoon minced garlic

1 teaspoon freshly ground
black pepper, or to taste

1/2 teaspoon lemon zest
(see Tip)

Traditionally, basil pesto is a rich green, highly aromatic blend of fresh basil, pine nuts, garlic, olive oil, and Parmesan cheese pulverized with a mortar and pestle—or with a food processor or electric mincer. This low-fat version also contains tofu, which adds creaminess. Try it as a dip for raw vegetables or as a stuffing for hollowed-out cherry tomatoes. The pesto also serves as a sauce for Mostaccioli and Plum Tomatoes (page 139) and as a dressing for a rice salad (page 69).

Put all the ingredients except the lemon zest into a food processor; process until the mixture is smooth. Stir in the lemon zest. Adjust the seasoning to taste.

Per tablespoon: Cal 35/Pro 1.8g/Carb 1g/Fat 2.6g/Chol 1mg/Sod 35mg

ADVANCE PREPARATION Covered and refrigerated, the pesto will keep for up to 4 days. Bring to room temperature before serving.

tips

Zesting is done with a kitchen gadget called a zester, which has a short, flat blade with a beveled end and 5 small holes. When drawn firmly over the skin of a lemon, lime, or orange, the tool removes long, thin strips of the colored zest. Ideally, do the zesting over the dish you are preparing to make use of the oils too; they are extremely fragrant and flavorful. (If you do not have a zester, use a vegetable peeler; cut the zest into thinner strips with a small knife.)

Grating citrus rind is done by rubbing the skin against the coarse, serrated surface of a grater, which reduces the rind to tiny bits. Lemons yield about 1 tablespoon grated rind; the thinner peels of limes yield about 1 teaspoon.

Before grating or zesting citrus rind, scrub the fruit well, then dry it thoroughly. Use only the outer colored part with its aromatic oils; the white portion beneath tastes bitter.

tofu guacamole

makes 1 cup

1 medium ripe avocado,
    peeled, pitted, and mashed
    (about 3/4 cup) (see Tip)

1/4 cup mashed silken firm tofu

2 tablespoons freshly squeezed
    lime juice

1 tablespoon minced onion

1/2 teaspoon minced garlic,
    or to taste

Dash of freshly ground black
    pepper, or to taste

Dash of hot pepper sauce,
    or to taste

Dash of salt, or to taste

garnish (optional) halved
cherry tomatoes

Enjoying guacamole made with tofu relieves some of the guilt, especially if it is accompanied by low-fat Baked Tortilla Chips (page 22). Also use Tofu Guacamole as a spread to add personality to sandwiches; see page 167.

Put all the ingredients (except the garnish, if using) into a food processor; process until smooth and creamy. Adjust the seasonings to taste.

Refrigerate in a covered container for at least 1 hour before serving.

Per tablespoon: Cal 22/Pro 0.5g/Carb 1.1g/Fat 1.8g/Chol 0mg/Sod 11mg

ADVANCE PREPARATION Covered and refrigerated, this mixture will keep for up to 3 days.

tip

The two most common varieties of avocados are the pebbly textured, almost black, rich-flavored Haas (my preference) and the Fuerte, which has a smooth green skin. Select fruits that are unblemished and heavy for their size. Most will require a few days of ripening after purchasing; place them in a pierced paper bag at room temperature for a day or two to speed up the process. When ripe, avocados will yield to gentle pressure; they are then ready to use. Store them in the refrigerator for up to 5 days. Once cut and exposed to the air, avocado flesh discolors rapidly; to minimize this, coat cut surfaces with lemon or lime juice and add these juices to recipes containing avocado.

hoisin peanut sauce

Remember celery sticks stuffed with peanut butter in your grade school lunchbox? Well, here's an updated version of the marriage spiked with spiciness to suit adult tastes; you can customize the liveliness by adjusting the amount of chili paste with garlic. Use this enticing update of a childhood favorite as an appetizer or snack dip for raw vegetables. It also serves as a sauce for three entrées: Spicy Asian Peanut Pasta (page 138), Vegetable Medley with Hoisin Peanut Sauce (page 117), and Tempeh-Rice Wraps (page 172).

makes 3/4 cup

1/2 cup mashed silken firm tofu

1/4 cup hoisin sauce
    (see Tip, page 147)

1 tablespoon creamy peanut
    butter

1 teaspoon chili paste with
    garlic, or to taste (see Tip)

1 teaspoon dark sesame oil

1 tablespoon water, or more as
    needed

garnish *(optional)* finely
chopped peanuts

Put all the ingredients except the water into a food processor; process until smooth and creamy. The consistency should resemble a thick, creamy salad dressing; add water as needed, depending upon the texture of the tofu and peanut butter. Adjust the seasoning to taste.

Per tablespoon: Cal 34/Pro 1.3g/Carb 3.9g/Fat 1.5g/Chol 0mg/Sod 182mg

ADVANCE PREPARATION Covered and refrigerated, this sauce will keep for up to 3 days. Bring to room temperature before serving. Because it thickens while standing, stir in water as needed.

tip

Chili paste with garlic, also called chili purée or Chinese chili sauce, is found in Asian markets and in the Asian foods section of most supermarkets.

parmesan-peppercorn dip

Serve this with fresh vegetables for dipping or use it as a deceptively rich-tasting sauce for Herbed Twice-Baked Potatoes (page 202).

makes 1 cup

1 cup mashed silken firm tofu

1/2 cup freshly grated Parmesan cheese

2 tablespoons freshly squeezed lemon juice

1 tablespoon tarragon white wine vinegar

1/2 teaspoon minced garlic

1/4 teaspoon freshly ground black pepper (coarse grind), or to taste (see Tip)

garnish *(optional)* sprigs of fresh flat-leaf parsley

Put all the ingredients into a food processor; process until smooth and creamy. Adjust the seasoning to taste. Stir before serving.

Per tablespoon: Cal 25/Pro 2.3g/Carb 0.8g/Fat 1.4g/Chol 2mg/Sod 63mg

ADVANCE PREPARATION Covered and refrigerated, this dip will keep for up to 2 days. If it thickens while standing, stir in a little milk or water as needed.

tip

Freshly ground or cracked whole dried peppercorns are more flavorful than preground pepper because, once cracked, the peppercorn immediately releases much of its oil as aroma and flavor. The best pepper grinders have settings for both coarse and fine grinds. To measure, grind the pepper onto a sheet of waxed paper and pour into a measuring spoon. For extra-coarse chunks of pepper, crack peppercorns by pressing them firmly on a cutting board with the side of a chef's knife.

peanut chili dip

This spicy dip is perfect for a variety of fresh vegetables, such as carrots, broccoli, green or red bell peppers, and cauliflower, or serve it atop strips of celery. Add more red pepper flakes or cayenne if you want to make the flavor zestier.

Put all the ingredients into a food processor; process until the mixture is smooth and creamy. (If the peanut butter is thick, it may be necessary to add some water.) Adjust the seasoning to taste.

Let stand in a covered container for 1 hour before serving.

Per tablespoon: Cal 62/Pro 3.5g/Carb 3.8g/Fat 4.2g/Chol 0mg/Sod 140mg

ADVANCE PREPARATION Covered and refrigerated, this dip will keep for up to 2 days; the flavors will blend. Bring to room temperature before serving. If it thickens while standing, stir in water as needed.

tips

In Mexican markets, chili powder is simply a powdered form of ancho, pasilla, or other dried red peppers. The domestic varieties often contain extra seasonings, such as cumin, oregano, garlic, coriander, black pepper, and paprika. If you want to make your chili powder hotter, just add cayenne.

Cayenne is the ground dried pod of the small, more pungent varieties of chili peppers. Use with caution, because it is very hot. Store it in a tightly closed container in the refrigerator to preserve the color and flavor.

makes 3/4 cup

1/3 cup smooth or crunchy peanut butter

1/2 cup mashed silken firm tofu

2 tablespoons low-sodium soy sauce

2 tablespoons freshly squeezed lemon juice

2 teaspoons honey

1 teaspoon minced garlic

1 tablespoon chili powder (see Tip)

1/8 teaspoon red pepper flakes, or to taste

garnish *(optional)* finely chopped peanuts, pinch of paprika

roasted garlic-tofu spread

Roasted garlic cloves are delicious as a spread for warm and crusty French bread, or mince and stir into mashed potatoes or use as a topping for baked potatoes. The roasted garlic cloves can be used as an ingredient in most recipes calling for garlic.

makes ³/4 cup

1 medium whole garlic bulb

1 teaspoon olive oil

¹/2 cup mashed silken firm tofu

2 tablespoons chèvre
    (goat cheese)

1 tablespoon balsamic vinegar

Dash of freshly ground black
    pepper, or to taste

Dash of salt, or to taste

garnish *(optional)* sprigs of
fresh flat-leaf parsley

Preheat the oven to 400°F. Line a baking sheet or small pan with aluminum foil.

To prepare the garlic bulb for roasting, gently remove the loose, excess papery skin, but leave the cloves intact. Trim off the top stem and ¹/4 to ¹/2 inch of the garlic head (exposing the cloves directly to the heat speeds up the roasting process). Brush the outer skin and top of the bulb with the olive oil; place on the prepared baking sheet or pan. Bake for 20 to 25 minutes, or until the cloves feel very soft when pierced with the tip of a knife. Remove from the baking sheet or pan and allow the bulb to cool.

Separate and remove 10 individual garlic cloves (save any remaining cloves to use in another recipe). Slice off the bottom from each and squeeze out the flesh. Put into a food processor with all the remaining ingredients; process until the mixture is smooth and creamy. Adjust the seasonings to taste.

Per tablespoon: Cal 14/Pro 1g/Carb 1.4g/Fat 0.5g/Chol 1mg/Sod 24mg

ADVANCE PREPARATION Covered and refrigerated, this spread will keep for up to 3 days.

VARIATION

To roast garlic in the microwave, place the prepared garlic bulb on a paper towel; microwave on high for 1 minute. Turn the bulb upside down, then microwave 1 minute more.

tofu baba ghanoush

This traditional Middle Eastern eggplant purée (with the nontraditional addition of tofu) makes a dynamite dip for raw vegetables, or use it as a spread for Pita Crisps (page 21) or sandwiches. And it's adaptable: serve it warm, at room temperature, or chilled.

Put the eggplant into a large microwave-proof dish; add about 1/4 cup water. Cover and microwave on high until softened, about 5 minutes; drain well. (Or cook the eggplant in a stovetop steamer.)

Put the cooked eggplant, tofu, tahini, lemon juice, and garlic into a food processor. Process until the mixture is smooth and creamy.

Stir in all the remaining ingredients. Adjust the seasonings to taste.

Per 1/4 cup: Cal 94/Pro 3.7g/Carb 6.1g/Fat 6.1g/Chol 0mg/Sod 24mg

ADVANCE PREPARATION The flavor matures if this mixture is made 1 or 2 days in advance; cover and refrigerate for up to 3 days. Bring to room temperature before serving.

tip

Tahini, a paste made of ground sesame seeds, is also called sesame butter. Although it is high in fat, the flavor is concentrated, so a little goes a long way. Light tahini is preferable to the more intensely flavored dark tahini, which is made from toasted sesame seeds. Stir before using to reincorporate the oil. Keep tahini refrigerated in a tightly closed container for up to 1 year; bring to room temperature before using.

makes 2 cups

1 medium eggplant, peeled and cut into 1/2-inch cubes (about 4 cups)

1/2 cup mashed silken firm tofu

1/4 cup tahini (see Tip)

2 tablespoons freshly squeezed lemon juice

2 teaspoons minced garlic

1/2 teaspoon freshly ground black pepper, or to taste

1/4 teaspoon ground cumin, or to taste

Dash of salt, or to taste

2 tablespoons toasted sesame seeds (see Tip, page 125)

1 tablespoon coarsely chopped fresh flat-leaf parsley

garnish *(optional)* sprig of fresh flat-leaf parsley, minced pistachios

fruit dip

For a quick and appealing appetizer or snack, serve this dip with fruit; my favorites are juicy fresh strawberries—especially visually appealing if they are large and long-stemmed—and crisp seedless green grapes.

makes 1 cup

1 cup Tofu Sour Cream
   (page 15)

2 tablespoons lightly packed
   light brown sugar, or to
   taste

Combine the Tofu Sour Cream and brown sugar in a small bowl. Adjust the sweetening to taste.

Refrigerate in a covered container for at least 1 hour before serving.

Per tablespoon: Cal 24/Pro 1g/Carb 2.2g/Fat 1.3g/Chol 0mg/Sod 14mg

ADVANCE PREPARATION Covered and refrigerated, this dip will keep for up to 3 days.

tip

Buy grapes that are firmly attached to their stems. Store them, unwashed, in a plastic bag in the refrigerator, where they will keep for up to a week. For the best flavor, remove them from the refrigerator about 30 minutes before serving.

tofu sour cream

Substitute this for dairy sour cream in your favorite appetizer dips. Used alone, it adds just the right amount of tartness when spread on thin slices of party rye bread; top with strips of roasted red bell peppers (see Tip, page 92). And don't overlook the pleasure of using this as a guilt-free topping for baked potatoes.

Put all the ingredients into a food processor; process until smooth and creamy. Adjust the seasoning to taste.

Per tablespoon: Cal 18/Pro 1g/Carb 0.5g/Fat 1.3g/Chol 0mg/Sod 13mg

ADVANCE PREPARATION Covered and refrigerated, this mixture will keep for up to 3 days.

tip

White rice vinegar, made from fermented rice, has a low acid content and is milder and sweeter than ordinary white vinegar. "Seasoned" white rice vinegar is used in recipes benefiting from the sugar and salt that it also contains. Both types of rice vinegar can be found in Asian markets and most supermarkets.

makes 1 cup

1 cup mashed silken firm tofu

1 tablespoon extra-virgin olive oil

2 tablespoons freshly squeezed lemon juice

1 teaspoon white rice vinegar (see Tip)

Dash of salt, or to taste

green goddess dip

makes 1 cup

1 cup packed sprigs of fresh
    flat-leaf parsley (see Tip)

1/2 cup chopped scallions (both
    green and white parts)

1/2 cup water

1 cup mashed silken firm tofu

2 tablespoons freshly squeezed
    lemon juice

1 tablespoon extra-virgin
    olive oil

1 teaspoon minced garlic

1/2 teaspoon sugar

1/2 teaspoon freshly ground
    black pepper, or to taste

Dash of salt, or to taste

garnish *(optional)* sprigs of
fresh flat-leaf parsley (see Tip)

Serve this dip with an assortment of fresh vegetables. It can also step in as a sandwich spread in place of mayonnaise. Or thin it with a little water and use as a dressing for green salads.

Put the cup of parsley sprigs, the scallions, and water into a small saucepan. Cover and bring the water to a boil over medium heat; simmer until the scallions are tender and the parsley is wilted, about 2 minutes. Drain well.

Transfer the cooked scallions and parsley to a food processor. Add the remaining ingredients and process until smooth. Adjust the seasonings to taste.

Refrigerate in a covered container for at least 30 minutes before serving.

Per tablespoon: Cal 21/Pro 1.2g/Carb 1.1g/Fat 1.3g/Chol 0mg/Sod 15mg

ADVANCE PREPARATION Covered and refrigerated, this dip will keep for up to 3 days.

tip

Flat-leaf parsley, also called Italian parsley, has a more pungent flavor than the more common curly-leaf parsley. Wash fresh parsley, shake off the excess moisture, and wrap first in paper towels, then in a plastic bag. Refrigerate for up to a week. Stay away from dried parsley, which has little of the distinctive parsley flavor.

Soybean Spreads and Dips

roasted red pepper hummus

I use this full-flavored Middle Eastern mixture to stuff hollowed-out cherry tomatoes and ribs of celery as appetizers. To accompany soups and salads, just spread it on crusty French bread or Pita Crisps (page 21). Also try it in place of ordinary mayonnaise to add both color and flavor to Sherried Tofu–Roasted Eggplant Sandwiches (page 164).

Prepare the roasted red bell peppers.

Heat the oil in a small nonstick skillet over medium heat. Add the onion and garlic; cook, stirring occasionally, until the onion is softened, about 2 minutes. Remove from the heat and set aside.

Put the roasted bell peppers, soybeans, and lemon juice into a food processor; process until well combined. Add the cooked onion and garlic; process until the mixture is smooth. Stir in the remaining ingredients. Adjust the seasonings to taste.

Refrigerate in a covered container for at least 1 hour before serving.

Per tablespoon: Cal 21/Pro 1.2g/Carb 1.5g/Fat 1.1g/Chol 0mg/Sod 6mg

ADVANCE PREPARATION The flavor matures if this mixture is made 1 or 2 days in advance; cover and refrigerate. Bring to room temperature before serving.

makes 1¹/2 cups

2 roasted red bell peppers
   (see Tip, page 92)

1 tablespoon olive oil

2 tablespoons coarsely
   chopped onion

2 teaspoons minced garlic

1 cup cooked soybeans

3 tablespoons freshly
   squeezed lemon juice

1/4 cup minced fresh basil
   (or 1 teaspoon dried)

1 teaspoon freshly ground
   black pepper, or to taste

Pinch of red pepper flakes,
   or to taste

Dash of salt, or to taste

garnish *(optional)* sprigs of
fresh basil

spinach-bean dip

makes 2 cups

One 10-ounce package frozen chopped spinach, thawed, drained, and squeezed dry (see Tip, page 207)

1 cup cooked soybeans

1 cup nonfat sour cream

1 tablespoon freshly squeezed lemon juice

1 teaspoon balsamic vinegar (see Tip)

$1/2$ teaspoon minced garlic

2 teaspoons minced fresh tarragon (or $1/2$ teaspoon dried)

$1/2$ teaspoon salt, or to taste

$1/4$ teaspoon freshly ground black pepper, or to taste

Pinch of red pepper flakes, or to taste

This garden-fresh dip looks spectacular presented in a small round loaf of hollowed-out bread or in a hollowed-out red cabbage; serve it with Pita Crisps (page 21), toasted small bread rounds, or a platter of assorted raw vegetables for dipping.

Put the spinach, soybeans, sour cream, lemon juice, and vinegar into a food processor; process until smooth. Add the remaining ingredients and process again. Adjust the seasonings to taste.

Refrigerate in a covered container for at least 1 hour before serving.

Per tablespoon: Cal 17/Pro 1.6g/Carb 1.8g/Fat 0.4g/Chol 0mg/Sod 39mg

ADVANCE PREPARATION Covered and refrigerated, this dip will keep for up to 3 days. Bring to room temperature before serving.

tip

Balsamic vinegar (the Italian aceto balsamico*) is an Italian red wine vinegar made by boiling the juice of white Trebbiano grapes in copper pots until it caramelizes. It is then aged for 3 to 30 years in barrels made from various woods (oak, chestnut, mulberry, and juniper), each adding a hint of its woody flavor. The result is a vinegar with a heavy, mellow, almost sweet flavor and a dark color. Store balsamic vinegar in a cool, dark place for up to 6 months after it has been opened. Balsamic vinegar is pricey, but a little goes a long way. Be aware of cheap imitations made with cane sugar, vanilla, licorice, and caramel flavoring. It pays to read the labels!*

soybean-salsa dip

Call on your favorite bottled salsa to make this dip. You can adjust its hotness by the style of salsa and the amount of black pepper and red pepper flakes you add. Serve with Baked Tortilla Chips (page 22), packaged tortilla chips, or Pita Crisps (page 21).

Put the soybeans, salsa, and sour cream into a food processor; process until smooth and creamy. Add the black pepper and red pepper flakes to taste.

Per tablespoon: Cal 24/Pro 1.9g/Carb 1.6g/Fat 1.1g/Chol 0mg/Sod 55mg

ADVANCE PREPARATION Covered and refrigerated, this dip will keep for up to 5 days.

tip

Commercial sour cream contains 18 to 20 percent fat; nonfat sour cream, which is thickened with stabilizers, still has the same characteristic tang. Refrigerated sour creams are good for up to 1 week after the expiration date on the container; discard if the surface becomes moldy.

makes 1 cup

1 cup cooked soybeans

1/2 cup prepared tomato salsa

1/4 cup nonfat sour cream
 (see Tip)

1/4 teaspoon freshly ground
 black pepper, or to taste

Pinch of red pepper flakes,
 or to taste

soybean hummus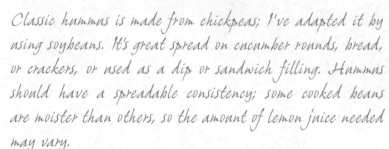

makes 1¹/2 cups

1 tablespoon safflower oil

2 tablespoons finely chopped onion

1 teaspoon minced garlic

¹/4 cup minced fresh flat-leaf parsley

1 teaspoon minced fresh basil (or ¹/4 teaspoon dried)

1 teaspoon minced fresh oregano (or ¹/4 teaspoon dried)

¹/2 teaspoon freshly ground black pepper, or to taste

Dash of ground cumin

Dash of salt, or to taste

1¹/2 cups cooked soybeans (one 15-ounce can, drained and rinsed)

3 tablespoons freshly squeezed lemon juice

2 tablespoons toasted sesame seeds (see Tip, page 125)

garnish (optional) halved cherry tomatoes, sprigs of fresh flat-leaf parsley

Classic hummus is made from chickpeas; I've adapted it by using soybeans. It's great spread on cucumber rounds, bread, or crackers, or used as a dip or sandwich filling. Hummus should have a spreadable consistency; some cooked beans are moister than others, so the amount of lemon juice needed may vary.

Heat the oil in a small nonstick skillet over medium heat. Add the onion and garlic; cook, stirring occasionally, until the onion is softened, about 2 minutes. Remove from the heat and add the parsley, fresh or dried basil, fresh or dried oregano, pepper, cumin, and salt; stir until the parsley is softened. Set aside.

Put the soybeans and lemon juice into a food processor; process until smooth. Transfer to the skillet; stir in the sesame seeds. Adjust the seasonings to taste.

Per tablespoon: Cal 33/Pro 2.1g/Carb 1.7g/Fat 2g/Chol 0mg/Sod 6mg

ADVANCE PREPARATION The flavor matures if this mixture is made 1 or 2 days in advance; cover and refrigerate. Bring to room temperature before serving.

tip

Don't wash fresh herbs before storage. Wrap the stem ends with a moist paper towel and refrigerate in a sealed plastic bag. Or place the bunch, stems down, in a glass of water and cover with a plastic bag, securing the bag to the glass with a rubber band; change the water every 2 days. With proper storage, fresh herbs will last for about a week, but for the best flavor, use them within a few days. After washing, dry herbs with paper toweling or in a salad spinner before using.

Other Appetizers

pita crisps

In place of store-bought crackers, serve these with Mushroom-Almond Spread (page 3), Roasted Red Pepper Hummus (page 17), Soybean Hummus (page 20), or Tofu Baba Ghanoush (page 13). You can also use them as an accompaniment to soups and salads.

makes 24 chips (4 servings)

Two 6-inch white or whole
  wheat pita breads

4 teaspoons olive oil

2 teaspoons dried oregano
  (do not substitute fresh)

4 tablespoons freshly grated
  Parmesan cheese

Set the oven rack 4 to 5 inches from the broiler heating element; preheat the broiler.

Slice the pita breads in half horizontally. Place the halves on an ungreased baking sheet, rough sides up. Using a pastry brush, lightly spread each with about 1 teaspoon of the olive oil, then sprinkle with about 1/2 teaspoon of the oregano and 1 tablespoon of the Parmesan cheese. Use kitchen shears to cut each pita half into 6 wedges.

Broil until the wedges are lightly browned and the cheese is melted, about 2 minutes. Watch closely! (The wedges will become more crispy as they cool.)

Per serving (6 wedges): Cal 121/Pro 4.6g/Carb 10.5g/Fat 6.7g/Chol 5mg/Sod 224mg

ADVANCE PREPARATION Pita Crisps are best when prepared just before serving. Cover and refrigerate extras for a day or two. Recrisp by heating on a baking sheet for about 5 minutes at 350°F.

VARIATION

❯ Substitute other dried herbs, such as basil or tarragon, for the oregano.

baked tortilla chips *v*

makes 24 chips (4 servings)

Four 6- or 7-inch flour tortillas

So who needs a package? All it takes is a few minutes in the oven, and you've got homemade tortilla chips. Serve these with Sweet Bean—Corn Salsa (page 23) or Tofu Guacamole (page 8). They also make a crispy accompaniment to Soybean Chili (page 54).

Preheat the oven to 400°F.

Use kitchen shears to cut each tortilla into 6 wedges. Arrange the wedges in a single layer on an ungreased baking sheet.

Bake until lightly browned and crisp, about 5 to 7 minutes. (The chips will continue to become crisp as they cool.)

Per serving (6 chips): Cal 127/Pro 4g/Carb 21g/Fat 3g/Chol 0mg/Sod 300mg

ADVANCE PREPARATION Stored in an airtight container at room temperature, these chips will keep for up to 2 days.

tip

When buying baking sheets, select stainless steel instead of aluminum. Aluminum sheets will bend and buckle when heated, resulting in an uneven surface.

sweet bean–corn salsa

Corn and beans have been compatible partners for centuries. The duo goes uptown with sweet beans and white corn kernels. Serve this chilled or at room temperature with Pita Crisps (page 21) or with packaged tortilla chips—or make your own low-fat chips using the recipe on page 22. This salsa also gets star billing in the tortilla salad on page 90.

Put the sweet beans into a small microwave-proof dish; add about 2 tablespoons water. Cover and microwave on high until crisp-tender, about 6 to 8 minutes; drain well. (Or cook the sweet beans in a stovetop steamer.)

Put the sweet beans into a small bowl; stir in the remaining ingredients. Adjust the seasonings to taste.

Refrigerate in a covered container for at least 1 hour before serving.

Per 1/4 cup: Cal 25/Pro 1.4g/Carb 4g/Fat 0.4g/Chol 0mg/Sod 13mg

ADVANCE PREPARATION Covered and refrigerated, this salsa will keep for up to 2 days if you begin with fresh ingredients.

tip

White shoepeg corn, named for its peglike shape, is available frozen. Its kernels are smaller and sweeter than those of yellow corn.

makes 2 cups

1/2 cup frozen sweet beans (see page xxvi)

2 plum tomatoes, cut into 1/4-inch cubes (about 3/4 cup)

1/2 cup frozen white shoepeg corn, thawed (see Tip)

1 medium scallion, coarsely chopped

1 tablespoon freshly squeezed lime juice

1 tablespoon coarsely chopped fresh cilantro, or to taste (do not used dried cilantro; if fresh is unavailable, substitute fresh basil or flat-leaf parsley)

2 teaspoons minced jalapeño pepper, or to taste

1/2 teaspoon minced garlic, or to taste

Dash of freshly ground black pepper, or to taste

batter-dipped tofu
with ginger sauce

For variety, this dish can double as a light entrée. Arrange the tofu atop Chinese wheat-flour noodles, add steamed asparagus spears or stir-fried vegetables, drizzle with the Ginger Sauce, and sprinkle with toasted sesame seeds (see Tip, page 125).

makes 4 servings

1 cup Ginger Sauce
    (page 26)

4 leaves red leaf lettuce

1/2 cup all-purpose white or
    unbleached flour

2 tablespoons toasted wheat
    germ (see Tip)

1/2 teaspoon dried thyme
    (do not substitute fresh)

1/4 teaspoon dried dill weed
    (do not substitute fresh)

1/4 teaspoon paprika

1/4 teaspoon freshly ground
    black pepper

1 large egg

1 tablespoon skim milk

1/4 teaspoon hot pepper sauce

12 ounces silken extra-firm
    tofu, cut into 1-inch
    squares about 1/2 inch
    thick (about 2 cups)

1 tablespoon safflower oil

Prepare the Ginger Sauce; cover and set aside.

Arrange a bed of the lettuce on a serving platter; set aside.

Combine the flour, wheat germ, thyme, dill weed, paprika, and pepper in a small shallow bowl.

Lightly beat the egg in a separate shallow bowl. Stir in the milk and hot pepper sauce.

Piece by piece, gently press the tofu cubes into the flour mixture, covering all sides; dip into the egg mixture and again into the flour mixture. As the cubes are prepared, place them in a single layer on a plate.

Heat the oil in a large nonstick skillet over medium-high heat. Arrange the cubes in a single layer in the skillet; cook until lightly browned, about 3 minutes on each side.

To serve, place the browned tofu cubes atop the lettuce. Pour the warm Ginger Sauce into a small bowl. Provide cocktail forks for dipping the tofu cubes into the sauce.

Per serving: Cal 260/Pro 13.9g/Carb 33.5g/Fat 7.8g/Chol 53mg/Sod 369mg

ADVANCE PREPARATION Covered and refrigerated, the sauce will keep for up to 2 days; reheat gently just before serving. For best results, sauté the tofu just before serving.

VARIATIONS

❯ Substitute $1/4$ cup cholesterol-free egg substitute or 2 egg whites for the egg.

❯ For a firmer texture, substitute pressed tofu (see page xxxii).

tip

Wheat germ, the embryo of the wheat berry, is rich in vitamins, minerals, and protein. Store it in the freezer. Toasted wheat germ, found in the cereal aisle of most supermarkets, is preferable to raw wheat germ in most recipes because of its nutty flavor and slightly crunchy texture. To prevent rancidity, store toasted wheat germ in a tightly closed container in the refrigerator.

ginger sauce   V

This fat-free sauce is one of my favorites because it is so versatile. Serve it with Batter-Dipped Tofu (page 24), Stuffed Mushrooms (page 27), or Vegetable Stir-Fry with Ginger Sauce (page 120). It also adds a special touch when drizzled over steamed vegetables and sprinkled with toasted sesame seeds (see Tip, page 125).

makes 1 cup

6 tablespoons white rice vinegar

6 tablespoons sugar

$3/4$ cup room-temperature water

2 tablespoons low-sodium soy sauce

1 tablespoon cornstarch (see Tip)

2 tablespoons cold water

1 tablespoon finely minced gingerroot

Stir together the vinegar, sugar, $3/4$ cup water, and soy sauce in a small saucepan. Bring the mixture to a boil over medium-high heat. Reduce the heat to medium-low and stir until the sugar is dissolved, about 3 minutes.

Stir together the cornstarch and cold water in a small bowl until smooth; pour into the saucepan. Stir constantly until the mixture is clear and thickened to maple syrup consistency.

Remove the pan from the heat; stir in the gingerroot. Set aside and cover to keep warm.

Per $1/4$ cup: Cal 92/Pro 1g/Carb 22.2g/Fat 0g/Chol 0mg/Sod 280mg

ADVANCE PREPARATION Covered and refrigerated, this sauce will keep for up to 2 days; bring to room temperature or reheat gently before serving.

tip

Cornstarch, a fine white flour obtained from corn, is used as a thickener. It gives sauces a glossy, almost transparent look rather than the cloudy appearance provided by flour thickening. Cornstarch works best when mixed with enough cold water to form a smooth, thin paste, which is then added to a hot mixture near the end of the cooking time. Stir constantly but gently as you add the cornstarch mixture; cook just long enough to thicken. Mixtures thickened with cornstarch will become thin if cooked too long, at too high a temperature, or if not stirred gently. (Also see arrowroot Tip, page 256.)

stuffed mushrooms

This classy appetizer can be readied well ahead. You can also serve these mushrooms as a vegetable accompaniment to entrées such as Curried Tofu en Papillote (page 204), Sherried Tofu Steaks (page 158), or Tofu-Walnut Loaf (page 214). Incidentally, this recipe is a good use for a small amount of leftover soybeans.

makes 12 stuffed mushrooms

Nonstick cooking spray

12 large white mushrooms

1 tablespoon safflower oil

1/4 cup diced red bell pepper

1 tablespoon minced shallot (see Tip)

1/4 cup cooked soybeans, mashed

2 tablespoons dry bread crumbs (see Tip, page 197)

1 tablespoon minced fresh flat-leaf parsley

1 tablespoon finely chopped pecans

2 teaspoons low-sodium soy sauce

2 tablespoons freshly grated Parmesan cheese

Preheat the oven to 350°F.

Oil a medium shallow baking dish with cooking spray.

Remove the mushrooms stems and coarsely chop 3 or 4 of them (to yield 1/3 cup). Discard the remaining stems (or reserve them for another use).

To make the stuffing, heat 2 teaspoons of the oil in a medium nonstick skillet over medium heat. Add the mushroom stems, bell pepper, and shallot; cook, stirring occasionally, until the vegetables are softened but not browned, about 4 minutes.

Remove from the heat. Stir in the soybeans, bread crumbs, parsley, pecans, and soy sauce.

Using your fingers, spread the remaining 1 teaspoon of oil over the mushroom caps and place them in the prepared baking dish. Fill each mushroom cap with the stuffing.

Bake for 15 minutes. Sprinkle with the Parmesan cheese and continue baking until the mushrooms are tender when pierced with a fork and the cheese is melted, about 5 minutes more. Serve warm.

Per mushroom: Cal 36/Pro 1.6g/Carb 2.2g/Fat 2.3g/Chol 1mg/Sod 58mg

ADVANCE PREPARATION Prepare the stuffing and fill the mushroom caps up to 2 hours in advance; cover and refrigerate. Bring to room temperature, bake, and serve immediately.

california rolls

makes 4 rolls (32 pieces)

For the rice

2 cups short-grain white rice
  (sushi rice)

6 cups water

1/4 cup seasoned white rice
  vinegar (see Tip, page 15)

For the wasabi paste

1 tablespoon *wasabi* powder
  (see Tip)

1 tablespoon water

To complete the recipe

1/4 cucumber, peeled and
  seeded, cut into 12 strips
  about 5 inches long by
  1/4 inch wide

1 avocado, cut into 12 strips
  about 5 inches long by
  1/4 inch wide

1 carrot, cut into 12 strips
  about 5 inches long by
  1/4 inch wide

6 ounces silken extra-firm tofu,
  cut into 12 strips about
  5 inches long by 1/4 inch
  wide

Four 7- by 8-inch sheets dried
  seaweed (see Tip)

1/4 cup toasted sesame seeds
  (see Tip, page 125)

Special equipment

plastic wrap

bamboo rolling mat (see Tip)

True sushi expertise requires years of apprenticeship to a master, but with this simplified procedure, "vegetarian sushi" can become a part of your repertoire. The ingredients may require a trip to an Asian market, but I guarantee the results of your efforts will be worthwhile.

Put the rice and water into a large saucepan; bring the water to a boil over high heat. Reduce the heat to low; cover and cook for about 15 to 20 minutes, or until the water is absorbed. Remove from the heat; set aside for 5 to 10 minutes to continue steaming the rice.

Meanwhile, in a small bowl, stir together the *wasabi* powder and water to form a thick paste. Cover and let stand to allow the flavor to mature.

While the rice is cooking, prepare the sushi filling ingredients (cucumber, avocado, carrot, and tofu). After chopping, put the carrot strips into a small microwave-proof dish; add about 2 tablespoons water. Cover and microwave on high until tender, about 3 minutes. (Or cook the carrot in a stovetop steamer.)

When the rice has finished steaming, transfer it to medium bowl. Use a rubber spatula to fold the seasoned rice vinegar into the rice. Set aside, uncovered, to allow the rice to reach room temperature.

Toast the sheets of seaweed over a stove burner: If using a gas stove, wave each sheet of seaweed back and forth about 7 to 8 inches above a medium flame for about 15 seconds on each side. If using an electric stove, turn a burner to high. As the burner heats, wave the seaweed back and forth about 4 to 5 inches above the burner for about 15 seconds on each side.

To assemble each California roll:

1. Place a sheet of seaweed, rough side up, on a cutting board, the longer edge facing you. Use a rubber spatula to spread the rice over the seaweed in an even layer

about $3/8$ inch thick. (Take care not to crush the rice grains.) Sprinkle the surface of the rice with about 1 tablespoon of the sesame seeds. Cover with a sheet of plastic wrap and press lightly.

accompaniments pickled ginger (see Tip), low-sodium soy sauce

2. Flip, turning the seaweed up, rice down. Spread about $1/8$ teaspoon of *wasabi* paste horizontally across the center. Then, also in the center, horizontally from edge to edge, arrange the strips of cucumber, avocado, carrot, and tofu.

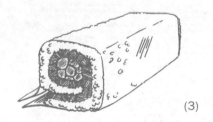

(1)

3. With the plastic wrap in place, roll up by hand, squeezing firmly as you roll. Firmly and evenly press down on each of 4 sides of the roll to form a square. (This can be done more easily by placing a bamboo rolling mat, or *sudare*, around the roll.) Flatten and firm the ends by pressing inward with your hands. Repeat up to this point with the remaining 3 rolls; keep the plastic wrap around the rolls to prevent them from drying out.

(2)

Just before serving, remove the plastic wrap. Place the rolls on a cutting board, seam sides down. Use a sawing motion to cut the rolls in half vertically; then cut each half into 4 equal slices. Moisten the knife with water or vinegar between cuts.

Arrange the California rolls on 4 serving plates. Accompany with small mounds of pickled ginger and the remaining *wasabi* paste. Serve immediately.

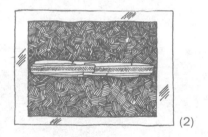

(3)

Eat by hand, dipping in soy sauce or soy sauce mixed with a small amount of the *wasabi* paste. Eating bites of pickled ginger along with the California rolls will enhance the flavors and cleanse the palate.

Per serving ($1/2$ roll = 4 pieces): Cal 226/Pro 6g/Carb 41g/Fat 4.2g/Chol 0mg/Sod 23mg

ADVANCE PREPARATION The rice can be cooked several hours in advance; cover with a damp towel and refrigerate. Bring the rice to room temperature and assemble the rolls just before serving.

VARIATION

❧ Substitute for the cucumber, avocado, and carrot or add other ingredients such as thin radish strips, slivers of scallion, or strips of steamed broccoli stalks.

tips

Authentic wasabi, *or Japanese horseradish, is very expensive and difficult to find. The canned powdered type commonly found in U.S. markets is actually horseradish with mustard powder added. When combined with water to form a thick paste, it develops an intense and pungent flavor. Use sparingly!*

Sheets of seaweed, called nori, *are available in Asian markets and in the gourmet section of some supermarkets. Store at room temperature and away from moisture.*

Pickled ginger is a cool, sharp condiment made from gingerroot that has been marinated in seasoned vinegar. Eat in small bites to cleanse the palate.

For shaping rolled sushi, sushi chefs use a sudare—*a bamboo rolling mat that is made from skewer-type bamboo sticks woven together with string. This inexpensive accessory is available in most Asian markets.*

roasted soybeans

Roasted soybeans can be purchased in health food stores and some supermarkets, but by using presoaked (not cooked or canned) soybeans, you can easily make them at home. Keep these on hand to serve as an appetizer, a crunchy snack, or a garnish for salads.

makes 6 cups

Nonstick cooking spray
    (see Tip)

3 cups whole dried soybeans,
    soaked using either the
    traditional or quick-soak
    method (see page xxiv)

Dash of salt, or to taste

Dash of chili powder,
    or to taste

Preheat the oven to 300°F.

Lightly oil a baking sheet.

Spread the soybeans in a single layer on the prepared baking sheet. Sprinkle with the salt and chili powder.

Bake, stirring the beans or shaking the pan every 15 minutes, for about 1 hour, or until the soybeans are crunchy and lightly browned.

Transfer the soybeans to a bowl and allow to come to room temperature before serving or storing.

Per 1/4 cup: Cal 62/Pro 4.9g/Carb 4.8g/Fat 2.6g/Chol 0mg/Sod 1mg

ADVANCE PREPARATION Stored in an airtight container at room temperature, Roasted Soybeans will keep for up to 2 weeks.

VARIATION

➘ Substitute curry powder for the chili powder.

tip

To make your own spray oil, pour an unflavored oil, such as safflower, canola, or soy, into a small container fitted with a pump sprayer. Use for oiling baking and cooking pans in place of commercially produced nonstick cooking sprays. Olive oil can also be used in this spray form for reduced-fat cooking and to apply a light touch of oil to green salads.

Soups

Chilled Soups

Roasted Red Bell Pepper Soup

Beet Soup

Soybean Gazpacho

Chilled Fresh Tomato Bisque

Puréed Soups

Fresh Pea Soup

Curried Corn and Pepper
   Chowder

Spicy Soybean Soup

Creamy Acorn Squash Soup

Creamy Tomato-Basil Soup

Parmesan Cream

Curried Sweet Potato Soup

Chunky Soups

Potage Mentonnaise

Chinese Noodle Soup

Soybean Chili

Carrot-Cashew Soup

Tuscan Soybean Soup

I have always loved soup. When I was a child, even the canned variety would satisfy the craving. But these days it definitely must be homemade. In the course of writing cookbooks and teaching cooking classes, I have developed recipes for hundreds of soups—soups that can be made in 15 minutes and the slow-simmered type; soups for one and to serve a crowd; vegetarian and chicken soups; chilled soups, hot soups; light first-course soups and hearty entrée soups. Until working on this assignment, I had not experimented with soy-based soups. These are now some of my favorites. Here's why.

Traditionally, creamy soups are thickened with a roux— a cooked mixture of flour and usually butter—to which cream is added. When puréed, tofu can create the same creamy texture, or "mouth feel," with a fraction of the calories and fat. I like to use silken firm tofu for its ease in puréeing and its delicate flavor; if you prefer, you can substitute regular soft tofu. My food processor or blender gets the job done in seconds. When puréeing the ingredients for use in recipes like Curried Sweet Potato Soup (page 50), it is important to push down the mixture several times from the sides of the work bowl or blender container in order to achieve a consistent texture. Like all of the soups in this chapter, tofu-thickened soups can be made in advance, but most become thicker while standing and need to be thinned before serving. Water or vegetable stock, or sometimes soy milk or tomato juice, will provide the necessary additional liquid. (When it is necessary to use this procedure, I have described it in the Advance Preparation information.)

For thinner cream-style soups such as Chilled Fresh Tomato Bisque (page 40), soy milk is the answer; it adds a lighter smooth texture with a slight sweetness. Because soy milk may curdle if boiled, especially when a soup contains an acidic ingredient like tomatoes, it's important to stir in the soy milk over medium heat at the end of the cooking time.

Chunky soups like chili and minestrone benefit from the addition of cooked whole soybeans to become a satisfying, down-to-earth meal. No need to simmer these soups for hours; using canned soybeans is perfectly acceptable and positions these bean soups in the quick-to-prepare category. Like other beans, soybeans can be puréed to serve as a soup thickener, as in Spicy Soybean Soup (page 44).

A tasty vegetable stock is the base for many of these soups. Making stock from scratch is simply not practical for most cooks today, but there are other good alternatives. My choice is to use a high-quality unsalted vegetable stock powder, which I buy in bulk at a natural foods store. It is made from ground dehydrated vegetables—no preservatives, no salt. It keeps forever in my kitchen cabinet. Since it is unseasoned, the mild flavor blends with the herbs and other soup ingredients. To make 1 cup of vegetable stock, I dissolve about 1 teaspoon of the powder in 1 cup of water. Some health food stores sell a similar product in cube form. Most vegetable stock powders from the supermarket contain salt along with flavor enhancers and preservatives, so read the small print. Some of my cooking class students tell me they prefer canned vegetable stock; there are many to choose from on the shelves of supermarkets and health food stores.

The first four soups in this chapter are meant to be served chilled; the first two are simply puréed and require no cooking; remember these on busy steamy summer days. I suggest serving them icy cold in chilled bowls. Among the warm soups, Soybean Chili (page 54) and Potage Mentonnaise (page 51) are two of my favorite winter entrée soups because they're so hearty and aromatic.

Soups are ideal when you're looking for do-ahead preparations, which is why I often choose them when I'll be entertaining. In fact, many of them, especially those that are tomato-based, like Soybean Gazpacho (page 38), actually benefit from being made one day before serving to allow time for the flavors to blend. While many of the lighter soups make a delicious first course, others are hearty enough to stand on their own as a main course. To round out the feast, make a generous green salad and add a basket of homemade muffins. Or you might choose complements like Bruschetta (page 163), Pita Crisps (page 21), Baked Tortilla Chips (page 22), or warm crusty bread. Serve them with a spread from the Appetizer chapter, such as Mushroom-Almond Spread (page 3) or Sun-Dried Tomato–Tofu Spread (page 4).

The soup garnish is important to both presentation and taste; sometimes this extra touch can also contribute crunchy texture, such as Herbed Garlic Croutons (page 65)—or creaminess, such as Parmesan Cream (page 49). Garnishes don't have to be fussy. Something as simple as a sprig of fresh herb or a dollop of yogurt will dress up the dish. I've provided suggestions with each recipe.

Soups recipes are especially adaptable. Many are an ideal destination for the odds and ends of vegetables you have on hand. Adapt, improvise, and enjoy!

Chilled Soups

roasted red bell pepper soup

Rather than roasting your own red bell peppers to make this uncooked chilled soup, for no-fuss preparation you can substitute a 12-ounce jar of roasted red bell peppers found at most supermarkets. Drain the peppers well and purée them with the other ingredients.

makes 4 servings

2 roasted red bell peppers (see Tip, page 92)

1 1/2 cups mashed silken firm tofu (12 ounces)

1 1/4 cups vegetable stock (see page 34)

3 tablespoons red wine vinegar

1 tablespoon extra-virgin olive oil

2 teaspoons minced garlic

1 teaspoon sugar, or to taste

1/2 teaspoon freshly ground black pepper, or to taste

1/4 teaspoon salt, or to taste

2 tablespoons minced fresh chives (see Tip)

1 tablespoon minced fresh thyme (or 1 teaspoon dried)

garnish (optional) nonfat sour cream or plain yogurt

Put the bell peppers, tofu, vegetable stock, vinegar, oil, garlic, sugar, pepper, and salt into a food processor; process until smooth and creamy. Stir in the chives and thyme. Adjust the seasonings to taste.

Refrigerate in a covered container for at least 3 hours before serving chilled.

Per serving (3/4 cup): Cal 110/Pro 6.7g/Carb 7.4g/Fat 6g/Chol 0mg/Sod 167mg

ADVANCE PREPARATION Covered and refrigerated, this soup will keep for up to 3 days. Since it thickens while standing, stir in water or vegetable stock as needed.

tip

Chives are a delicately flavored member of the onion family. Given a choice, buy potted chives; they are fresher than cut. Use scissors to snip off what you need, cutting off whole blades rather than chopping the tops off all the blades. If you buy cut chives, look for those with a uniform green color and no signs of wilting; wrap them in damp paper towels, seal in a plastic bag, and refrigerate for up to a week. When using in cooked dishes, add chives near the end of the cooking time to retain their flavor. Avoid dried chopped chives, which have lost their characteristic flavor and aroma. If fresh chives are unavailable, substitute scallion greens cut into julienne strips.

beet soup

This bright red soup gains extra pizzazz when garnished with dollops of nonfat plain yogurt or nonfat sour cream; top with orange zest and toasted chopped walnuts (see Tip, page 50) to add texture, color, and compatible flavors. I like Beet Soup best chilled, but on cool days, serve it warm.

Put the beets into a medium saucepan; cover with water. Bring the water to a boil over high heat. Reduce the heat to medium and cook until tender, about 20 to 25 minutes.

Rinse the beets under cold water; then drain, slip off the skins, and quarter.

Put the beets and the remaining ingredients into a food processor; process until smooth. Adjust the seasonings to taste.

To serve chilled, refrigerate in a covered container for at least 3 hours before serving.

Per serving (1 cup): Cal 116/Pro 5.1g/Carb 12.2g/Fat 5.2g/Chol 0mg/Sod 79mg

ADVANCE PREPARATION Covered and refrigerated, this soup will keep for up to 3 days. Serve chilled or reheat.

tip

Purchase beets with green tops that are crisp and bright, but because they pull moisture from the beets, the greens should be removed before storage (leave about 1 inch of the stem attached). Store beets, refrigerated in a plastic bag, for up to 3 weeks. Just before cooking, wash the surface gently without piercing the skin; to minimize nutrient loss, peel after cooking.

makes 4 servings

4 medium beets, trimmed, leaving 1 inch of stem, and rinsed (see Tip)

1 tablespoon olive oil

1/4 cup coarsely chopped yellow onion

1 cup mashed silken firm tofu

1 cup freshly squeezed orange juice

1 teaspoon grated orange rind

Dash of ground nutmeg, or to taste

Dash of freshly ground black pepper, or to taste

Dash of salt, or to taste

garnish *(optional)* nonfat sour cream or plain yogurt

soybean gazpacho

With the addition of soybeans, my favorite chilled soup from The 15-Minute Vegetarian Gourmet *(Macmillan, 1987) becomes a light but filling summer entrée. It is quite thick; if you prefer a thinner consistency, stir in tomato juice or water when mixing the soup or after refrigerating.*

makes 4 servings

One 15-ounce can tomato sauce

2 tablespoons extra-virgin olive oil

2 tablespoons red wine vinegar

1 teaspoon honey

1 1/2 cups cooked soybeans (one 15-ounce can, drained and rinsed)

1 medium tomato, cut into 1/2-inch cubes

1/2 cucumber, seeded and cut into 1/2-inch cubes

1/2 cup coarsely chopped green bell pepper

1/2 cup coarsely chopped red bell pepper

1 rib celery, finely chopped

1/2 teaspoon minced garlic (see Tip)

1/2 teaspoon freshly ground black pepper, or to taste

1/2 teaspoon hot pepper sauce, or to taste

garnish *(optional)* Herbed Garlic Croutons (page 65), plain yogurt or nonfat sour cream topped with minced fresh chives

Combine the tomato sauce, olive oil, vinegar, and honey in a medium bowl. Stir in the remaining ingredients. Adjust the seasonings to taste.

Refrigerate in a covered container for at least 2 hours before serving.

Per serving (1 cup): Cal 250/Pro 14.2g/Carb 18.5g/Fat 13.3g/Chol 0mg/Sod 633mg

ADVANCE PREPARATION Covered and refrigerated, this soup will keep for up to 4 days. Since it thickens while standing, stir in water or tomato juice as needed.

tips

Select garlic heads that are clean and firm to the touch. Store them in a cool, dark, well-ventilated place such as a garlic cellar (a ceramic pot with holes and a lid), or seal in a plastic bag and refrigerate. Unbroken bulbs will keep for up to 2 months; once broken from the bulb, individual cloves will keep for up to 10 days. Sprouted garlic cloves are fine to use but less flavorful.

To peel garlic, place the flat blade of a chef's knife on a garlic clove; pound with your fist to flatten the clove. This separates the skin and automatically crushes the garlic. Crushing, pressing, or puréeing garlic releases the essential oils and flavor better than slicing the cloves or leaving them whole.

Marinated minced garlic is an acceptable alternative to fresh garlic. It is sold in the produce department of most supermarkets. Always use a clean spoon when measuring it from the jar and refrigerate after opening to prevent bacteria growth. (For reasons of food safety, it is not recommended to mince your own garlic and store it in olive oil.) Avoid using dried garlic, which is bitter and will not provide the distinctive garlic flavor and aroma.

Garlic develops a bitter taste if permitted to brown, so add it near the end of the cooking period unless there is an abundance of moisture in the pan.

chilled fresh tomato bisque

makes 6 servings

1 tablespoon safflower oil

1/4 cup finely chopped onion

2 teaspoons minced garlic

4 large tomatoes, peeled and
    chopped (about 5 cups)
    (see Tip, page 45)

2 cups vegetable stock
    (see page 34)

1 tablespoon minced fresh
    oregano (or 1 teaspoon
    dried)

1/2 teaspoon ground cumin
    (see Tip)

1/4 teaspoon freshly ground
    black pepper, or to taste

Pinch of red pepper flakes,
    or to taste

Dash of salt, or to taste

1 cup soy milk

1/4 cup tomato paste
    (see Tip, page 4)

2 tablespoons freshly
    squeezed lime juice

garnish (optional) sprigs of
fresh flat-leaf parsley or
cilantro

Here soy milk replaces the cream that typically adds texture and richness. Plan ahead to allow chilling time before serving. It's heaven-sent on hot midsummer days when fresh tomatoes are at their juicy best. (On cool days I serve the bisque hot.)

Heat the oil in a large saucepan or Dutch oven over medium-high heat. Add the onion and garlic; cook, stirring constantly, until softened but not browned, about 2 minutes.

Stir in the tomatoes, vegetable stock, fresh or dried oregano, cumin, pepper, red pepper flakes, and salt. When the liquid comes to a boil, reduce the heat to medium; cover and cook until the tomatoes are softened, about 10 minutes. Remove the pan from the heat and allow to cool.

Pour the soy milk and tomato paste into a food processor or blender; process until smooth. Add half of the tomato-stock mixture; process until smooth. Transfer to a refrigerator container. Process the remaining tomato-stock mixture until smooth; stir into the soup. Adjust the seasonings to taste.

Cover the container and refrigerate the soup for at least 3 hours. Stir in the lime juice just before serving.

Per serving (1 cup): Cal 80/Pro 3g/Carb 9.5g/Fat 3.3g/Chol 0mg/Sod 77mg

ADVANCE PREPARATION Covered and refrigerated, this soup will keep for up to 3 days.

tip

Cumin is the dried fruit of a plant in the parsley family. Available in both seed and ground forms, it provides an aromatic, nutty, and peppery flavor that is widely used in Mexican and Indian cooking. It is an essential ingredient in chili powder and curry powder. Like all seeds, herbs, and spices, cumin should be stored in a cool, dark place, where it will keep for up to 6 months.

Puréed Soups

fresh pea soup

When we think of pea soup, we usually think of a slow-cooked soup made with dried split peas and flavored with ham. This vegan version, made with frozen fresh peas, is quicker and fresher tasting. It's adapted from my pea soup recipe in The 15-Minute Single Gourmet (Macmillan, 1994).

Heat the oil in a large saucepan or Dutch oven over medium-high heat. Add the celery and onion; cook, stirring occasionally, until the vegetables are crisp-tender, about 4 minutes. Add the garlic during the last minute.

Stir in the vegetable stock and peas. When the liquid begins to boil, reduce the heat to medium; cover and cook until the vegetables are tender, about 5 minutes.

Meanwhile, put the carrots into a small microwave-proof dish; add about 2 tablespoons water. Cover and microwave on high until tender, about 5 minutes; drain well. (Or cook the carrots in a stovetop steamer.)

Transfer the pea-stock mixture to the bowl of a food processor; add $1/2$ cup of the soy milk and process until smooth.

Pour the puréed mixture into the pan; stir in the remaining 1 cup of soy milk, the cooked carrots, white pepper, and nutmeg. Stir gently over medium heat until the mixture is heated through, about 5 minutes. Adjust the seasonings to taste.

Per serving (1 cup): Cal 216/Pro 10.8g/Carb 31.1g/Fat 5.4g/Chol 0mg/Sod 184mg

ADVANCE PREPARATION Covered and refrigerated, this soup will keep for up to 3 days. Since it thickens while standing, stir in soy milk or vegetable stock as needed when reheating.

makes 4 servings

1 tablespoon safflower oil

2 ribs celery, finely chopped

$1/2$ cup finely chopped onion

$1/2$ teaspoon minced garlic

$1 1/2$ cups vegetable stock
(see page 34)

One 16-ounce bag frozen baby peas (see Tip, page 107)

4 carrots, cut into $1/8$-inch-thick slices

$1 1/2$ cups soy milk

Dash of white pepper,
or to taste

Dash of nutmeg (preferably fresh ground), or to taste
(see Tip, page 239)

garnish (optional) Herbed Garlic Croutons (page 65), Parmesan Cream (page 49), chopped fresh flat-leaf parsley, freshly grated Parmesan cheese

curried corn and pepper chowder ✓

makes 4 servings

2 tablespoons safflower oil

$1/2$ cup diced green bell pepper

$1/2$ cup diced red bell pepper

$1/4$ cup minced shallots

2 teaspoons curry powder,
    or to taste

One 16-ounce bag frozen corn,
    thawed (about 3 cups)

1 cup vegetable stock
    (see page 34)

$1/2$ teaspoon freshly ground
    black pepper, or to taste

3 cups soy milk

garnish *(optional)* paprika,
shredded cheddar cheese

This is a perfect way to use corn in or out of season. When fresh corn is available, use about 3 cobs in place of the frozen corn; cook and then cut from the cob. Roasted corn is especially tasty. See the Tips for cooking instructions.

Heat the oil in a large saucepan or Dutch oven over medium-high heat. Add the bell peppers; cook, stirring occasionally, until tender, about 4 minutes. Add the shallots during last minute; stir until tender but not browned. Add the curry powder; stir for about 30 seconds.

Stir in the corn, vegetable stock, and pepper. When the liquid begins to boil, reduce the heat to medium; cover and cook until the vegetables are tender, about 5 minutes.

Transfer 2 cups of the corn-pepper mixture to the bowl of a food processor. Add 1 cup of the soy milk. Process until the mixture is nearly smooth.

Pour the puréed mixture into the saucepan; stir in the remaining soy milk. Stir gently over medium heat until the mixture is heated through, about 5 minutes. Adjust the seasonings to taste.

Per serving (1$1/4$ cups): Cal 293/Pro 11.8g/Carb 38.8g/Fat 10.1g/Chol 0mg/Sod 89mg

ADVANCE PREPARATION Covered and refrigerated, this soup will keep for up to 2 days.

VARIATION

⟍ For a spicier soup, stir in a pinch of cayenne or red pepper flakes along with the black pepper.

tips

Because the sugar immediately begins to convert to starch when corn is picked, it is best to buy fresh corn for immediate use. To make the most of corn's natural sweetness, refrigerate it for no more than 1 day before using.

To cook corn on the cob, remove the husks and snap off the ends of the cobs; pull off the silk. Add the husked ears to a pot of boiling water; cover and allow the water to return to a boil. (Adding salt will toughen the corn; a little sugar will enhance the corn's sweetness.) Cook only long enough to tenderize the kernels, about 3 to 5 minutes.

To microwave, secure the ends of the husks with string or individually wrap husked corn in waxed paper and cook for 3 to 5 minutes; or place it in a covered dish with about 2 tablespoons water and cook for about 5 to 7 minutes.

To steam, place whole or cut-up ears of corn in a vegetable steamer. Cover and cook over boiling water until tender, about 8 to 10 minutes.

To oven-roast corn, loosen the top of the husks and pull out the silk; then replace the husks and twist the tops to keep them in place or tie them with kitchen string. Soak the corn in cold water for 5 minutes. Set the corn on a baking sheet or directly on the oven rack; roast at 375°F until tender and lightly browned, about 20 to 30 minutes.

makes 4 servings

1 tablespoon olive oil

1/2 cup coarsely chopped
    celery

1/4 cup coarsely chopped onion

1 teaspoon minced garlic

2 cups vegetable stock
    (see page 34)

1 1/2 cups cooked soybeans
    (one 15-ounce can,
    drained and rinsed)

2 large tomatoes, peeled and
    cut into 1/2-inch cubes
    (about 1 1/2 cups) (see Tip)

1 tablespoon minced jalapeño
    pepper, or to taste

1 teaspoon ground cumin

1 tablespoon minced fresh
    oregano (or 1 teaspoon
    dried)

1/2 teaspoon freshly ground
    black pepper, or to taste

Dash of salt, or to taste

1 tablespoon minced fresh
    cilantro (do not use
    dried cilantro; if fresh is
    unavailable, substitute
    minced fresh flat-leaf
    parsley) (see Tip)

garnish *(optional)* plain
yogurt, diced red bell peppers,
minced hard-cooked eggs,
sprigs of fresh cilantro

spicy soybean soup

Although this nourishing soup is easy to make, its flavors are anything but simple. You can adjust the amount of jalapeño pepper to suit your addiction or aversion to heat.

Heat the oil in a large saucepan or Dutch oven over medium-high heat. Add the celery and onion; cook, stirring occasionally, until the vegetables are tender, about 4 minutes. Add the garlic during the last minute.

Reduce the heat to medium. Stir in the vegetable stock, soybeans, tomatoes, jalapeño pepper, cumin, dried oregano (if using), pepper, and salt. Stir occasionally until the tomatoes and jalapeño pepper are softened, about 5 minutes. Stir in the fresh oregano (if using) and cilantro.

Use a ladle to transfer 1/2 cup of the soup mixture to a blender or food processor; process until smooth. Pour back into the pan; stir until the soup is heated through. Adjust the seasonings to taste.

Per serving (1 1/2 cups): Cal 187/Pro 12.6g/Carb 11.9g/Fat 9.9g/Chol 0mg/Sod 87mg

ADVANCE PREPARATION Covered and refrigerated, this soup will keep for up to 2 days. Since it thickens while standing, stir in water as needed when reheating.

VARIATIONS

For a milder flavor, substitute 1 tablespoon minced Anaheim pepper or 1 tablespoon canned diced mild green chilies (drained) for the fresh jalapeño pepper.

For a spicier soup, add a pinch of chili powder and/or cayenne when stirring in the cumin and oregano.

tips

To peel a tomato, first core it with a paring knife, removing the stem end and white center; cut an "X" on the bottom of the tomato, carefully cutting just through the skin. Immerse it in a pot of boiling water just long enough to loosen the skin without cooking the tomato (5 seconds for a very ripe tomato, 10 to 20 seconds for a firmer tomato). Remove the tomato with a slotted spoon and immediately plunge it into a bowl of very cold water; let stand about 1 minute. When the tomato is cool enough to handle, use a paring knife to slip off the skin (which will be very loose).

Seeding is really not necessary, but if you prefer your tomato soups and sauces seedless, here's how: cut tomatoes in half crosswise and, holding each half in the palm of your hand, gently squeeze out the seeds.

Cilantro, often sold as "fresh coriander" or "Chinese parsley," is a cornerstone of Vietnamese, Thai, Asian, Indian, and Mexican cuisines. The ancient herb has a distinctive pungent flavor and fragrance that enhance highly spiced foods. Choose leaves with a bright, even color and no sign of wilting. (See page 20 for tips on the storage of fresh herbs.) The leaves are often used uncooked; their interesting appearance makes them an attractive garnish. If adding to a cooked recipe, do so near the end of the cooking period to retain full flavor. The dried leaves lack fresh cilantro's distinctive flavor and are an unacceptable substitution; instead use fresh flat-leaf parsley. Ground coriander, an ingredient in most curry powders, is made from the ground seeds of the plant and serves a different purpose from coriander leaves in cooking.

creamy acorn squash soup

Acorn squash is available year-round, but it is at its best early in the fall through the winter. For variety, try substituting other types of winter squash (see Tip).

makes 6 servings

2 tablespoons safflower oil

1 cup coarsely chopped onion

1 tablespoon curry powder
(see Tip)

3 cups vegetable stock
(see page 34)

2 large acorn squash, peeled,
seeded, and cut into
1-inch cubes (about
6 cups) (see Tips)

2 apples, peeled, cored,
and chopped

1 cup mashed silken firm tofu

1 cup apple juice

1/4 teaspoon freshly ground
black pepper, or to taste

Dash of salt, or to taste

garnish *(optional)* thin apple
slices

Heat the oil in a large saucepan or Dutch oven over medium-high heat. Add the onion; cook, stirring occasionally, until tender but not browned, about 4 minutes. Add the curry powder; stir for about 30 seconds.

Stir in the vegetable stock, squash, and apples; increase the heat to high. When the liquid comes to a boil, reduce the heat to medium; cover and cook until the squash and apples are very tender, about 20 minutes. Remove from the heat.

Transfer the soup to a large bowl. Put 2 cups of the soup and 1/4 cup of the tofu into a food processor or blender; process until the mixture is smooth. Then pour the puréed mixture into the pan. Repeat with the remaining soup and tofu.

Add the apple juice, pepper, and, salt to the pan. Stir over medium heat until the soup is warmed through. Adjust the seasonings to taste.

Per serving (1 1/3 cups): Cal 258/Pro 5.5g/Carb 44.9g/Fat 6.3g/Chol 0mg/Sod 50mg

ADVANCE PREPARATION Covered and refrigerated, this soup will keep for up to 2 days.

tips

Curry powder, a combination of many herbs and spices, is blended in literally thousands of versions. Domestic curry powders are usually quite mild. Imported brands often are more flavorful; some provide several choices labeled mild, medium, or hot.

Squash are divided into two categories, summer squash and winter squash. Summer squash (such as zucchini, pattypan, and crookneck) have thin, edible skins and soft seeds; they cook quickly because of their high water content. Winter squash (such as acorn, butternut, and Hubbard) have hard, thick skins and seeds that should be removed for cooking. Their deep yellow to orange flesh is very firm and requires lengthy cooking to become tender.

Summer squash should be refrigerated in a plastic bag for no more than 5 days. The hard skin of a winter squash allows for longer storage; it does not need to be refrigerated and will keep in a cool, dark place for a month or more.

creamy tomato-basil soup

makes 4 servings

One 28-ounce can Italian (plum) tomatoes, with juice (see Tip, page 119)

1$\frac{1}{2}$ cups mashed silken firm tofu (12 ounces)

1 teaspoon sugar

1 tablespoon olive oil

$\frac{1}{2}$ cup finely chopped onion

1 teaspoon minced garlic

$\frac{1}{4}$ cup minced fresh basil (or 1 teaspoon dried)

1 teaspoon freshly ground black pepper, or to taste

Dash of salt, or to taste

garnish *(optional)* Parmesan Cream (following page) or Tofu-Chèvre Spread (page 5), Herbed Garlic Croutons (page 65), sprigs of fresh basil

This is tomato soup for grown-ups. A hint of tartness and cheese makes Parmesan Cream the perfect flavor complement and garnish. Accompany this soup with Bruschetta (page 163) for a light but satisfying meal.

Put the tomatoes with juice, tofu, and sugar into a food processor or blender; process until the mixture is creamy and smooth. Set aside.

Heat the oil in a large saucepan or Dutch oven over medium-high heat (see Tip). Add the onion; cook, stirring occasionally, until tender but not browned, about 4 minutes. Add the garlic during the last minute.

Reduce the heat to medium. Pour the tomato-tofu mixture and the dried basil (if using) into the pan; stir constantly until the soup is heated through. Stir in the fresh basil (if using), pepper, and salt. Adjust the seasonings to taste.

Per serving (1 cup): Cal 150/Pro 8.4g/Carb 14.4g/Fat 6.5g/Chol 0mg/Sod 390mg

ADVANCE PREPARATION Covered and refrigerated, this soup will keep for up to 2 days.

tip

Avoid cooking tomatoes in untreated aluminum or cast-iron pans. A chemical reaction will give the tomatoes a brownish color and will affect the flavor.

parmesan cream

Use this versatile uncooked creamy mixture as a garnish for creamy soups, such as Curried Sweet Potato Soup (page 50) and Creamy Tomato-Basil Soup (previous page), to add visual appeal, flavor, and texture. Make this in advance, since it can be refrigerated for up to a week; ideally, bring to room temperature before using.

makes ¹/₂ cup

¹/₂ cup nonfat plain yogurt
   (see Tip)

2 tablespoons freshly grated
   Parmesan cheese

¹/₄ teaspoon freshly ground
   black pepper, or to taste

Stir together all the ingredients in a small bowl. Adjust the seasoning to taste.

Per tablespoon: Cal 15/Pro 1.4g/Carb 1.1g/Fat 0.5g/Chol 2mg/Sod 38mg

ADVANCE PREPARATION Covered and refrigerated, this will keep for up to 1 week.

tip

Check the expiration date when buying yogurt; if refrigerated, it will keep for 1 week beyond that date. The watery layer in yogurt cartons is simply the whey rising to the top. Stir it back in; it has nothing to do with the age or quality of the yogurt.

yumm......

curried sweet potato soup

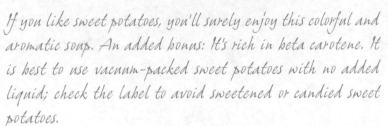

makes 4 servings

3 cups vegetable stock
(see page 34)

One 18-ounce can sweet
potatoes, drained (a
15-ounce can will do)

1 1/2 cups mashed silken firm
tofu (12 ounces)

1 tablespoon safflower oil

1/4 cup minced shallots

1 tablespoon curry powder,
or to taste

1/4 teaspoon freshly ground
black pepper, or to taste

Pinch red pepper flakes,
or to taste

garnish *(optional)* freshly
ground black pepper, plain
yogurt or Parmesan Cream
(page 49), toasted chopped
walnuts (see Tip)

If you like sweet potatoes, you'll surely enjoy this colorful and aromatic soup. An added bonus: It's rich in beta carotene. It is best to use vacuum-packed sweet potatoes with no added liquid; check the label to avoid sweetened or candied sweet potatoes.

Pour the vegetable stock, sweet potatoes, and tofu into a food processor; process until the mixture is smooth and creamy. Set aside.

Heat the oil in a large saucepan or Dutch oven over medium heat. Add the shallots; cook, stirring constantly, until tender but not browned, about 2 minutes. Add the curry powder; stir for about 30 seconds.

Add the sweet potato mixture, pepper, and red pepper flakes; stir constantly until the soup is heated through. Adjust the seasonings to taste.

Per serving (1 cup): Cal 218/Pro 8.6g/Carb 31.6g/Fat 6.4g/Chol 0mg/Sod 105mg

ADVANCE PREPARATION Covered and refrigerated, this soup will keep for up to 2 days.

tip

Toasting enhances the flavor of most nuts, allowing you to achieve more intense flavors with fewer nuts—and less fat. To toast nuts on the stovetop, put them into a dry skillet over medium-high heat. Watch closely as you stir or toss them until they are golden brown, about 4 to 5 minutes. If you prefer, nuts can be toasted on a baking sheet or pie plate in a 375°F oven for about 5 to 10 minutes, stirring frequently. Prevent burning by removing the nuts from the skillet or baking pan as soon as they are toasted.

Chunky Soups

potage mentonnaise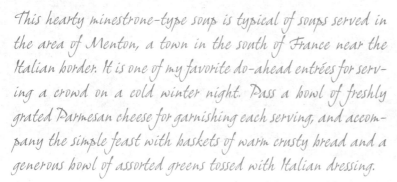

This hearty minestrone-type soup is typical of soups served in the area of Menton, a town in the south of France near the Italian border. It is one of my favorite do-ahead entrées for serving a crowd on a cold winter night. Pass a bowl of freshly grated Parmesan cheese for garnishing each serving, and accompany the simple feast with baskets of warm crusty bread and a generous bowl of assorted greens tossed with Italian dressing.

Heat the oil in a large saucepan or Dutch oven over medium-high heat. Add the onion and 1 teaspoon of the garlic; cook, stirring constantly, until softened but not browned, about 3 minutes. Stir in the vegetable stock, tomatoes with juice, potatoes, zucchini, green beans, and cauliflower. Increase the heat to high; when the liquid comes to a boil, reduce the heat to medium and stir in the soybeans. Cook, uncovered, until the vegetables are tender, about 25 minutes.

Stir in the spaghetti; continue to cook, uncovered, until the spaghetti is tender, about 10 to 12 minutes.

Meanwhile, in a small bowl, stir together the tomato paste, parsley, fresh or dried basil and oregano, pepper, and remaining 1 teaspoon of garlic. Set aside.

Whisk 1/2 cup of the soup into the tomato paste mixture, then add it to the soup and stir gently until heated through. Adjust the seasonings to taste.

Per serving (1 1/2 cups): Cal 222/Pro 10.6g/Carb 28.5g/Fat 7.2g/Chol 0mg/Sod 246mg

ADVANCE PREPARATION If this soup is made one day in advance and refrigerated, the flavors will blend and develop. Covered and refrigerated, it will keep for up to 3 days. Since it thickens while standing, stir in water, vegetable stock, or tomato juice as needed when reheating.

makes 8 servings

2 tablespoons olive oil

1/2 cup finely chopped onion

2 teaspoons minced garlic

6 cups vegetable stock (see page 34)

One 28-ounce can Italian tomatoes, with juice, tomatoes halved (see Tip, page 119)

2 potatoes, cut into 1/2-inch cubes (about 4 cups)

2 medium zucchini, coarsely chopped (about 2 cups)

2 cups green beans in 2-inch lengths

2 cups cauliflower florets

1 1/2 cups cooked soybeans (one 15-ounce can, drained and rinsed)

4 ounces spaghetti, broken into 2-inch lengths

One 6-ounce can tomato paste

3/4 cup chopped fresh flat-leaf parsley

1/4 cup minced fresh basil (or 2 tablespoons dried)

2 tablespoons minced fresh oregano (or 1 tablespoon dried)

1/2 teaspoon freshly ground black pepper, or to taste

Dash of salt, or to taste

garnish *(optional)* freshly grated Parmesan cheese

chinese noodle soup

makes 6 servings

8 cups vegetable stock
(see page 34)

8 ounces Chinese wheat-flour
noodles

4 ounces oyster mushrooms,
stems removed and
discarded, tops cut
into $1/4$-inch-wide strips
(see Tip)

20 snow peas, stems and
strings removed

$1/2$ cup coarsely shredded carrot

2 medium scallions, chopped

$1/4$ cup diced red bell pepper

2 tablespoons low-sodium soy
sauce, or to taste

1 teaspoon minced garlic

$1/2$ teaspoon red pepper
flakes, or to taste

$1/8$ teaspoon ground white
pepper, or to taste

12 ounces silken extra-firm
tofu, cut into $1/2$-inch
cubes (about 2 cups)

2 teaspoons dark sesame oil

garnish (optional) chopped
scallions, toasted sesame
seeds (see Tip, page 125)

The typical proportion of broth to solid ingredients is reversed in this soup. Here a large helping of noodles fills the bowls, then the spicy broth, tofu, and vegetables are poured atop. Make nothing else for dinner! Serve the soup in large bowls with chopsticks and Chinese soupspoons. Adjust the amount of red pepper flakes if you prefer your soup less fiery.

Pour the vegetable stock into a large saucepan or Dutch oven; cover and heat over high heat just until the liquid comes to a boil.

Stir in the noodles, mushrooms, snow peas, carrot, scallions, bell pepper, soy sauce, garlic, red pepper flakes, and white pepper. When the liquid returns to a boil, reduce the heat to medium; cover and cook until the noodles and vegetables are tender, about 5 minutes.

Gently stir in the tofu cubes and sesame oil; heat until the tofu is warm. Adjust the seasonings to taste.

To serve, use tongs to fill large soup bowls with the cooked noodles. Ladle the broth, tofu, and vegetables over the noodles.

Per serving ($1^{1/3}$ cups): Cal 125/Pro 8.2g/Carb 13g/Fat 4.5g/Chol 0mg/Sod 370mg

ADVANCE PREPARATION This soup is best when prepared just before serving. Covered and refrigerated, it will keep for up to 1 day. After standing, the stock becomes absorbed into the noodles; add more as needed when reheating.

VARIATIONS

Substitute white or shiitake mushrooms for the oyster mushrooms.

❧ With the noodles, add other vegetables, such as $1/2$ cup sliced bok choy, including coarsely chopped leaves (see Tip, page 123), or frozen baby peas (see Tip, page 107).

❧ Substitute 1 teaspoon hot sesame oil (or to taste) for the sesame oil and red pepper flakes.

❧ With the sesame oil, stir in about 2 tablespoons minced fresh cilantro.

tip

Oyster mushrooms (also called oyster caps, tree mushrooms, tree oyster mushrooms, or summer oyster mushrooms) are graceful fluted oyster shell–shaped mushrooms that vary in color from pale gray to dark brownish gray. The flavor of raw oyster mushrooms is robust and slightly peppery but becomes much milder when cooked; add them toward the end of cooking to preserve their graceful appearance. Oyster mushrooms are available in some markets year-round, particularly in specialty produce and Asian markets. Look for young mushrooms, $1^{1}/2$ inches or less in diameter, which are considered the best.

soybean chili

Why open a can when you can have homemade chili in minutes? In fall and winter, enjoy this topped with dollops of Tofu-Chèvre Spread (page 5). For variety in both flavor and texture, try substituting texturized vegetable protein (TVP) for the soybeans (see Variation).

makes 6 servings

2 tablespoons olive oil

2 carrots, coarsely shredded

1/2 green bell pepper, coarsely chopped

1/2 cup coarsely chopped onion (see Tips)

1 rib celery, coarsely chopped

1 teaspoon minced garlic

1 cup water

One 6-ounce can tomato paste

One 28-ounce can Italian tomatoes, with juice, tomatoes halved (see Tip, page 119)

1 1/2 cups cooked soybeans (one 15-ounce can, drained and rinsed)

2 teaspoons chili powder, or to taste

1 teaspoon sugar

1 tablespoon minced fresh basil (or 1 teaspoon dried)

1 tablespoon minced fresh oregano (or 1 teaspoon dried)

1/2 teaspoon freshly ground black pepper, or to taste

1/2 teaspoon ground cumin

1/4 teaspoon hot pepper sauce, or to taste

Heat the oil in a large saucepan or Dutch oven over medium-high heat. Add the carrots, bell pepper, onion, and celery; cook, stirring occasionally, until the vegetables are tender, about 5 minutes. Add the garlic during the last minute.

Meanwhile, combine the water and tomato paste in a small bowl; pour into the saucepan. Stir in the remaining ingredients (except the fresh basil and oregano, if using). Increase the heat to high; stir occasionally. When the liquid comes to a boil, reduce the heat to medium-low; cover and cook until heated through, about 5 minutes. Add the fresh basil and oregano (if using) during the last minute or two. Adjust the seasonings to taste.

Per serving (1 cup): Cal 205/Pro 10.5g/Carb 19.9g/Fat 9.3g/Chol 0mg/Sod 308mg

ADVANCE PREPARATION Covered and refrigerated, this chili will keep for up to 3 days. The flavors will blend, and it reheats well. Since it thickens while standing, stir in water, vegetable stock, or tomato juice as needed when reheating.

VARIATIONS

When sautéing the vegetables, substitute for the carrots, bell pepper, or celery or add other vegetables (up to 3 cups total) such as sliced mushrooms, sliced zucchini, or 1 seeded and chopped jalapeño pepper; or when stirring in the tomatoes, add steamed broccoli florets, steamed potato cubes, corn, or canned diced mild green chilies (drained).

⟩ Substitute texturized vegetable protein (TVP) for the soybeans: Stir together $3/4$ cup TVP and $1/2$ cup hot water; allow to stand until the water is absorbed and the TVP is softened, about 5 minutes. Stir into the chili with the tomato paste and canned tomatoes.

⟩ For a spicier chili, when stirring in the chili powder, add a pinch of cayenne or a pinch of red pepper flakes.

⟩ Substitute 1 teaspoon dried epazote (see page xxvii) for the dried basil and oregano.

⟩ After refrigerating, warm the chili without thinning; spoon the thickened chili over baked potato halves.

garnish *(optional)* corn, chopped scallions, raw cashews, shredded cheddar or Monterey Jack cheese, Tofu-Chèvre Spread (page 5), Baked Tortilla Chips (page 22)

tips

When you need only part of an onion, do not peel it before cutting. The unused portion will keep better in the refrigerator if the skin is left on. Wrap it tightly in plastic wrap or store it in a screw-top jar. If you prefer, chop leftover onion and store it in a refrigerator container or a zip-top plastic bag. Use within 4 days. Frozen in a plastic bag, chopped onion will keep for months.

When chopping an onion, cut it in half through the root but don't remove the root end. Place, cut side down, on a cutting board. Slice lengthwise to, but not through, the root. Then make crosswise cuts through the onion. For speedy chopping, use a food processor. Tear-producing vapors can be reduced by refrigerating an onion for several hours or freezing it for 20 minutes before chopping.

To remove onion odor, rub your hands with salt, vinegar, or lemon juice. Rinse with cold water, then wash with warm water and soap.

carrot-cashew soup

Rather than roasted and salted cashews, select raw nuts for this recipe. Both the nuts and the raisins will soften as they cook, adding unexpected texture and sweetness to your soup.

makes 6 servings

2 tablespoons olive oil

1 cup finely chopped onion

2 cups shredded white or
    green head cabbage

2 cups coarsely shredded
    carrots

3 cups vegetable stock
    (see page 34)

One 15-ounce can tomato
    sauce

1 apple, peeled, cored, and cut
    into 1/2-inch chunks

1/3 cup uncooked brown rice

1/2 teaspoon freshly ground
    black pepper, or to taste

Dash of salt, or to taste

1/2 cup raw cashews
    (see Tip, page 126)

1/2 cup golden raisins (see Tip)

2 cups soy milk

Heat the oil in a large saucepan or Dutch oven over medium-high heat. Add the onion and cook, stirring occasionally, until softened, about 2 minutes. Stir in the cabbage and carrots; continue to cook, stirring occasionally, until the cabbage is wilted and the carrots are softened, about 3 minutes.

Stir in the vegetable stock, tomato sauce, apple, rice, pepper, and salt. When the liquid comes to a boil, reduce the heat to medium; cover and cook until the carrots are tender and the rice is done, about 25 minutes.

Stir in the cashews and raisins; cover and continue to cook until the raisins are softened and plumped, about 5 minutes.

Reduce the heat to medium; add the soy milk and stir until heated through. Adjust the seasonings to taste.

Per serving (1 1/3 cups): Cal 300/Pro 8.5g/Carb 40.3g/Fat 11.7g/Chol 0mg/Sod 496mg

ADVANCE PREPARATION Covered and refrigerated, this soup will keep for up to 3 days. Since it thickens while standing, stir in water, tomato juice, or soy milk as needed when reheating.

tips

Slender young carrots are sweeter for eating fresh. Older ones are thicker and tougher, ideal for soups.

Both dark and golden seedless raisins are made from Thompson seedless grapes. The dark raisins are sun-dried for several weeks. Golden raisins are treated with sulfur dioxide to prevent them from darkening, then dried with artificial heat, which produces a moister, plumper raisin. Store all raisins at room temperature for several months or refrigerate them in a tightly sealed plastic bag for up to a year.

tuscan soybean soup

Pass baskets of warm country-style sourdough bread and a bowl of freshly grated Parmesan cheese to garnish each serving of soup the way they do in Tuscany, where simple eating is an art form.

Heat the oil in a large saucepan or Dutch oven over medium-high heat. Add the carrots, celery, and onion; cook, stirring occasionally, until the vegetables are crisp-tender, about 4 minutes. Add the garlic during the last minute.

Stir in the vegetable stock, kale, soybeans, mushrooms, dried thyme (if using), pepper, and salt. Increase the heat to high; when the liquid comes to a boil, reduce the heat to medium-low. Cover and cook until the kale is wilted and the vegetables are tender, about 10 minutes.

Stir in the fresh thyme (if using), lemon juice, and red pepper flakes. Adjust the seasonings to taste.

Per serving (1 cup): Cal 157/Pro 10g/Carb 13.8g/Fat 6.9g/Chol 0mg/Sod 126mg

ADVANCE PREPARATION Covered and refrigerated, this soup will keep for up to 3 days.

tip

Kale is a member of the cabbage family. Ornamental varieties come in shades of blue and purple; for cooking, choose dark green kale, avoiding any limp or yellowing leaves. Store it in the coldest section of the refrigerator for no longer than 2 or 3 days; after that, the flavor becomes quite strong and the leaves turn limp. Because the center stalk is tough, remove it before cooking.

makes 6 servings

1 tablespoon olive oil

2 carrots, halved lengthwise and cut into $1/4$-inch-thick slices

2 ribs celery, cut into $1/4$-inch-thick slices

$1/2$ cup diced onion

2 teaspoons minced garlic

4 cups vegetable stock (see page 34)

4 cups chopped fresh kale (see Tip)

$1 1/2$ cups cooked soybeans (one 15-ounce can, drained and rinsed)

3 cups sliced cremini mushrooms (see Tip, page 3)

2 tablespoons minced fresh thyme (or 2 teaspoons dried)

$3/4$ teaspoon freshly ground black pepper, or to taste

$1/4$ teaspoon salt, or to taste

1 tablespoon freshly squeezed lemon juice, or to taste

Pinch of red pepper flakes, or to taste

garnish *(optional)* freshly ground black pepper, freshly grated Parmesan cheese

3 Salads

Salads with Greens

Romaine Lettuce Salad with
Blue Cheese Dressing

Chinese Tofu Salad with
Sesame-Ginger Dressing

Lemon Caesar Salad

Herbed Garlic Croutons

Salads with Grains

Wild Rice and Apricot Salad
with Marinated Tempeh

Soybean Tabbouleh

Tofu Pesto–Rice Salad

Couscous Salad with Lemon-
Cinnamon Vinaigrette

Thai Noodle Salad with Tofu
Teriyaki

Riso–Sweet Bean Salad with
Sun-Dried Tomato–Basil
Vinaigrette

Pepper-Bean Pasta Salad with
Italian Dressing

Marinated Salads

Two-Bean Salad in Walnut
Vinaigrette

Marinated French Herb Bean
Salad

Sweet Beans and Corn in
Sesame-Soy Dressing

Greek Tofu Salad

Salads with Vegetables

Tempeh–Green Bean Salad
with Creamy Peanut-Chutney
Dressing

Tofu-Chèvre-Stuffed Roasted
Red Bell Peppers with Shallot
and Caper Dressing

Tomato Slices with Creamy
Avocado Dressing

Dijon Potato Salad

Orange-Caraway Coleslaw

Tofu "Egg Salad"

Tortilla-Salsa Salad with
Roasted Sweet Red Pepper
Dressing

*Roasted Sweet Red Pepper
Dressing*

Fruit Salad

Maple-Walnut Apple Salad

Warm Salads

Warm Soybean and Sweet Red
Pepper Salad with Basil-Sherry
Vinaigrette

Tempeh Stir-Fry Salad with
Gingered Plum Vinaigrette

With the ever-increasing array of enticing components now available in supermarkets, salad has come of age—no longer merely a side dish of wilted iceberg lettuce topped with bottled dressing. In fact, salads are some of my favorite meals. Thanks to soy, there's more good news. We can count on soy to accompany fresh produce and take our salads beyond the garden variety, turning them into satisfying and nutritious main courses partnered simply with crusty bread or muffins. Or served in smaller portions, these salads can become side dish salads of distinction aside a light entrée.

As the author of *The Complete Book of Dressings* (Macmillan, 1995), I spent months developing recipes for dressings and salads. In the process I experimented with dozens of vinegars, oils, herbs, and ethnic flavorings served atop greens, vegetables, fruits, and grains. I must admit, I overlooked the possibilities of tofu, tempeh, and soybeans. This chapter just might reinvent your idea of "salad," as it did mine.

Tofu makes thick, full-bodied dressings when quickly puréed with other ingredients until the mixture is smooth. Always begin with very fresh silken firm or soft tofu; I like to use aseptically packaged tofu. Some of these dressings improve in flavor if allowed to stand for a while before using. Some may thicken after standing and need to be thinned. Tofu variations of classic dressings, like Caesar and blue cheese, cut the fat and cholesterol content while adding protein and top-notch flavors.

In some salad recipes in this chapter, soy products are brought to life with the addition of homemade vinaigrettes. The secret to success is beginning with quality ingredients. Call on extra-virgin olive oil, dark sesame oil, roasted nut oils, flavorful vinegars, and fresh herbs (when possible) for their distinctive personalities. In some salads the vinaigrette is drizzled over the salad, such as Chinese Tofu Salad with Sesame-Ginger Dressing (page 62). In others, such as Two-Bean Salad in Walnut Vinaigrette (page 77), the dressing is used as a marinade, allowing the salad ingredients to absorb the vibrant flavors.

Many salad dressing flavorings are added "to taste." Tasted from a spoon, most dressings seem very strong, so it is best to taste by dipping a salad ingredient, such as a leaf of lettuce, into the dressing; then adjust the seasonings if necessary. Because oil and vinegar separate after standing, whisk, shake, or stir these dressings before adding them to your salad.

Vegetables, fruits, pasta, and rice add variety to soy salads made with tofu, tempeh, whole soybeans, and sweet beans. Some of these salads can be tossed quickly and served immediately. Others, like Marinated French Herb Bean Salad (page 78), are best if made in advance. For variety, some salads are served warm rather than chilled. Tempeh Stir-Fry Salad with Gingered Plum Vinaigrette (page 96) is an unusual entrée salad that breaks stir-fry tradition. With salads like Tofu-Chèvre-Stuffed Roasted Red Bell Peppers with Shallot and Caper Dressing (page 84) or Tortilla-Salsa Salad with Roasted Sweet Red Pepper Dressing (page 90), delight your guests with impressive composed presentations, the components arranged on the plate with style.

Salad recipes are especially adaptable, so call on your imagination. Most of these dressings can be used on other salads; they're speedy to make and are a pleasant change of pace from bottled dressings, which often contain artificial colors and flavorings, as well as preservatives. Make these soy-based salads a part of your repertoire. Serve them any time of the year, not just in summer.

Most important, when it comes to salads, use the freshest ingredients available and unleash your creativity. Few dishes offer more visual appeal or possibilities for variations.

Salads with Greens

romaine lettuce salad with blue cheese dressing

Juicy grapes, crunchy chopped walnuts, and freshly ground black pepper bring just the right complements to the blue cheese dressing.

Put the tofu, blue cheese, lemon juice, vinegar, olive oil, Worcestershire sauce, garlic, pepper, and hot pepper sauce into a food processor; process until smooth. Stir in the fresh or dried dill and summer savory. (If you prefer a thinner consistency, stir in some water, milk, or soy milk.) Adjust the seasonings to taste.

Toss the lettuce, grapes, and 2 tablespoons of the walnuts in a large salad bowl. Add all the dressing and toss again.

Transfer the salad to individual plates; top the salads with the remaining walnuts and sprinkle with pepper.

Per serving: Cal 179/Pro 7.4g/Carb 11.8g/Fat 11.4g/Chol 6mg/Sod 148mg

ADVANCE PREPARATION If possible, allow the dressing to stand for 15 to 30 minutes in the refrigerator before using. Covered and refrigerated, it will keep for up to 2 days. Since it thickens while standing, stir in water, milk, or soy milk as needed. Toss the dressing with the lettuce, grapes, and walnuts just before serving.

tips

Blue cheeses are strong in flavor and aroma, both of which intensify with aging. Commonly available varieties include Danablu, Gorgonzola, Roquefort, and Stilton.

Never soak lettuce in water; rinse under cool water and drain completely or blot with a paper towel to remove any excess moisture. Or use a salad spinner to remove water from the leaves.

---

makes 4 servings

For the Blue Cheese Dressing

$1/2$ cup mashed silken firm tofu

$1/4$ cup crumbled blue cheese (see Tip)

2 tablespoons freshly squeezed lemon juice

2 tablespoons white wine vinegar

1 tablespoon extra-virgin olive oil

1 teaspoon Worcestershire sauce

$1/2$ teaspoon minced garlic, or to taste

$1/8$ teaspoon freshly ground black pepper, or to taste

Dash of hot pepper sauce, or to taste

1 teaspoon minced fresh dill (or $1/4$ teaspoon dried dill weed)

1 teaspoon minced fresh summer savory (or $1/4$ teaspoon dried)

For the salad

6 cups torn romaine lettuce hearts (see Tip)

1 cup halved seedless green or red grapes

$1/4$ cup toasted chopped walnuts (see Tip, page 50)

Dash freshly ground black pepper, or to taste

chinese tofu salad with sesame-ginger dressing

Leave well enough alone? Not here! This refreshing entrée salad lends itself to countless variations by substituting other vegetables or fruits.

makes 4 servings

For the Sesame-Ginger Dressing

2/3 cup white rice vinegar

2 tablespoons low-sodium soy sauce

2 teaspoons dark sesame oil

2 teaspoons finely minced gingerroot

2 teaspoons sugar

1 teaspoon minced garlic

1 teaspoon toasted sesame seeds (see Tip, page 125)

Dash of ground white pepper, or to taste

For the salad

2 teaspoons safflower oil

1 teaspoon minced garlic

1 teaspoon minced gingerroot

1 cup 1/2-inch cubes silken extra-firm tofu

Dash of freshly ground black pepper, or to taste

24 snow peas, stems and strings removed

6 cups coarsely shredded Chinese cabbage (see Tip)

Bring a medium saucepan of water to a boil over high heat.

In a small bowl, whisk together the dressing ingredients, making certain the sugar is dissolved. Adjust the seasoning to taste. Set aside.

Heat the safflower oil in a large nonstick skillet over medium-high heat. Stir in the garlic and gingerroot. Add the tofu cubes; cook until they are lightly browned, about 2 minutes on each side. Sprinkle with pepper. Use a slotted spatula to transfer the tofu to a plate; set aside to cool.

Blanch the snow peas by immersing them for about 30 seconds in the saucepan of boiling water. Pour into a mesh strainer and then rinse under cold running water (see Tip, page 61). Drain well.

Toss together the Chinese cabbage, snow peas, bok choy, and scallions in a large mixing bowl. Whisk the dressing; add half to the salad and toss again.

Divide the salad mixture among 4 individual serving plates. Arrange the tofu and mandarin orange sections on top. Whisk the remaining dressing; drizzle over the salads. Garnish and serve immediately.

Per serving: Cal 154/Pro 8.1g/Carb 16.3g/Fat 6.3g/Chol 0mg/Sod 318mg

ADVANCE PREPARATION The dressing will keep for up to 1 week in a tightly closed container in the refrigerator. The salad can be made early on the day it is to be served; cover and refrigerate. Add the dressing to the salad just before serving.

VARIATIONS

❧ Add about 2 tablespoons chopped fresh cilantro to the dressing.

❧ Substitute shredded romaine lettuce or fresh salad spinach leaves for the Chinese cabbage.

❧ Substitute celery, water chestnuts, or strips of jícama for the bok choy.

❧ Substitute for the snow peas or bok choy or add other vegetables (up to 3 cups total) such as bean sprouts, sliced mushrooms, peas, or red or green bell pepper strips.

❧ Substitute grapes or pineapple for the mandarin orange sections.

❧ When tossing the salad, add up to $1/2$ cup raisins or currants.

tips

Chinese cabbage, sometimes called Napa cabbage or celery cabbage, can be recognized by its solid oblong heads of long smooth stalks with crinkly, thick-veined, pale green leaves. Unlike head cabbage, Chinese cabbage is mild and delicate; it can be used raw or in stir-fries. In most supermarkets it is available year-round. Refrigerate, tightly wrapped, for up to 3 days.

Blanching *means to plunge food quickly into simmering water and then immediately into cold water to stop the cooking. Blanching enhances the colors and flavors of vegetables and also loosens the skins of tomatoes, peaches, and nuts (such as almonds), making them easy to peel.*

4 ribs bok choy, coarsely chopped; include green tops (see Tip, page 123)

3 medium scallions, finely chopped

1 cup canned mandarin orange sections, drained

garnish *(optional)* toasted sesame seeds (see Tip, page 125), toasted sliced or slivered almonds (see Tip, page 50)

lemon caesar salad

makes 4 servings

For the Parmesan Dressing

1/4 cup Parmesan-Peppercorn Dip (page 10)

1 tablespoon skim milk

1 tablespoon freshly squeezed lemon juice

1 tablespoon minced fresh flat-leaf parsley

1/2 teaspoon Worcestershire sauce

Few drops of hot pepper sauce, or to taste

For the salad

6 cups loosely packed torn romaine lettuce hearts

2 tomatoes, each cut into 8 wedges

2 hard-cooked eggs, each cut into 6 wedges (see Tip)

garnish (optional) freshly ground black pepper, Herbed Garlic Croutons (page 65)

Hail, Caesar! These days it's everyone's favorite salad, it seems. Parmesan-Peppercorn Dip can be transformed into a low-fat Caesar dressing with the addition of just a few ingredients. Double this recipe to provide enough for 4 entrée salads.

Stir together the dressing ingredients in a medium bowl. Adjust the seasoning to taste.

Put the romaine lettuce in a large salad bowl; add the dressing and toss.

Arrange the dressed greens on salad plates; arrange the tomato and egg wedges around the edges. Sprinkle with freshly ground black pepper and top with croutons.

Per serving: Cal 95/Pro 7.5g/Carb 6.6g/Fat 4.3g/Chol 109mg/Sod 116mg

ADVANCE PREPARATION The dressing will keep for up to 2 days in a tightly closed container in the refrigerator. Since it thickens while standing, stir in milk, soy milk, or water as needed. Cook the hard-cooked eggs at least 1 hour or up to 2 days in advance; chill. Toss and assemble the salads just before serving.

tips

To hard-cook eggs, place them in a single layer in a pan and cover with at least 1 inch of water. Cover and bring the water to a full rolling boil over medium-high heat. Remove the pan from the heat and let the eggs stand in the water, covered, for about 15 minutes. (For larger or smaller eggs, adjust the time up or down by about 3 minutes for each size variation.) Drain off the hot water and immediately cover the eggs with cold water; let stand until the eggs are completely cool. This cooling process prevents a dark gray-green surface from forming around the yolk. (If it does occur, the greenish color is harmless and does not alter the nutritional value or flavor of the egg.)

herbed garlic croutons

These croutons are the "little extra" that adds flavor and texture when used to garnish salads, such as Lemon Caesar Salad (previous page). They're also a big hit on soups, such as Soybean Gazpacho (page 38).

Heat the oil in a small nonstick skillet over medium heat. Add the garlic, basil, and oregano; stir constantly for about 30 seconds to soften the herbs. Increase the heat to medium-high. Add the bread cubes; stir until lightly browned and crispy, about 4 to 5 minutes.

Transfer the croutons to a plate and set aside to cool. (The croutons will become crisper as they cool.)

Per serving (1/4 cup): Cal 48/Pro .7g/Carb 3.1g/Fat 3.7g/ Chol 0mg/Sod 40mg

ADVANCE PREPARATION The croutons can be stored in a covered tin at room temperature for up to 2 days (they become soggy in a covered plastic container). To recrisp, spread the croutons in a single layer on a baking sheet and heat at 350°F for about 5 minutes.

VARIATION

Substitute other dried herbs, such as dried thyme, for the basil and oregano.

tip

Buy a true whole wheat bread by selecting one that contains mostly whole wheat, stone-ground whole wheat, whole-grain, multigrain, or cracked-wheat flour. Some dark breads are made from white flour with caramel coloring added.

makes 1 cup

1 tablespoon olive oil

1/2 teaspoon minced garlic

1/4 teaspoon dried basil
(do not substitute fresh)

1/4 teaspoon dried oregano
(do not substitute fresh)

1 cup 1/2-inch bread cubes,
preferably whole wheat
(see Tip)

Salads with Grains

wild rice and apricot salad with marinated tempeh 🌿

I think you'll agree that this entrée salad is both elegant and unusual. Plan ahead to allow time for cooking the wild rice, marinating the tempeh, and allowing the salad to stand for at least an hour before serving.

makes 4 servings

For the Sesame-Orange Vinaigrette

1/4 cup white rice vinegar

1/4 cup water

2 tablespoons dark sesame oil

1 tablespoon low-sodium soy sauce

1 teaspoon orange zest (see Tip, pages 6–7)

Dash of freshly ground black pepper, or to taste

Dash of salt, or to taste

For the Sesame-Soy Marinade

1/4 cup white rice vinegar

1/4 cup low-sodium soy sauce

2 tablespoons dark sesame oil

1 teaspoon ground coriander (see Tip, page 45)

To complete the recipe

8 ounces tempeh, cut into 1/2-inch cubes

1 cup uncooked wild rice, cleaned (see Tip)

Whisk together the vinaigrette ingredients in a small bowl; set aside. Adjust the seasonings to taste.

Combine the marinade ingredients in a small bowl. Pour half of the marinade into a shallow glass baking dish. Place the tempeh cubes in the marinade; cover with the remaining marinade. Cover and set aside at room temperature for 30 minutes or refrigerate for up to 4 hours.

Meanwhile, combine the rice, water, and salt in a medium saucepan; bring the liquid to a boil over high heat. Reduce the heat to medium-low; cover and cook for about 40 to 50 minutes, or until the rice is tender and most of the grains have split slightly. Drain and discard any liquid that remains in the pan.

Preheat the oven to 400°F. Bake the tempeh in the marinade for 20 minutes. Drain well; discard the marinade.

Heat the safflower oil in a small nonstick skillet over medium-high heat. Add the scallions and shallots; cook, stirring constantly, until tender, about 4 minutes.

Combine the tempeh, rice, scallions, and shallots in a medium bowl. Add the apricots, parsley, and vinaigrette; toss again.

Allow to stand at room temperature for 1 hour before serving.

Per serving: Cal 400/Pro 18.6g/Carb 44.8g/Fat 16.3g/Chol 0mg/Sod 458mg

ADVANCE PREPARATION This salad is best when prepared the day it is to be served. Covered and refrigerated, it will keep for up to 3 days.

tips

Wild rice really isn't a rice at all; it's actually a long-grain marsh grass that is native to the northern Great Lakes area. Store it in an airtight container in a cool, dark place where it will keep almost indefinitely. Before cooking, it is important to clean wild rice; place it in a bowl, fill with cold water, stir, and set aside. Drain the water and any debris that floats to the surface. Wild rice is a slow-cooking rice; check it near the end of the cooking period, since overcooking will result in a starchy product.

Dried apricots are pitted, unpeeled apricot halves that have had a large percentage of their moisture removed. To preserve their vivid color, they are usually treated with sulfur dioxide. In addition to being rich in vitamin A, dried apricots are also a source of iron and calcium. Stored in an airtight container in a dry place, dried fruit will keep its flavor, color, and nutritional value for up to 6 months. Chopping dried apricots is most easily done using kitchen shears.

3 cups water

Dash of salt

1 teaspoon safflower oil

$1/2$ cup thinly sliced scallions (both green and white parts)

$1/4$ cup minced shallots

$1/3$ cup dried apricots in $1/4$-inch-wide strips (see Tip)

2 tablespoons minced fresh flat-leaf parsley

soybean tabbouleh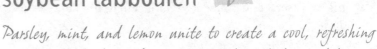

Parsley, mint, and lemon unite to create a cool, refreshing antidote to the heat of summer. But this salad is so delicious, I serve it all year long. Try it atop a bed of lettuce or spinach or use it as a do-ahead sandwich filling for pita bread pockets.

makes 6 servings

For the salad

2 cups vegetable stock (see page 34)

1 cup bulgur wheat (see Tip)

1 cup cooked soybeans

1 cup minced fresh flat-leaf parsley

2 plum tomatoes, cut into 1/2-inch cubes

1/2 cup finely chopped celery

1/2 cup finely chopped cucumber

1/2 cup finely chopped scallions (both green and white parts)

For the Lemon-Mint Dressing

1/2 cup freshly squeezed lemon juice

1/4 cup extra-virgin olive oil

1/4 cup chopped fresh mint (or 2 teaspoons dried)

1/4 teaspoon freshly ground black pepper, or to taste

1/8 teaspoon ground cinnamon

Dash of ground allspice

Dash of ground nutmeg

Dash of salt, or to taste

Heat the vegetable stock in a small saucepan over high heat. When the liquid comes to a boil, remove the pan from the heat. Stir in the bulgur wheat; cover and set aside until the bulgur is softened and the liquid is completely absorbed, about 30 minutes.

Meanwhile, whisk together the dressing ingredients in a small bowl. Adjust the seasonings to taste. Set aside.

When it has softened, transfer the bulgur wheat to a large bowl; add the remaining salad ingredients and toss. Whisk the dressing, add it to the salad, and toss again.

Refrigerate in a covered container for at least 1 hour before serving.

Per serving: Cal 240/Pro 8.2g/Carb 24.6g/Fat 12.1g/Chol 0mg/Sod 41mg

ADVANCE PREPARATION Covered and refrigerated, this salad will keep for up to 3 days.

tip

The "rice" of the Middle East is granulated wheat called bulgur wheat, or cracked wheat. In processing, the wheat is parboiled (steamed and dried) and then cracked into small pieces. It is sold in bulk in specialty food stores and health food stores or in boxes in supermarkets, where it is usually stocked with either the rice or hot cereal. Bulgur, which has a unique nutty flavor, is available in coarse, medium, or fine fragments; select the smallest fragments for use in tabbouleh. Store it in an airtight container in a cool, dry place.

tofu pesto-rice salad

This do-ahead salad can be varied by substituting white rice, wild rice, or a combination. It's especially nice served on beds of mesclun (see Tip). The greens serve both as a flavor and a visual complement.

Put the asparagus into a medium microwave-proof dish; add about 2 tablespoons water. Cover and microwave on high until crisp-tender, about 4 minutes; drain well. (Or cook the asparagus in a stovetop steamer.)

Toss the asparagus, rice, bell pepper, scallions, and parsley in a medium bowl. Add the pesto and red pepper flakes; toss again. Adjust the seasonings to taste.

Per serving: Cal 294/Pro 10.2g/Carb 48g/Fat 6.8g/Chol 2mg/Sod 84mg

ADVANCE PREPARATION The pesto will keep for up to 4 days in a tightly closed container in the refrigerator. Covered and refrigerated, the completed salad will keep for up to 4 days if the pesto is freshly made; it will keep just 1 day if the pesto was made in advance.

VARIATION

❧ Substitute small broccoli florets for the asparagus.

tip

Mesclun is a salad mix found in specialty produce markets and most supermarkets. It is a mixture of young, tender salad greens, which may include arugula, frisée, mizuna, baby spinach, oak leaf, radicchio, sorrel, or any combination of these. If refrigerated in a plastic bag, it will keep for up to 5 days. Wash and gently pat dry before using.

makes 4 servings

2 cups asparagus in 2-inch lengths

3 cups cooked brown rice

1/2 cup diced red bell pepper

2 medium scallions, finely chopped

2 tablespoons finely chopped fresh flat-leaf parsley

1/2 cup Tofu-Basil Pesto (page 6)

Pinch of red pepper flakes, or to taste

garnish *(optional)* freshly ground black pepper, freshly grated Parmesan cheese, toasted pine nuts (see Tip, page 75)

couscous salad with
lemon-cinnamon vinaigrette

makes 6 servings

For the Lemon-Cinnamon Vinaigrette

1/2 cup freshly squeezed lemon juice

3 tablespoons extra-virgin olive oil (see page 200)

1/2 teaspoon ground cinnamon

1/2 teaspoon freshly ground black pepper

1/4 teaspoon ground turmeric

Few drops of hot pepper sauce, or to taste

For the salad

1 cup vegetable stock (see page 34)

1 cup couscous (see Tip)

1 teaspoon olive oil

1/4 cup pine nuts

1 rib celery, finely chopped

1 medium scallion, finely chopped

1/3 cup dried currants

1/4 cup minced red bell pepper

2 tablespoons minced fresh flat-leaf parsley

1 cup silken extra-firm tofu 1/2-inch cubes

Morocco is the inspiration for this salad; cinnamon is the secret ingredient in the dressing. Serve this on beds of red leaf lettuce. If you care to make the salad more substantial, arrange steamed slender asparagus spears over the couscous.

Whisk together the vinaigrette ingredients in a small bowl. Adjust the seasoning to taste. Set aside.

Pour the vegetable stock into a small saucepan; cover and bring nearly to a boil over medium-high heat. Remove from the heat; stir in the couscous. Let stand, covered, until the liquid is completely absorbed, about 5 to 10 minutes.

Meanwhile, heat the olive oil in a small nonstick skillet over medium heat. Add the pine nuts and stir constantly until lightly browned, about 2 minutes Use a slotted spoon to transfer the nuts to a bowl; set aside to cool.

When the couscous has softened, toss it with a fork. Toss in the pine nuts and the remaining salad ingredients except the tofu. Add the tofu and toss gently.

Whisk the dressing and gently stir it into the salad just before serving.

Per serving: Cal 285/Pro 8.4g/Carb 33.8g/Fat 12.9g/Chol 0mg/Sod 43mg

ADVANCE PREPARATION Store the vinaigrette and salad separately; covered and refrigerated, they will keep for up to 2 days. Toss the dressing with the salad just before serving.

Couscous, sometimes called Moroccan pasta, is a tiny beadlike pasta made from semolina flour. It is available in both white and whole wheat varieties in most supermarkets, usually in the rice aisle. Couscous keeps almost indefinitely in a tightly closed container in a dark, dry place. This quick-cooking pasta is prepared by combining equal amounts of couscous and hot (nearly boiling) liquid. (Water is often used, but chicken broth, vegetable stock, or even tomato juice will add flavor.) Then simply let it stand in a covered bowl until the couscous is tender and the liquid completely absorbed, about 5 to 10 minutes. (Couscous will double in volume as it absorbs the liquid.) Before serving, fluff with a fork. Serve as is or drizzle with a little olive oil, or add vegetables such as diced carrots (steamed or raw) or minced parsley. In addition to performing as a tasty side dish, couscous can substitute for rice when served with stir-fries or in salads calling for rice.

thai noodle salad with tofu teriyaki

Is this salad tasty? Well, let's just say I've been known to sneak into the kitchen at midnight to polish off the leftovers. But plan ahead when serving this out-of-the ordinary salad; the Tofu Teriyaki and the noodles with Peanut-Ginger Dressing are best if the spicy flavors are allowed to develop for several hours before serving.

makes 4 servings

For the salad

1 recipe Tofu Teriyaki (page 160)

4 ounces cellophane noodles (see Tip)

2 tablespoons coarsely chopped fresh basil (fresh is essential)

For the Peanut-Ginger Dressing

1/2 cup unsalted dry-roasted peanuts

One piece gingerroot 2 inches long by 1 inch thick, peeled and cut into 1/2-inch chunks (or 2 tablespoons minced gingerroot)

1 teaspoon hot red chili pepper (seeds removed), or to taste (see Tip, page 137)

1/4 cup freshly squeezed lime juice

2 tablespoons low-sodium soy sauce

2 tablespoons sugar

garnish (optional) finely chopped unsalted dry-roasted peanuts

After marinating, sauté the Tofu Teriyaki. Set aside to cool.

Bring a small pot of water to a boil over high heat; remove from the heat. Add the cellophane noodles, cover, and soak until they are softened and clear, about 8 to 10 minutes; drain well. Transfer the noodles to a large bowl; use kitchen shears to cut the them into shorter lengths. Set aside to cool.

To prepare the dressing, put all of the dressing ingredients into a food processor or electric mincer; process until the gingerroot is finely chopped and the peanuts are slightly chunky.

Pour the dressing over the noodles and toss gently until it is evenly distributed. Add the basil and toss. Adjust the amount of hot pepper to taste. Allow to stand at room temperature for 1 hour before serving.

To serve, spread a layer of noodles on 4 large salad plates; top each with 4 tofu triangles.

Per serving: Cal 350/Pro 12.7g/Carb 39.6g/Fat 15.7g/Chol 0mg/Sod 491mg

ADVANCE PREPARATION The tofu should be marinated for at least 1 hour or up to 8 hours. It can be cooked up to 1 day in advance; cover and refrigerate. The noodles with Peanut-Ginger Dressing should stand at room temperature for at least 1 hour before serving; or cover and refrigerate for up to 8 hours. Assemble the salads with the sautéed Tofu Teriyaki just before serving.

VARIATIONS

❧ For a milder flavor, substitute a green chili pepper or jalapeño pepper for the hot red chili pepper.

❧ Substitute $1/2$ teaspoon red pepper flakes, or to taste, for the fresh chili pepper.

❧ Substitute fresh cilantro or mint for the basil.

❧ Substitute freshly squeezed lemon juice or white rice vinegar for the lime juice.

tip

Available in Asian markets and some supermarkets, cellophane noodles (also called bean threads, mung bean sticks, Chinese vermicelli, glass noodles, or harusame *noodles) are translucent threads made from the starch of green mung. Store the noodles, wrapped airtight, in a cool, dry place for up to 6 months. Sold dried, they must be soaked in hot water before adding to most dishes; presoaking is not necessary when they are added to soups.*

riso-sweet bean salad with sun-dried tomato-basil vinaigrette

I'm always tempted to make a double recipe of this enticing salad. First it shows up aside Spicy Soybean Patties (page 171) or Veggie Burgers (page 170). The next day it doubles as a luncheon salad served atop arugula.

makes 6 servings

For the salad

1 cup riso pasta (see Tip)

1 1/2 cups frozen sweet beans (see page xxvi)

2 plum tomatoes, cut into 1/2-inch cubes (about 3/4 cup)

1/4 cup toasted pine nuts (see Tip)

For the Sun-Dried Tomato–Basil Vinaigrette

1/4 cup drained and coarsely chopped oil-packed sun-dried tomatoes

1/4 cup extra-virgin olive oil

3 tablespoons freshly squeezed lemon juice

1 teaspoon Dijon mustard

1 tablespoon minced fresh basil (or 1 teaspoon dried)

1/8 teaspoon freshly ground black pepper, or to taste

Dash of salt, or to taste

garnish *(optional)* freshly ground black pepper, crumbled mild feta cheese

Bring a saucepan of water to a boil over high heat; add the riso. When the water returns to a boil, stir once to separate the riso. Reduce the heat to medium-high and cook until tender, about 10 to 12 minutes.

Put the sweet beans into a microwave-proof dish; add about 1/4 cup water. Cover and microwave on high until crisp-tender, about 6 to 8 minutes; drain well. (Or cook the sweet beans in a stovetop steamer.)

While the riso and sweet beans are cooking, whisk together the vinaigrette ingredients in a small bowl. Adjust the seasonings to taste.

When the riso is done, drain well. Put it into a medium bowl; add the sweet beans and the remaining salad ingredients. Toss to combine. Whisk the dressing; add to the salad and toss again.

Per serving: Cal 329/Pro 9.8g/Carb 39.5g/Fat 14.7g/Chol 0mg/Sod 44mg

ADVANCE PREPARATION If fresh basil is used, the vinaigrette will keep for up to 2 days in a tightly closed container in the refrigerator; if dried basil is used, it will keep for up to 1 week. Covered and refrigerated, the completed salad will keep for up to 3 days.

➤ Substitute Shallot and Caper Dressing (page 84) for the Sun-Dried Tomato-Basil Vinaigrette; omit the pine nuts.

➤ Substitute orzo (see Tip) for the riso.

tips

Riso and orzo, available in most supermarkets, are tiny, rice-shaped pastas; cooking doubles the volume. They can be used as a substitute for rice.

Pine nuts (also called pignoli nuts, pignolia, or piñons) are the seeds from the cone of certain pine trees. Their natural oil turns rancid very quickly, so they should be refrigerated for no more than 1 month or frozen for up to 3 months. Like other nuts, they are high in fat: use them in moderation.

The sweet, mild flavor of pine nuts is enhanced by toasting. Place them in a small skillet over medium heat, stirring constantly and watching carefully; the nuts will brown in about 4 to 5 minutes. Or toast them in the oven: spread a single layer on an ungreased baking sheet; bake at 375°F for about 4 to 5 minutes, stirring frequently. Immediately remove the nuts from the pan when they are browned. For efficiency, toast 1 or 2 cups at a time and freeze the nuts until they are needed.

Because of their high fat content, nuts quickly become rancid at room temperature. Shelled nuts can be refrigerated in an airtight container for up to 4 months or frozen for up to 6 months. To freshen their flavor, spread the nuts on a baking sheet and heat in a 150°F oven for a few minutes.

pepper-bean pasta salad with italian dressing ✓

For a change of pace, instead of serving this salad chilled, try serving it warm, just after preparing. To do so, do not rinse the corkscrew pasta with cold water after it is cooked; also, briefly heat the soybean—bell pepper mixture in the sauté pan after adding the Italian Dressing.

makes 6 servings

For the Italian Dressing

1/2 cup white wine vinegar

1/2 cup drained and minced oil-packed sun-dried tomatoes

1/4 cup extra-virgin olive oil (see page 200)

1 tablespoon minced shallot

1 tablespoon minced fresh flat-leaf parsley

2 teaspoons minced fresh oregano (or 1/2 teaspoon dried)

1/2 teaspoon freshly ground black pepper, or to taste

Pinch of red pepper flakes

Pinch of dry mustard (see Tip)

Dash of salt, or to taste

For the salad

8 ounces rotini pasta (about 3 cups)

1 tablespoon olive oil

1 red bell pepper, cut into strips about 2 inches long by 1/2 inch wide

1 green bell pepper, cut into strips about 2 inches long by 1/2 inch wide

1 1/2 cups cooked soybeans (one 15-ounce can, drained and rinsed)

garnish *(optional)* crumbled mild feta or goat cheese

Bring a large pot of water to a boil over high heat.

Meanwhile, whisk together the dressing ingredients in a small bowl. Adjust the seasonings to taste. Set aside.

When the water comes to a boil, add the rotini. When the water returns to a boil, stir once to separate the rotini. Reduce the heat to medium-high and cook until *al dente*, about 8 to 10 minutes. Drain, rinse with cool water, then drain well again.

While the pasta is cooking, heat the olive oil in a large non-stick sauté pan over medium-high heat. Add the bell peppers. Cook, stirring occasionally, until tender, about 5 minutes. Reduce the heat to medium; stir in the soybeans and the dressing. Add the pasta and toss.

Allow to cool, then refrigerate in a covered container for at least 1 hour before serving.

Per serving: Cal 313/Pro 12.2g/Carb 30.1g/Fat 16g/Chol 13mg/Sod 26mg

ADVANCE PREPARATION If dried oregano is used, the dressing will keep for up to 1 week in a tightly closed container in the refrigerator; if fresh oregano is used, it will keep for up to 4 days. Covered and refrigerated, the completed salad will keep for up to 2 days.

tip

Dry mustard is made from finely ground mustard seed; it can be stored in a dry, dark place for up to 6 months.

Marinated Salads

two-bean salad in walnut vinaigrette

For the best flavor, use walnut oil made from roasted walnuts. This exceptional salad deserves it.

Whisk together the dressing ingredients in a small bowl. Adjust the seasonings to taste. Set aside.

Put the green beans into a medium microwave-proof dish; add about 2 tablespoons water. Cover and microwave on high until crisp-tender, about 4 to 6 minutes; drain well. (Or cook the green beans in a stovetop steamer.)

Toss the green beans, soybeans, bell pepper, and onion in a medium bowl. Whisk the dressing; add 1/4 cup of the dressing to the salad and toss.

Arrange the endive leaves and pear wedges, alternating them in pinwheel fashion, on 4 salad plates. Using a slotted spoon, mound the salad in the center of each plate. Drizzle the remaining dressing over the pears and endive leaves.

Per serving: Cal 337/Pro 13.5g/Carb 24.8g/Fat 20.4g/Chol 0mg/Sod 80mg

ADVANCE PREPARATION The vinaigrette will keep for up to 1 week in a tightly closed container in the refrigerator. Covered and refrigerated, the salad will keep for up to 2 days. Assemble with the endive and pears just before serving.

tips

Walnuts are 60 percent oil; the oil has a pleasant but strong, nutty taste and is used mainly for salads rather than as a cooking medium. Because walnut oil turns rancid quickly, refrigerate after opening; it will keep for up to 3 months. Roasted walnut oil is available from Loriva Supreme Foods; for more information, call 1-800-94LORIV.

makes 4 servings

For the Walnut Vinaigrette

1/4 cup red wine vinegar

3 tablespoons walnut oil, preferably roasted walnut oil (see Tip)

1 tablespoon extra-virgin olive oil (see page 200)

1 teaspoon Dijon mustard

1/4 teaspoon freshly ground black pepper, or to taste

1/8 teaspoon salt, or to taste

For the salad

1 1/2 cups green beans in 2-inch lengths

1 1/2 cups cooked soybeans (one 15-ounce can, drained and rinsed)

1/4 cup diced red bell pepper

1/4 cup coarsely chopped red onion

20 leaves Belgian endive

2 large ripe pears (preferably red d'Anjou), at room temperature, each cut into 8 wedges

garnish *(optional)* toasted chopped walnuts (see Tip, page 50)

marinated french herb bean salad

makes 4 servings

For the French Herb Dressing

1/4 cup extra-virgin olive oil

1/4 cup freshly squeezed lemon juice

1/4 cup white wine vinegar

1 tablespoon honey

1 tablespoon Dijon mustard

1 teaspoon herbes de Provence (see Tip)

1/2 teaspoon grated lemon peel (see Tip, pages 6–7)

1/2 teaspoon minced garlic

1/8 teaspoon freshly ground black pepper, or to taste

Dash of salt, or to taste

For the salad

2 cups green beans in 2-inch lengths

2 cups frozen sweet beans (see page xxvi)

1 medium cucumber, seeded and coarsely chopped (about 1 cup)

1/2 cup coarsely chopped red bell pepper

This slightly sweet dressing scented with herbes de Provence accentuates the flavor of sweet beans and pleasantly contrasts the bitterness of endive. Serve this as a light lunch accompanied by French bread slices and Mushroom-Almond Spread (page 3). Or serve smaller portions as a side salad.

Whisk together the dressing ingredients in a small bowl. Adjust the seasonings to taste. Set aside.

Put the green beans and sweet beans into large microwave-proof dish; add about 1/4 cup water. Cover and microwave on high until crisp-tender, about 6 minutes; drain well (see Tip). (Or cook the green beans and sweet beans in a stovetop steamer.)

Put the green beans and sweet beans into a medium bowl; add the remaining salad ingredients except the Belgian endive and toss. Whisk the dressing; add to the salad and toss again. Cover and refrigerate for at least 1 hour before serving.

When ready to serve, arrange 5 Belgian endive leaves in a pinwheel on each salad plate. Use a slotted spoon to place a mound of bean salad in the centers. Drizzle the exposed endive leaves with additional dressing, about 1 tablespoon per salad.

Per serving: Cal 218/Pro 11.9g/Carb 19.8g/Fat 10.1g/Chol 0mg/Sod 54mg

ADVANCE PREPARATION The dressing will keep for up to 1 week in a tightly closed container in the refrigerator. Covered and refrigerated, the bean salad will keep for up to 3 days. Assemble the salads with the endive just before serving.

Herbes de Provence is an assortment of dried herbs commonly containing basil, fennel seed, lavender, marjoram, rosemary, sage, summer savory, and thyme. The blend can be found in small clay crocks in gourmet shops and some supermarkets; it is most often imported from the south of France, where it is a traditional flavoring.

Microwave cooking time depends on the wattage and size of the microwave oven. It is also affected by the freshness, moisture content, maturity, and quantity of vegetables being cooked. To hold in the steam, cover the cooking dish with a lid or heavy-duty plastic wrap. Test for doneness at the minimum suggested cooking time; if necessary, microwave further in 1-minute increments. Food continues to cook after it is removed from the microwave, so remove it a minute or so before it would be done. Drain well before using.

1 medium scallion, finely
    chopped

2 tablespoons coarsely
    chopped celery

2 tablespoons minced fresh
    flat-leaf parsley

20 leaves Belgian endive
    (2 heads)

sweet beans and corn in sesame-soy dressing

This is delicious served as a side dish with Curried Tofu-Carrot Sloppy Joes (page 169). Or turn it into an entrée salad by adding rice (see Variation). To make the salad even more zesty, add 1/4 teaspoon Chinese hot oil or a pinch of red pepper flakes to the dressing.

makes 4 servings

For the salad

2 cups frozen sweet beans (see page xxvi)

1 cup frozen corn, thawed

1/4 cup diced red bell pepper

4 large leaves red leaf lettuce

For the Sesame-Soy Dressing

1/3 cup white rice vinegar

2 tablespoons low-sodium soy sauce (see Tip)

1 teaspoon dark sesame oil (see Tip)

1 teaspoon minced gingerroot

1 teaspoon sugar

1 teaspoon toasted sesame seeds (see Tip, page 125)

1/2 teaspoon minced garlic

Dash of ground white pepper, or to taste

garnish *(optional)* toasted sesame seeds (see Tip, page 125)

Put the sweet beans into a medium microwave-proof dish; add about 1/4 cup water. Cover and microwave on high until crisp-tender, about 6 to 8 minutes; drain well. (Or cook the sweet beans in a stovetop steamer.)

Meanwhile, whisk together the dressing ingredients in a small bowl, making certain the sugar is dissolved. Adjust the seasoning to taste. Set aside.

Put the sweet beans into a medium bowl; add the corn and bell pepper. Whisk the dressing; add it to the salad and toss.

To serve, arrange lettuce leaves on individual serving plates; use a slotted spoon to mound the salad mixture atop the greens.

Per serving: Cal 143/Pro 9.8g/Carb 18.7g/Fat 3.2g/Chol 0mg/Sod 148mg

ADVANCE PREPARATION The dressing will keep for up to 1 week in a tightly closed container in the refrigerator. Covered and refrigerated, the bean and corn salad will keep for up to 3 days. Assemble the salads with the lettuce just before serving.

VARIATION

When tossing the salad, add about 1 cup cooked brown, white, or basmati rice.

tips

Low-sodium, or "lite," soy sauce contains less sodium than traditional soy sauce or tamari, but it provides nearly the same flavor. Soy sauce will keep almost indefinitely if refrigerated.

Buy dark, amber-colored sesame oil made from toasted sesame seeds rather than light-colored sesame oil. The light oils are extracted from raw sesame seeds and lack the distinctive strong flavor. Because dark sesame oil is so volatile, it is used as a flavoring oil rather than as a cooking oil and is usually added as one of the last steps in a cooked recipe.

greek tofu salad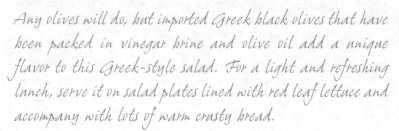

Any olives will do, but imported Greek black olives that have been packed in vinegar brine and olive oil add a unique flavor to this Greek-style salad. For a light and refreshing lunch, serve it on salad plates lined with red leaf lettuce and accompany with lots of warm crusty bread.

makes 4 servings

For the Balsamic-Garlic Vinaigrette

3 tablespoons extra-virgin olive oil

2 tablespoons balsamic vinegar

2 tablespoons freshly squeezed lemon juice

1 teaspoon minced garlic

1/4 teaspoon freshly ground black pepper, or to taste

Dash of salt, or to taste

For the salad

12 ounces silken extra-firm tofu, cut into 1/2-inch cubes (about 2 cups)

2 tomatoes, cut into 1/2-inch cubes

1 medium cucumber, peeled, seeded, and cut into 1/2-inch cubes (about 1 1/2 cups)

12 pitted Greek black olives, halved (see Tip)

garnish *(optional)* crumbled mild feta cheese

Whisk together the vinaigrette ingredients in a medium bowl. Adjust the seasonings to taste. Gently stir in the tofu cubes; allow to stand at room temperature for about 15 minutes.

Add the tomatoes, cucumber, and olives; toss gently.

Refrigerate in a covered container for at least 1 hour before serving.

Per serving: Cal 203/Pro 8.1g/Carb 12g/Fat 13.6g/Chol 0mg/Sod 549mg

ADVANCE PREPARATION The vinaigrette will keep for up to 2 days in a tightly closed container in the refrigerator. Covered and refrigerated, the assembled salad will keep for up to 2 days.

tip

Greek black olives are the traditional olive of Greece. These round olives are actually brownish gray in color. The flavor is mild and meaty; the texture is semifirm. They can be found with imported products in gourmet shops and many supermarkets. Unopened jars of olives can be stored at room temperature for up to 2 years; once opened, refrigerate the olives in their own liquid for several weeks.

Salads with Vegetables

tempeh–green bean salad with creamy peanut-chutney dressing

The combination of tangy, sweet-sharp chutney with rich, nutty peanut butter can't be beat.

Put the dressing ingredients into a food processor; process until smooth and creamy. Adjust the seasonings to taste. Set aside.

Put the green beans into a medium microwave-proof dish; add about 1/4 cup water. Cover and microwave on high until crisp-tender, about 4 to 6 minutes; drain well. (Or cook the green beans in a stovetop steamer.)

Meanwhile, heat the oil in a medium nonstick skillet over medium-high heat. Add the tempeh and cook, turning occasionally, until the chunks are lightly browned, about 5 to 8 minutes. Transfer to a plate and set aside to cool.

Toss the green beans and tempeh in a medium bowl. Add the dressing and toss again.

Per serving: Cal 184/Pro 11.6g/Carb 14.8g/Fat 8.7g/Chol 0mg/Sod 43mg

ADVANCE PREPARATION The dressing can be made up to 1 day in advance; cover and refrigerate. Since it thickens while standing, stir in water as needed. The green beans and tempeh can be cooked and refrigerated up to 1 day in advance. Toss the salad with the dressing just before serving.

tip

Chutney is a mixture of fruit and/or vegetables cooked with vinegar, sugar, and spices. Most often made with mango, chutney is found in most supermarkets; look for it shelved with either the condiments or the dressings.

makes 6 servings

For the Creamy Peanut-Chutney Dressing

1/2 cup mashed silken firm tofu

1/4 cup white rice vinegar

2 tablespoons creamy peanut butter

2 tablespoons mango chutney (see Tip)

2 teaspoons curry powder, or to taste

Dash of freshly ground black pepper, or to taste

For the salad

3 cups green beans in 2-inch lengths

1 tablespoon safflower oil

8 ounces tempeh, cut into chunks about 1 inch square by 1/2 inch thick

tofu-chèvre-stuffed roasted red bell peppers with shallot and caper dressing

The sweetness of red bell peppers is the flavor we're celebrating here. For the best texture, I recommend roasting your own rather than using the roasted peppers available in jars. Roast the peppers as your first step in preparing this salad. Next make the Tofu-Chèvre Spread and then proceed with the recipe.

makes 4 servings

For the Shallot and Caper Dressing

1/4 cup red wine vinegar

1/4 cup extra-virgin olive oil

1 tablespoon minced shallot (see Tip)

1 tablespoon capers, drained and rinsed (see Tip)

Dash of freshly ground black pepper, or to taste

Dash of salt, or to taste

For the salad

4 cups mesclun (see Tip, page 69)

1/2 cup Tofu-Chèvre Spread (page 5)

4 roasted red bell peppers (see Tip, page 92)

garnish *(optional)* toasted pine nuts (see Tip, page 75)

Whisk together the dressing ingredients in a small bowl. Adjust the seasonings to taste. Set aside.

Divide the mesclun among 4 salad plates. Set aside.

Spoon 1 tablespoon of the Tofu-Chèvre Spread into the center of a roasted bell pepper half; carefully roll the pepper around the filling. Place, seam side down, on top of the mesclun. Repeat; prepare 2 stuffed bell pepper halves for each salad.

Whisk or shake the dressing. Drizzle about 2 tablespoons over each salad.

Per serving: Cal 202/Pro 4.3g/Carb 8.5g/Fat 16.7g/Chol 12mg/Sod 150mg

ADVANCE PREPARATION The flavor of the dressing improves after standing overnight or longer; it will keep for up to 1 week in a tightly closed container in the refrigerator. The peppers can be roasted early the day the salad is to be served. Stuff the peppers and assemble the salads just before serving.

Capers are the unopened flower buds of a shrub native to the Mediterranean and parts of Asia. The buds are dried in the sun and then pickled in a vinegar brine. Capers come in several sizes; the largest have the strongest flavor. The smallest, called nonpareil, are subtle in taste but are the most tender and most expensive. Capers should be rinsed before using to remove excess salt. Once opened, store in the refrigerator for up to 3 months.

Shallots, a member of the onion family, are small bulbous herbs with a mild onion–garlic flavor. Always use fresh shallots; dehydrated or powdered products will not do. (If unavailable, substitute some fresh onion and fresh garlic.) Fresh shallots will keep for a month in the bottom bin of your refrigerator; use before they begin to sprout. When cooking, don't allow shallots to brown or they will taste bitter.

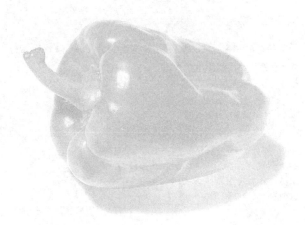

tomato slices with creamy avocado dressing

makes 6 servings

For the Creamy Avocado Dressing

1 small ripe avocado, peeled, pitted, and mashed (about $1/2$ cup)

$1/4$ cup mashed silken firm tofu

$1/4$ cup white wine vinegar (see Tip)

2 tablespoons extra-virgin olive oil

1 tablespoon freshly squeezed lime juice

Dash of freshly ground black pepper, or to taste

Dash of salt, or to taste

For the salad

8 leaves leaf lettuce

2 large ripe beefsteak tomatoes (at room temperature), cut into $3/8$-inch-thick slices

garnish *(optional)* roasted and unsalted sunflower seeds, sprigs of fresh flat-leaf parsley

Here's the perfect salad for the height of summer. Spoon the Creamy Avocado Dressing over slices of juicy homegrown beefsteak tomatoes and serve as an accompaniment to Mexican-inspired menus. The dressing recipe makes more than you will need for 4 salads; store the remainder. Another time, toss it with romaine lettuce and top with plum tomato slices and Herbed Garlic Croutons (page 65).

Put the dressing ingredients into a food processor; process until smooth and creamy. Adjust the seasonings to taste. Cover and set aside.

Arrange the lettuce on 4 salad plates; top with the tomato slices. Drizzle each salad with about 2 tablespoons of the dressing.

Per serving ($1/2$ tomato with 2 tablespoons dressing): Cal 91/Pro 2g/Carb 6.7g/Fat 6.2g/Chol 0mg/Sod 31mg

ADVANCE PREPARATION The dressing will keep, covered and refrigerated, for up to 3 days. Since it thickens while standing, stir in water as needed. Assemble the salads just before serving.

tip

Wine vinegars are produced from the acetic fermentation of wine; they are mellow in flavor and retain the aroma of the wine from which they are made. The name vinegar *comes from the French* vin aigre, *which means "sour wine."*

dijon potato salad

No need to peel the new potatoes for potato salad; just scrub them well with a vegetable brush before cooking. The creamy dressing with zesty Dijon mustard brings this salad to life.

Put the dressing ingredients into a food processor; process until smooth and creamy. Adjust the seasonings to taste. Set aside.

Bring a large pot of salted water to a boil over high heat. Meanwhile, scrub the potatoes; add to the pot. When the water returns to a boil, reduce the heat to medium; cover and cook until the potatoes are just tender, about 10 to 12 minutes (or about 20 to 25 minutes if the potatoes are large). Drain well.

When the potatoes are cool enough to handle, cut into quarters; transfer to a large bowl. Add the scallions, celery, and bell pepper; toss gently. Add the dressing and toss again.

Per serving: Cal 197/Pro 4.5g/Carb 32.8g/Fat 5.3g/Chol 0mg/Sod 53mg

ADVANCE PREPARATION The dressing will keep for up to 2 days in a tightly closed container in the refrigerator. Since it thickens while standing, stir in milk or water as needed. The salad can be made early the day it is to be served; cover and refrigerate. To prepare the day ahead, cover and refrigerate the dressing and salad ingredients separately; add the dressing to the salad just before serving.

tip

Red new potatoes are young potatoes that are harvested before maturity. They are small, thin-skinned, low in starch, and sweet in flavor. They cook rapidly when boiled or steamed; they are not recommended for baking or mashing. New potatoes are preferable for potato salads because mature baking potatoes break apart too easily and absorb too much of the dressing. Store new potatoes at room temperature in a cool, dark place; use them within 1 or 2 weeks.

makes 6 servings

For the Creamy Dijon Dressing

1/2 cup mashed silken
firm tofu

3 tablespoons freshly
squeezed lemon juice

2 tablespoons extra-virgin
olive oil

1 tablespoon Dijon mustard

1/2 teaspoon celery seed

1/2 teaspoon freshly ground
black pepper, or to taste

Dash of paprika, or to taste

Dash of salt, or to taste

For the salad

2 pounds medium size new
potatoes (about 16),
quartered (see Tip)

3 medium scallions, thinly
sliced

2 ribs celery, diced

1/2 red bell pepper, diced

garnish *(optional)* paprika

orange-caraway coleslaw

Serve this bright new version of the deli staple as a side dish with your favorite sandwich.

makes 4 servings

For the Orange-Caraway Dressing

1/2 cup mashed silken firm tofu

1/4 cup freshly squeezed orange juice

1 tablespoon white rice vinegar

1 teaspoon honey

Dash of freshly ground black pepper, or to taste

Dash of salt, or to taste

1/2 teaspoon caraway seeds (see Tip)

For the salad

2 cups shredded white or green head cabbage

1 large carrot, coarsely grated (about 1 cup)

Put the dressing ingredients except the caraway seeds into a food processor; process until smooth and creamy. Stir in the caraway seeds. Adjust the seasonings to taste.

Toss the cabbage and carrot in a medium bowl. Add the dressing and toss again.

Per serving: Cal 54/Pro 2.9g/Carb 8.3g/Fat 1g/Chol 0mg/Sod 58mg

ADVANCE PREPARATION The dressing will keep for up to 2 days in a tightly closed container in the refrigerator. The salad is best when prepared just before serving.

tip

Caraway seeds, from an herb in the parsley family, have a nutty, delicate anise flavor. Store them in an airtight container in a cool, dark place for up to 6 months.

tofu "egg salad"

This virtuous salad makes an excellent filling for pita bread pockets or hollowed-out tomato shells, or it can be used in "egg salad" sandwiches. To serve as an appetizer, dice the carrot and green bell pepper; spread the mixture on whole-grain crackers and top each with half a cherry tomato or a sprig of parsley.

makes 6 servings

Stir together the ingredients in a medium bowl. Adjust the seasonings to taste.

Per serving: Cal 53/Pro 5g/Carb 4.1g/Fat 1.8g/Chol 0mg/Sod 130mg

ADVANCE PREPARATION Covered and refrigerated, this salad will keep for up to 2 days.

VARIATIONS

❯ Add other vegetables such as 1/4 cup chopped red bell pepper or zucchini.

❯ Add 1 or 2 chopped hard-cooked eggs.

tip

Dijon mustard, which originated in Dijon, France, is made from brown mustard seeds, spices, and white wine, making it more flavorful (and more expensive) than ordinary yellow mustard.

- 1 1/2 cups mashed silken extra-firm tofu (12 ounces)
- 3 tablespoons nonfat plain yogurt
- 1 rib celery, finely chopped
- 1 carrot, finely chopped
- 1/4 cup finely chopped green bell pepper
- 1 medium scallion, minced
- 1 tablespoon Dijon mustard (see Tip)
- 1 tablespoon low-sodium soy sauce
- 1/2 teaspoon minced garlic
- 1/2 teaspoon ground turmeric
- 1/2 teaspoon freshly ground black pepper, or to taste
- Dash of ground cumin, or to taste
- Dash of salt, or to taste

tortilla-salsa salad with roasted sweet red pepper dressing

This light entrée salad takes a little advance planning in order to prepare several of its components ahead of time so flavors can mellow. Once assembled, the colorful presentation is quite impressive. Most of all, I relish the alluring flavor contrasts of sweet and tart and the play of soft against crispy textures.

makes 4 servings

1/4 cup Roasted Sweet Red Pepper Dressing (page 92)

1/4 cup Tofu-Chèvre Spread (page 5)

2 cups Sweet Bean–Corn Salsa (page 23)

Four 6- or 7-inch flour tortillas

4 teaspoons olive oil

1/4 cup crumbled mild feta cheese (see Tip)

garnish *(optional)* sprigs of fresh cilantro, basil, or flat-leaf parsley

At least 1 hour prior to serving this salad, prepare the Roasted Red Pepper Dressing, Tofu-Chèvre Spread, and Sweet Bean–Corn Salsa. (Advance preparation of these recipes will allow the flavors to develop.) Cover and refrigerate separately.

At least 15 minutes before serving the salad, toast the tortillas: Preheat the oven to 400°F. Lightly brush both sides of each tortilla with olive oil, about 1/2 teaspoon per side. Prick the surfaces of the tortillas several places with a fork. Place the tortillas directly on the oven rack; toast in the preheated oven until lightly browned, about 2 minutes. Turn and toast the other sides until lightly browned, about 1 minute. Watch closely! (Since tortillas differ in thickness, toasting time may vary.) Remove the tortillas from the oven; cool on a wire rack.

Assemble the salads just before serving. For each tortilla, spread 1 tablespoon of the Tofu-Chèvre Spread in the center, leaving a 1-inch border uncovered. Top the spread with a mound of 1/2 cup of the salsa. Stir the Roasted Sweet Red Pepper Dressing and drizzle 1 tablespoon over each salad; sprinkle with 1 tablespoon feta cheese. Garnish and serve immediately.

Per serving: Cal 305/Pro 11.6g/Carb 31.9g/Fat 14.5g/Chol 17mg/Sod 539mg

ADVANCE PREPARATION Prepare the Roasted Sweet Red Pepper Dressing, Tofu-Chèvre Spread, and Sweet Bean–Corn Salsa at least 1 hour or up to 2 days before serving the salad. Cover and refrigerate separately. Toast the tortillas at least 15 minutes or up to 1 day before serving the salad; set aside, uncovered, at room temperature. (More than 15 minutes advance preparation is not recommended on a humid day, since the tortillas may lose their crispness.) Assemble the salads just before serving.

tip

Feta cheese is a white Greek cheese with a rich, tangy flavor. Traditionally, it is made with goat's milk or sheep's milk or a combination; today it is also often made with cow's milk. Fresh feta is crumbly with whey; when mature it becomes drier and saltier.

roasted sweet red pepper dressing ✓

makes 1/2 cup

1 roasted red bell pepper
   (see Tip)

1 tablespoon red wine vinegar

1 tablespoon roasted garlic–
   infused extra-virgin olive oil
   (see Tip, page 200)

1/4 teaspoon freshly ground
   black pepper, or to taste

Dash of salt, or to taste

This is a favorite recipe from my cookbook The Complete Book of Dressings (Macmillan, 1995). It stars as the topping for Tortilla-Salsa Salad (page 90), or warm it gently to serve over Spicy Soybean Patties (page 171) or Garden Frittata (page 150).

Put the ingredients into a food processor; process until smooth. Adjust the seasonings to taste. Stir before serving.

Per tablespoon: Cal 19/Pro 0.1g/Carb 0.8g/Fat 1.7g/Chol 0mg/Sod 17mg

ADVANCE PREPARATION This dressing will keep for up to 2 days in a tightly closed container in the refrigerator.

tip

To roast a bell pepper: Position the oven broiler rack about 3 inches from the heating element and preheat the broiler. Remove the stem and cut the bell pepper in half lengthwise; discard the seeds and membranes. Place the pepper halves, skin sides up, on a foil-lined baking sheet; flatten each with the palm of your hand. Broil until the skins are blackened, charred, and blistered, about 5 to 10 minutes. While still hot, transfer the pepper halves to a heavy-duty zip-top plastic bag and seal; set aside for 10 to 15 minutes. (The steam will loosen the skins.) Remove from the bag; peel and discard the skins.

Fruit Salad

maple-walnut apple salad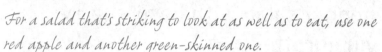

For a salad that's striking to look at as well as to eat, use one red apple and another green-skinned one.

Put the tofu, maple syrup, and lemon juice into a food processor; process until smooth and creamy. Stir in the celery seeds, mustard, paprika, and salt. Adjust the seasoning to taste. Set aside.

Toss together the apples, raisins, and walnuts in a medium bowl. Add the dressing and toss.

Per serving: Cal 121/Pro 4g/Carb 20.1g/Fat 2.7g/Chol 0mg/ Sod 50mg

ADVANCE PREPARATION Covered and refrigerated, this salad will keep for up to 1 day.

tips

Celery seeds are the seeds from lovage, a wild celery that comes from India. Since they have a strong flavor, use them sparingly.

Pick apples with firm, unblemished skin and stems attached. Best-selling red and golden Delicious apples lack tartness; however, after being cut, they (as well as Cortlands) tend to darken less readily than many other apples. For the best crisp texture and tart flavor, select Granny Smith, Winesap, or McIntosh. Avoid waxed apples if you plan to eat the skin. Since apples are picked at peak ripeness, additional "ripening" means "spoiling"; store apples in a plastic bag in the refrigerator crisper for up to 6 weeks.

makes 4 servings

For the Maple Dressing

3/4 cup mashed silken firm tofu

2 tablespoons pure maple syrup

2 tablespoons freshly squeezed lemon juice

1/4 teaspoon celery seeds (see Tip)

1/4 teaspoon dry mustard

Dash of paprika

Dash of salt, or to taste

For the salad

2 large apples, cored and cut into 1-inch cubes (see Tip)

1/4 cup raisins

1 tablespoon toasted chopped walnuts (see Tip, page 50)

Warm Salads

warm soybean and sweet red pepper salad with basil-sherry vinaigrette ✓

Once you have tasted balsamic vinegar, you'll never want to be without it. Here its sweet, intense flavor is mingled with arugula, soybeans, and feta cheese. Served warm, this unusual winter salad is hearty enough to stand on its own. Or you can make it in advance to serve chilled or at room temperature.

makes 4 servings

For the Balsamic Vinaigrette

1/4 cup balsamic vinegar

2 tablespoons extra-virgin olive oil

2 tablespoons water

1 teaspoon Dijon mustard

1 tablespoon minced fresh basil (or 1 teaspoon dried)

1 teaspoon light brown sugar

1/2 teaspoon minced garlic

1/8 teaspoon freshly ground black pepper, or to taste

Dash of salt, or to taste

For the salad

12 leaves romaine lettuce, shredded

8 leaves arugula (see Tip)

1 tablespoon olive oil

1 cup coarsely shredded carrot

Whisk together the Balsamic Vinaigrette ingredients in a small bowl; make certain the brown sugar is dissolved. Adjust the seasonings to taste. Set aside.

Spread a layer of shredded lettuce on 4 large salad plates. Arrange the arugula leaves atop the lettuce, radiating from the center pinwheel fashion.

Heat the olive oil in a medium nonstick skillet over medium heat. Add the carrot, bell pepper, celery, scallions, and garlic; cook, stirring occasionally, until the vegetables are tender, about 4 minutes. Add the soybeans; stir until warm, about 2 minutes. Stir in the vinaigrette (do not allow it to evaporate).

Spoon the warm salad mixture over the arugula. Garnish and serve immediately.

Per serving: Cal 241/Pro 13.6g/Carb 16.6g/Fat 13.4g/Chol 0mg/Sod 51mg

ADVANCE PREPARATION If dried basil is used, allow the dressing to stand for 15 to 30 minutes before serving; it will keep for up to 1 week in a tightly closed container in the refrigerator. If fresh basil is used, the dressing will keep for up to 4 days. The bean and vegetable mixture can be prepared early on the day it is to be served; cover and refrigerate. Serve chilled or at room temperature; assemble the plates with the romaine lettuce and arugula just before serving.

VARIATION

❧ Substitute cooked sweet beans (see page xxvi) for the soybeans.

tip

Arugula, also called roquette or rocket, is rich in iron and beta carotene; compared to most greens, it is also high in vitamin C. The long spear-shaped leaves resemble dandelion greens; they have a spicy, peppery, mustardlike bitterness and aroma. Select dark green leaves 3 to 5 inches long; the more mature the green, the stronger the flavor. Wrap the roots in moist paper towels and put them in a plastic bag; store in the refrigerator for up to 2 days. Wash the sandy leaves thoroughly before using.

1 red bell pepper, cut into strips about 2 inches long by 1/4 inch wide

1/4 cup diced celery

2 medium scallions, finely chopped

1/2 teaspoon minced garlic

1 1/2 cups cooked soybeans (one 15-ounce can, drained and rinsed)

garnish *(optional)* freshly ground black pepper, crumbled mild feta cheese

tempeh stir-fry salad with gingered plum vinaigrette

Go ahead, break tradition! It's not necessary for salads to be served chilled or for stir-fries to be dished out over rice. This warm stir-fry can be served on greens or noodles. The Gingered Plum Vinaigrette imparts delicate Asian flavors.

makes 4 servings

For the Gingered Plum Vinaigrette

1 teaspoon orange zest (see Tips, pages 6–7)

1/2 cup freshly squeezed orange juice

1/4 cup Chinese plum sauce (see Tip)

2 tablespoons freshly squeezed lime juice

2 tablespoons white rice vinegar

1 teaspoon minced gingerroot

1 teaspoon Dijon mustard

1 teaspoon minced garlic

Pinch of red pepper flakes, or to taste

To complete the recipe

2 tablespoons safflower oil

2 cups asparagus in 2-inch lengths

8 ounces tempeh, cut into strips about 2 inches long by 1/2 inch wide

1 red bell pepper, cut into strips about 2 inches long by 1/4 inch wide

2 medium scallions, coarsely chopped

6 cups shredded Chinese cabbage (see Tip, page 63)

Whisk together the vinaigrette ingredients in a small bowl. Adjust the seasoning to taste. Set aside.

Heat the oil in a large nonstick sauté pan over medium-high heat. Add the asparagus and tempeh; stir-fry until the asparagus is crisp-tender and the tempeh is lightly browned, about 5 minutes. Add the bell pepper and scallions; stir-fry until the bell pepper is crisp-tender, about 3 minutes. Remove the pan from the heat; stir in 1/2 cup of the vinaigrette. Cover and set aside.

Toss the Chinese cabbage and the remaining vinaigrette in a medium bowl.

Divide the cabbage among 4 large salad plates. Top with the warm tempeh-vegetable mixture.

Per serving: Cal 292/Pro 17g/Carb 29.4g/Fat 11.8g/Chol 0mg/Sod 42mg

ADVANCE PREPARATION The vinaigrette will keep for up to 2 days in a tightly closed container in the refrigerator. Stir-fry the tempeh and vegetables and assemble the warm salads just before serving.

VARIATIONS

❯ Add 1 tablespoon chopped fresh cilantro (or more, to taste) to the vinaigrette.

❯ Substitute 4 cups cooked Chinese wheat-flour noodles (see Tip, page 162), at room temperature, for the shredded Chinese cabbage.

Chinese plum sauce is a thick sweet-and-sour sauce made from plums, apricots, chili peppers, sugar, vinegar, and spices. It is usually used as a condiment but also makes a tasty ingredient in other sauces. Look for it in the Asian section of most supermarkets. Store in the refrigerator after opening.

Shredding means to cut food into narrow strips.

garnish *(optional)* sprigs of
fresh cilantro

4

Entrées

Soy with Sauces

Tofu with Chinese Tahini Sauce

Tofu and Portobello
Mushrooms Marsala

Tofu and Vegetable Curry

Soybeans Bourguignonne

Tempeh Strips and Broccoli
with Ancho Chili Sauce

Ancho Chili Sauce

Tofu-Mushroom Stroganoff

Tofu and Fruit in Mango
Chutney Sauce

Tempeh with Spicy Peanut
Sauce

Tofu Newburg

Vegetable Medley with Hoisin
Peanut Sauce

Tempeh with Black Bean–Tomato
Sauce

Stir-Fries

Vegetable Stir-Fry with Ginger
Sauce

Sweet Bean Stir-Fry with
Hoisin-Orange Sauce

Sweet-and-Sour Tofu

Spicy Cashew Stir-Fry

Rice Dishes

Tempeh Paella

Italian Tempeh, Vegetable, and
Rice Skillet

Tofu Fried Rice

Soybean-Mushroom Risotto

Chili-Rice Skillet

Stovetop Pasta Dishes

Penne with Cremini
Mushrooms and
Tomato-Tofu Pesto

Udon Noodles with Tempeh
and Hijiki

Spaghetti with Tempeh in
Mexican Chili Sauce

Spicy Asian Peanut Pasta

Mostaccioli and Plum
Tomatoes with
Tofu-Basil Pesto

Penne Rigate with Parmesan-
Peppercorn Sauce

Rotini with Parsley-Nut
Pesto

Bell Pepper–Soybean Toss
with Pasta

Cabbage and Noodles
with Tofu

Stovetop Dishes

Curried Acorn Squash Ragout

Mu Shu Tofu

Romaine Spring Rolls with
    Five-Spice Soybeans

Garden Frittata

Huevos Rancheros

Scrambled Tofu

Tofu Tacos

Grilled Tofu-Vegetable
    Towers with Parmesan
    Vinaigrette

Sherried Tofu Steaks

Tofu Teriyaki

Chinese Wheat-Flour
    Noodles with Sesame-
    Pepper Dressing

Sandwiches

Bruschetta

Sherried Tofu–Roasted
    Eggplant Sandwiches

Roasted Vegetable Pitas

Tempeh-Yam Sandwiches

Tempeh Reubens

Curried Tofu Carrot
    Sloppy Joes

Burgers

Veggie Burgers

Spicy Soybean Patties

Wraps

Tempeh-Rice Wraps with Hoisin
    Peanut Sauce

Broccoli Burritos

Rice Paper Spring Rolls

Entrée Pies, Tartlets, and Pita and Tortilla Crusts

Chili Custard Pie

Asparagus-Mushroom Quiche

Whole Wheat Pastry

Soybean Confetti Pie with
    Cornmeal Crust

Vegetable Tartlets with Herbed
    Tomato Sauce

Soybean Pita Pizzas

Tofu Tostada

Pepper-Bean Quesadillas

Stuffed Vegetables

Stuffed Acorn Squash

Bell Peppers Stuffed with
    Herbed Tofu and Rice

Zucchini with Herbed Tomato-
    Soybean Stuffing

Baked Vegetable Dishes

Spinach and Leek Ring

Garlic Mashed Potatoes

Rosemary-Parmesan Potato Bake

Herbed Twice-Baked Potatoes

Caribbean Squash and Soybean
  Casserole

Curried Tofu en Papillote

Baked Pasta Dishes

Tofu Stuffed Shells with
  Tomato-Basil Sauce

Tofu-Spinach Lasagna

Vegetarian Pastitsio

Loaves and Accompanying Sauces

Vegetable-Soybean Loaf

Tofu-Walnut Loaf

Cremini Mushroom Sauce

Tomato–Red Pepper Sauce

Entrées for Brunch

Tofu-Nut Pancakes

Noodle Pudding

*T*oday there are far more vegetarian entrées than the bland rice and beans of the past. Supermarket shelves are full of vegetarian-friendly products, not to mention the colorful fresh vegetables and aromatic herbs just waiting to be cooked. Ethnic flavors make the options for soy entrées almost endless. With the 75 recipes in this chapter, many of which include suggested variations, you can enjoy a couple of new soy entrées every week of the year.

This chapter features dishes that are substantial enough to serve as a main course; many of them, such as Romaine Spring Rolls with Five-Spice Soybeans (page 148), make a meal in themselves by satisfying several food groups at once. In other entrées the nutrients, flavors, textures, or colors are enhanced by a complement, so I've included a few side dishes, such as Garlic Mashed Potatoes (page 200), and sauces, such as Cremini Mushroom Sauce (page 216). Often a side salad and bread are all that's necessary.

Most of the recipes are quick enough to prepare on busy weeknights. Surprise your family with such simple pleasures as Veggie Burgers (page 170), Tofu Tacos (page 155), and Soybean Pita Pizzas (page 188). For a special Sunday breakfast, prepare Tofu-Nut Pancakes (page 218) or have weekend visitors awake to the comforting aroma of Noodle Pudding (page 219). Several dishes are elegant enough to please your most discriminating guests, such as Tofu-Mushroom Stroganoff (page 112) and Soybean-Mushroom Risotto (page 130). For nonvegetarians some of the creations can be served as an accompaniment to meat, such as Stuffed Acorn Squash (page 193).

In these recipes you will find tofu, whole soybeans, tempeh, and texturized vegetable protein (TVP) prepared with a variety of cooking methods. Some dishes are cooked on the stovetop using a skillet, sauté pan, or stovetop grill pan (see Tip, page 157); others are baked, such as the stuffed vegetables, lasagnas, and the soybean and tofu loaves. There are sauces made with soy milk, light coconut milk, vegetable stock, fruit juice, and tomato juice and brought to life with dried chilies, chutney, hoisin sauce, peanut butter—and even a couple made with wine to reserve for elegant evenings, such as Tofu and Portobello Mushrooms Marsala (page 104). Rice dishes are anything but mundane when flavored with saffron or made with Arborio rice. For speedy preparation, select stir-fries; embellished with spicy sauces or sweet sauces, they're as tasty as they are quick.

Before beginning to prepare your entrée, it's important to read the recipe. Plan your accompaniment, and preheat the water for cooking pasta or cook the rice. Then keep in mind one of the principles of French cooking, *mise en place,* which means "everything in place." Put this principle into action before you begin by setting out the necessary pans and utensils and preheating the oven or broiler if necessary. Set out all of the items in the ingredient list, then clean and chop the vegetables. Follow the cooking procedure as described; for kitchen efficiency, sometimes you will be doing more than one procedure at a time, such as mixing a sauce while pasta or vegetables cook.

As you become familiar with making soy entrées, feel free to improvise and substitute. When using the suggested variations from the original recipe, be certain quantities are in keeping with the original recipe, however. And always begin by sautéing or stir-frying the firmest vegetables first so everything will be cooked to just the right consistency at the same time.

When your healthful, appetizing soy creation is ready, simply add an attractive garnish and serve it proudly with style.

Soy with Sauces

tofu with chinese tahini sauce

Some like it hot. Some like it mild. Simply adjust the "heat" by varying the amount of chili paste with garlic to suit your taste. Serve this colorful veggie combination over rice, couscous, or buckwheat noodles.

To prepare the sauce, combine the tahini and chili paste in a small bowl. Add the water gradually and stir until smooth. (The sauce should have a cake-batter consistency; it may be necessary to add more water if the tahini is thick.) Set aside.

Put the broccoli, carrot, and bell pepper into a large microwave-proof dish; add about $1/4$ cup water. Cover and microwave on high until crisp-tender, about 4 to 6 minutes; drain well. (Or cook the vegetables in a stovetop steamer.)

Transfer the vegetables to a large nonstick skillet; stir in the sauce. Warm over medium heat, stirring occasionally. Adjust the seasoning to taste. Gently stir in the tofu; heat until warm, about 3 minutes.

Per serving: Cal 266/Pro 15.7g/Carb 13.1g/Fat 16.7g/Chol 0mg/Sod 143mg

VARIATIONS

❧ Substitute for the broccoli and carrot or add other vegetables (up to 5 cups total) such as cut green beans or asparagus.

❧ For a firmer texture, substitute pressed tofu (see page xxxii).

makes 4 servings

For the Chinese Tahini Sauce

$1/3$ cup tahini (see Tip, page 13)

1 tablespoon chili paste with garlic, or to taste (see Tip, page 9)

1 cup water, or as needed

To complete the recipe

4 cups broccoli florets

1 carrot, halved lengthwise and cut into $1/8$-inch-thick slices

$1/2$ red bell pepper, coarsely chopped

12 ounces silken extra-firm tofu, cut into $1/2$-inch cubes (about 2 cups)

garnish *(optional)* toasted sesame seeds (see Tip, page 125), sprigs of fresh cilantro

tofu and portobello mushrooms marsala

Portobello mushrooms, shallots, and Marsala wine are ingredients with distinctive flavors, intoxicating aromas, and elegance. Serve this to your most discriminating guests.

makes 4 servings

1/2 cup all-purpose white or unbleached flour

1/8 teaspoon freshly ground black pepper

Dash of salt

1 large egg

12 ounces silken extra-firm tofu, cut into 2 × 3/4 × 3/8-inch strips

1 tablespoon olive oil

For the Marsala sauce

1 tablespoon cold water

1 tablespoon cornstarch

1 1/4 cups sweet Marsala wine (preferably Italian) (see Tip)

1/4 cup freshly squeezed lemon juice

1/8 teaspoon freshly ground black pepper, or to taste

Dash of salt, or to taste

Bring a large saucepan of water to a boil over high heat.

To prepare the tofu, combine the flour, pepper, and salt in a shallow bowl.

Lightly beat the egg in a separate shallow bowl.

Gently press the tofu strips into the flour, covering all sides; dip them into the egg and press again into the flour. As the strips are prepared, place them in a single layer on a plate.

Heat the tablespoon of oil in a large nonstick skillet over medium-high heat. Arrange the tofu strips in a single layer; cook until lightly browned, about 2 minutes on each side. Use a slotted spatula to transfer the tofu to a plate; cover to keep warm.

To prepare the Marsala sauce, stir together the water and cornstarch in a small bowl until smooth. Stir in the wine, lemon juice, pepper, and salt. Set aside.

To complete the recipe, heat the remaining 1 tablespoon of oil in the same large skillet over medium heat. Add the mushrooms; cook, turning occasionally, until they are lightly browned and tender, about 2 minutes. Add the shallots and cook for 1 minute more. Stir the Marsala sauce and add it to the pan; stir constantly until the sauce thickens slightly, about 1 minute. Reduce the heat to low; cover and cook for about 5 minutes. Adjust the seasonings to taste. Gently stir in the tofu strips.

Meanwhile, add the noodles to the boiling water. When the water returns to a boil, stir once to separate the noodles. Reduce the heat to medium-high and cook until tender, about 5 to 7 minutes; drain well.

To assemble the servings, divide the noodles among 4 plates. Top with tofu strips and mushroom slices; drizzle with the remaining sauce. Garnish and serve.

Per serving: Cal 357/Pro 15g/Carb 46.9g/Fat 12.1g/Chol 76mg/Sod 88mg

VARIATIONS

❧ Substitute $1/4$ cup cholesterol-free egg substitute for the egg.

❧ For a firmer texture, substitute pressed tofu (see page xxxii).

❧ Substitute tempeh for the tofu: Cut 8 ounces tempeh crosswise into 12 even-size strips; sauté the strips (flour and egg are not necessary) in 1 tablespoon olive oil in a medium nonstick skillet over medium-high heat until the strips are lightly browned, about 4 to 5 minutes per side. Remove from the heat; cover and set aside to keep warm. After the Marsala sauce has thickened, stir the tempeh strips into the sauce and mushrooms. Reduce the heat to low; cover and cook for about 5 minutes.

tips

Portobello mushrooms are large dark brown mushrooms with an open, flat cap; the tops can easily measure 6 inches in diameter. Because of a long growing cycle, the portobello's gills are fully exposed, which means that some of the moisture has evaporated; this concentrates and enriches the flavor and creates a dense, meaty texture. Portobellos can be found in many supermarkets and in gourmet produce markets.

The best Marsala wine is imported from Sicily. It has a rich, smoky flavor that can range from sweet to dry. Like port, sherry, and other dessert wines, Marsala is a "fortified" wine, which means brandy or another spirit has been added, increasing the alcohol content and enhancing the flavor.

To complete the recipe

1 tablespoon olive oil

4 portobello mushrooms, stems removed, caps cut into $1/2$-inch-wide slices (see Tip)

$1/4$ cup minced shallots

8 ounces wide egg noodles (about 4 cups)

garnish *(optional)* freshly ground black pepper, thin lemon slices, sprigs of flat-leaf parsley

tofu and vegetable curry

Traditionally, curries are accompanied by an assortment of condiments to enhance the curries' flavors and provide a cooling element. I usually select two or three from these options: plain yogurt, chutney, cucumber slices, tomato wedges, or unsalted dry-roasted peanuts. I also like to serve this curry atop basmati rice (see Tip, page 114).

makes 6 servings

2 tablespoons safflower oil

2 carrots, thinly sliced

1 red bell pepper, cut into
    1/2-inch squares

1 small onion, cut into
    1/4-inch-thick wedges

2 cups sliced mushrooms

1 teaspoon minced garlic

1 tablespoon curry powder, or
    to taste (see Tip, page 46)

1 1/2 cups light coconut milk
    (see Tip)

3/4 cup unsweetened apple
    juice

2 teaspoons minced gingerroot

1/2 teaspoon ground cumin

1/2 teaspoon freshly ground
    black pepper, or to taste

Dash of salt, or to taste

2 tablespoons cold water

2 tablespoons cornstarch

12 ounces silken extra-firm
    tofu, cut into 1/2-inch
    cubes (about 2 cups)

1 cup frozen baby peas,
    thawed (see Tip)

garnish *(optional)* sprigs of
fresh cilantro or mint

Heat the oil in a large nonstick skillet over medium-high heat. Add the carrots, bell pepper, and onion; cook, stirring occasionally, until the carrot slices are crisp-tender, about 5 minutes. Add the mushrooms and garlic; continue to cook until the carrots and mushrooms soften, about 3 minutes. Add the curry powder; stir for about 30 seconds.

Stir in the coconut milk, apple juice, gingerroot, cumin, pepper, and salt. When the liquid begins to simmer, reduce the heat to medium; stir occasionally.

Meanwhile, stir together the water and cornstarch in a small bowl or measuring cup until smooth; add to the curry mixture. Cook over medium heat, stirring constantly, until the mixture thickens, about 3 minutes.

Add the tofu and peas; stir gently until heated through. Adjust the seasonings to taste.

To serve, spoon rice onto each serving plate; top with the curry mixture. Garnish as desired and serve with accompaniments.

Per serving: Cal 223/Pro 8g/Carb 19.1g/Fat 12.7g/Chol 0mg/Sod 106mg

ADVANCE PREPARATION This dish is best when served immediately after cooking, but it can be refrigerated for up to 1 day. The sauce will thicken while standing; stir in water as needed when reheating. The flavor of curry often intensifies when a dish is allowed to stand.

VARIATIONS

❯ Substitute for the carrots, bell pepper, or mushrooms or add other vegetables (up to 4 cups in total) such as thin potato slices, green beans, snap peas, cauliflower florets, or broccoli florets; plum tomato wedges may be stirred in with, or in place of, the peas.

❯ For a firmer texture, substitute pressed tofu (see page xxxii).

tips

Do not confuse canned unsweetened coconut milk with "cream of coconut," used mainly for desserts and mixed drinks. Light (or "lite") coconut milk, available in health food stores, Asian markets, and some supermarkets, contains less than half the calories and fat of regular coconut milk. In both products the coconut fat naturally separates from the coconut milk; shake well before using.

Generally, the flavor of frozen baby peas (or petit pois) is preferable to that of standard-size peas. Harvested when young, baby peas remain especially sweet after picking; they also retain a brighter green color and a firmer texture.

soybeans bourguignonne

makes 6 servings

3 tablespoons olive oil

3/4 cup coarsely chopped onion

1 teaspoon minced garlic

1 1/4 cups water, or more as needed

One 6-ounce can tomato paste

1 large russet (baking) potato, peeled and cut into 1-inch cubes

1 large carrot, halved lengthwise and cut into 1/4-inch-thick slices

1 tablespoon minced fresh thyme (or 1 teaspoon dried)

2 bay leaves

1 1/4 cups dry red wine

1 1/2 cups cooked soybeans (one 15-ounce can, drained and rinsed)

3 cups sliced mushrooms

1/4 teaspoon freshly ground black pepper, or to taste

Dash of salt, or to taste

Bourguignonne means "as prepared in Burgundy." Burgundy, in eastern France, is noted for its superb wines, which are robust and full-bodied. When preparing this dish, which I've adapted from the original that calls for beef, use a good-quality dry red table wine, not "cooking wine." If possible, prepare it an hour or so before serving; standing improves the flavor. This is meant to be served as a hearty stew, but sometimes, for variety, I serve it in a nontraditional manner over pasta.

Heat 1 tablespoon of the oil in a large nonstick sauté pan over medium-high heat. Add the onion and garlic; cook, stirring occasionally, until tender but not browned, about 4 minutes.

Meanwhile, stir together 1 1/4 cups water and half of the tomato paste in a small bowl; add to the sauté pan. Stir in the potato, carrot, dried thyme (if using), and bay leaves. When the liquid comes to a boil, reduce the heat to medium; cover and cook until the potato and carrot begin to turn tender but are not thoroughly cooked, about 20 minutes. (Check occasionally; if the water is cooking away, add more, 1/4 cup at a time.)

Stir in the wine, remaining tomato paste, soybeans, and fresh thyme (if using); increase the heat to high. When the liquid returns to a boil, reduce the heat to medium. Cook, uncovered, until the potato and carrot are tender and the sauce is reduced by about one-half and thickened, about 10 minutes (see Tip).

Meanwhile, heat the remaining 2 tablespoons of oil in a medium nonstick skillet over medium heat. Add the mushrooms; cook, stirring occasionally, until they are tender but not browned, about 4 minutes. Remove from the heat.

Remove the bay leaf from the sauté pan; stir in the mushrooms, pepper, and salt. Adjust the seasonings to taste.

Per serving: Cal 224/Pro 10.4g/Carb 20.3g/Fat 11.2g/Chol 0mg/Sod 103mg

ADVANCE PREPARATION Covered and refrigerated, this dish will keep for up to 2 days; it is delicious reheated.

tip

Stocks and sauces are "reduced" by boiling rapidly, uncovered, until the volume is reduced by evaporation. This thickens the consistency and intensifies the flavors.

tempeh strips and broccoli with ancho chili sauce

makes 4 servings

2 cups Ancho Chili Sauce
(recipe follows)

2 tablespoons olive oil

4 cups broccoli florets

1/2 cup coarsely chopped
red bell pepper

8 ounces tempeh, cut crosswise into 12 even-size
slices

garnish *(optional)* sprigs of
fresh cilantro

For variety, substitute cauliflower florets for part of the broccoli. Arrange the tempeh strips and vegetables over rice and top with the Ancho Chili Sauce.

Prepare or reheat the chili sauce; cover and keep warm over very low heat.

Heat 1 tablespoon of the oil in a medium nonstick skillet over medium-high heat. Add the broccoli and bell pepper; cook, stirring occasionally, until the broccoli is tender, about 5 minutes.

While the broccoli is cooking, heat the remaining 1 tablespoon of oil in a separate medium nonstick skillet over medium-high heat. Arrange the tempeh strips in a single layer; cook until lightly browned, about 4 to 5 minutes per side.

To serve, arrange the tempeh strips and vegetable mixture on beds of rice; top each serving with about 1/2 cup sauce.

Per serving: Cal 269/Pro 16.1g/Carb 24.6g/Fat 11.8g/Chol 0mg/Sod 548mg

ADVANCE PREPARATION Covered and refrigerated, the sauce will keep for up to 3 days. Reheat before serving with freshly sautéed tempeh strips and vegetables.

ancho chili sauce

When fresh green poblano chilies have been dried, they are called ancho, which means "wide" in Spanish. The flavor of the reddish-brown dried chilies is slightly fruity and sweet; hotness ranges from mild to pungent. Because of this natural variation, it's best to prepare the sauce without the red pepper flakes. Taste after it has been puréed, then add the red pepper flakes, just a pinch at a time, since their flavor is fiery. Serve this sauce spooned over Broccoli Burritos (page 174), Tempeh Strips and Broccoli with Ancho Chili Sauce (previous page), or Spicy Soybean Patties (page 171).

makes 2 cups

2 large ancho chilies (see Tip)

2 cups tomato juice

1 large tomato, peeled and quartered (see Tip, page 45)

1/4 cup coarsely chopped onion

1 teaspoon minced garlic

1/4 teaspoon ground cumin

Pinch of red pepper flakes (optional)

Rinse the ancho chilies; put them into a medium bowl and cover with boiling water. Soak until softened, about 30 minutes; drain well. Remove the stems, rinse to remove and discard the seeds, and coarsely chop the chilies.

Put the chopped chilies into a medium saucepan; stir in the remaining ingredients except the red pepper flakes. Cover and bring the mixture to a boil over high heat. Reduce the heat to low and cook until the chilies are tender, about 20 minutes.

Transfer the mixture to a blender or food processor; process until smooth. Return to the saucepan. Taste; add red pepper flakes if you prefer a hotter flavor. Serve warm.

Per 1/2 cup: Cal 55/Pro 1.4g/Carb 12g/Fat 0.2g/Chol 0mg/Sod 524mg

ADVANCE PREPARATION Covered and refrigerated, this sauce will keep for up to 3 days.

tip

The best dried chilies are sun-dried; oven drying makes the skins bitter. Dried chilies will keep indefinitely at room temperature.

tofu-mushroom stroganoff

A wide variety of elegant and earthy mushrooms is available in the marketplace. Rather than limiting yourself solely to cremini mushrooms, try substituting or adding morels (see Tip) or oyster mushrooms (see Tip, page 53).

makes 4 servings

1¹/2 cups Tofu Sour Cream (page 15)

¹/2 cup mashed silken firm tofu

¹/4 cup dry sherry (see Tip, page 159)

2 tablespoons low-sodium soy sauce

¹/4 teaspoon freshly ground black pepper, or to taste

1 tablespoon minced fresh flat-leaf parsley

2 teaspoons minced fresh thyme (or ¹/2 teaspoon dried)

8 ounces wide egg noodles (see Tip)

2 tablespoons olive oil

1 red bell pepper, finely chopped

4 cups sliced cremini mushrooms (see Tip, page 3)

¹/2 cup finely chopped shallots

garnish *(optional)* paprika, snipped fresh chives

Bring a large pot of water to a boil over high heat.

Put the Tofu Sour Cream, tofu, sherry, soy sauce, and pepper into a food processor; process until smooth. Stir in the parsley and fresh or dried thyme. Set aside.

When the water comes to a boil, add the noodles. When the water returns to a boil, reduce the heat to medium-high. Stir once to separate the noodles and cook until tender, about 7 minutes.

While the noodles are cooking, heat the oil in a large nonstick sauté pan over medium-high heat. Add the bell pepper; cook, stirring occasionally, until tender but not browned, about 4 minutes. Add the mushrooms and shallots; continue to cook, stirring occasionally, until the mushrooms are softened, about 4 minutes. Reduce the heat to medium-low; add the Tofu Sour Cream mixture. Stir gently until the mixture is heated through. Adjust the seasoning to taste.

When the noodles are done, drain well. Spoon them onto individual serving plates and top with the stroganoff mixture.

Per serving: Cal 278/Pro 11.7g/Carb 26.6g/Fat 13.9g/Chol 19mg/Sod 352mg

ADVANCE PREPARATION Covered and refrigerated, the Tofu Sour Cream will keep for up to 3 days. Prepare the stroganoff mixture and noodles just before serving.

VARIATION

Serve the stroganoff mixture over rice rather than egg noodles.

Morels are edible wild mushrooms belonging to the truffle family. Their flavor is smoky, earthy, and nutty; in general, the darker the mushroom, the stronger the flavor. Choose mushrooms with a firm yet spongy texture. Refrigerate in a single layer, covered with a damp towel; avoid airtight plastic bags. Do not eat raw morels; they must be cooked. Dried morels, available year-round, have a smokier, more intense flavor than fresh; they can be substituted in recipes after being rehydrated. (To rehydrate, soak in warm water or warm sherry, brandy, or broth for about 30 minutes, or boil for about 2 to 5 minutes; drain well before using.) To remove traces of sand, rinse both fresh and dried morels well before use.

In addition to the flour and water in pasta, egg noodles also contain whole eggs or egg yolks, which impart a tender texture and slightly sweet flavor. For the cholesterol-conscious, "yolk-free" egg noodles made with egg whites only are available in most supermarkets.

tofu and fruit in mango chutney sauce

Pear and mango flavor tofu slices in this exceptionally quick-to-prepare fruity but savory topping. Serve this over fluffy basmati rice (see Tip) or couscous with steamed asparagus spears on the side.

makes 4 servings

1/2 cup soy milk

1/4 cup mango chutney (see Tip, page 83)

1/4 teaspoon freshly ground black pepper, or to taste

Dash of salt, or to taste

2 tablespoons margarine

1 pear (at room temperature), peeled, cored, halved, and cut crosswise into 1/4-inch-thick slices

12 ounces silken extra-firm tofu cut into 2 × 1/2 × 1/4-inch strips

1 mango (at room temperature), peeled, halved, and seeded, each half cut crosswise into 1/4-inch-thick slices

1/4 cup finely snipped fresh chives

garnish (optional) sprigs of fresh flat-leaf parsley, finely chopped scallions, or snipped chives

Combine the soy milk, chutney, pepper, and salt in a small bowl. Set aside.

Melt the margarine in a large nonstick skillet over medium-high heat. Add the pear; cook, stirring occasionally, until tender, about 3 minutes.

Reduce the heat to medium; gently stir in the soy milk mixture, tofu, mango, and chives. Cover and heat until warmed through, about 5 minutes. Adjust the seasonings to taste.

Per serving: Cal 227/Pro 8.9g/Carb 28.7g/Fat 8.5g/Chol 0mg/Sod 178mg

VARIATIONS

Substitute skim milk for the soy milk.

Substitute butter for the margarine.

Substitute finely chopped scallions for the chives; sauté with the pear.

tip

Basmati, the most famous aromatic rice, is grown in the foothills of the Himalayas; less aromatic varieties are grown in the United States, primarily in the Southwest and California. In both brown and white forms, it has a nutlike fragrance during cooking and a delicate, almost buttery flavor. Lower in starch than other long-grain rices, basmati rice grains cook up flaky and separate in just 15 minutes.

tempeh with spicy peanut sauce ✓

The tempeh absorbs the rich, mellow flavor of the peanut sauce. Serve this aromatic mélange over rice or couscous and accompany with steamed vegetables such as broccoli florets, green beans, or carrot slices.

Combine the sauce ingredients in a small nonstick saucepan over low heat. (The amount of water needed will vary, depending on the thickness of the peanut butter; the sauce should be cake-batter consistency.) Stir occasionally until the sauce is heated through. Adjust the seasoning to taste. Remove the pan from the heat; cover and set aside.

Heat the oil in large nonstick skillet over medium-high heat. Add the tempeh; cook until lightly browned, about 4 to 5 minutes per side.

For each serving, arrange 3 tempeh strips over rice or couscous; drizzle each serving with about 3 tablespoons of the sauce.

Per serving: Cal 272/Pro 15.4g/Carb 13.6g/Fat 17.3g/Chol 0mg/Sod 218mg

ADVANCE PREPARATION Covered and refrigerated, the sauce will keep for up to 3 days. Since it thickens while standing, stir in water as needed. Reheat the sauce and brown the tempeh just before serving.

VARIATION

➘ Substitute 1/4 teaspoon red pepper flakes for the jalapeño pepper.

tip

Buy natural peanut butter with the oil on top; stir in the oil before using. Many processed peanut butters are hydrogenated to prevent separation and have sugars, salt, and stabilizers added.

makes 4 servings

For the Spicy Peanut Sauce

3 tablespoons smooth peanut butter (see Tip)

1 tablespoon dark sesame oil

1 tablespoon low-sodium soy sauce

2 teaspoons honey

2 teaspoons minced jalapeño pepper, or to taste

1 teaspoon minced garlic

1/2 cup water, or as needed

To complete the recipe

1 tablespoon safflower oil

8 ounces tempeh, cut crosswise into 12 even-size slices

garnish *(optional)* ➚ sprigs of fresh cilantro or flat-leaf parsley

tofu newburg

I call this "Sunday supper" food—simple, warm, and comforting. Serve the creamy mixture atop brown rice or, for variety, over whole wheat toast.

makes 4 servings

2 tablespoons margarine

1 green bell pepper, coarsely chopped

1/4 cup finely chopped onion

1/4 cup minced scallion (both green and white parts)

1 teaspoon minced garlic

2 tablespoons all-purpose white or unbleached flour

1 1/2 cups soy milk

1/2 cup dry sherry (see Tip, page 159)

1 tablespoon minced fresh flat-leaf parsley (see Tip)

1 tablespoon minced fresh thyme (or 1 teaspoon dried) (see Tip)

1/4 teaspoon white pepper, or to taste

Dash of cayenne, or to taste

12 ounces silken extra-firm tofu, cut into 1/2-inch cubes (about 2 cups)

1 cup frozen baby peas, thawed (see Tip, page 107)

garnish (*optional*) paprika

Melt the margarine in a medium nonstick sauté pan over medium heat. Add the bell pepper, onion, scallion, and garlic; cook, stirring occasionally, until the bell pepper is tender, about 5 minutes. Add the flour and stir constantly until the mixture is bubbly. Gradually add the soy milk; stir constantly until the sauce is smooth and thickened, about 2 to 3 minutes.

Reduce the heat to low. Stir in the sherry, parsley, fresh or dried thyme, white pepper, and cayenne. Adjust the seasonings to taste. Gently stir in the tofu and peas; heat until warm, about 2 minutes.

Per serving: Cal 224/Pro 12.9g/Carb 20.7g/Fat 9.9g/Chol 0mg/Sod 173mg

VARIATION

Substitute butter for the margarine.

tips

To mince parsley very finely, be sure to dry it well with a paper towel or dish towel after cleaning it under cool running water. Wet or damp parsley will stick together in clumps as you mince it. Minced parsley can be frozen in small freezer containers and spooned out as needed for cooked recipes; always use fresh for garnishing.

To use fresh thyme leaves, hold a sprig between your thumb and forefinger, and gently strip the leaves from the stem. Use the leaves whole or minced, or crush them with a mortar and pestle. Thyme is pungent whether it is fresh or dried, so use moderate amounts.

vegetable medley with hoisin peanut sauce 🗸

I've come to love the peanut sauces in many Szechuan Chinese restaurants. Experimenting at home, I tried tossing my Hoisin Peanut Sauce with green beans, carrots, and red pepper—a winning combination. I like this dish equally well served warm or cold.

Put the green beans and carrots into a large microwave-proof dish; add about $1/4$ cup water. Cover and microwave on high until crisp-tender, about 6 minutes. (Or cook the green beans and carrots in a stovetop steamer.)

While the vegetables are cooking, prepare the Hoisin Peanut Sauce. Adjust the seasoning to taste. Set aside.

When the green beans and carrots are done, drain well; transfer to a medium bowl. Add the bell pepper and scallions; toss. Add the peanut sauce; toss again.

To assemble the servings, place a layer of lettuce on each plate. Top with the green bean–carrot mixture.

Per serving: Cal 173/Pro 6.8g/Carb 25.6g/Fat 4.8g/Chol 0mg/Sod 578mg

ADVANCE PREPARATION Covered and refrigerated, this dish will keep for up to 3 days.

VARIATION

➘ Substitute cut asparagus or broccoli florets for the green beans.

makes 4 servings

4 cups green beans in 2-inch lengths

2 carrots, cut into strips about 2 inches long by $1/4$ inch wide

$3/4$ cup Hoisin Peanut Sauce (page 9)

1 red bell pepper, finely chopped

2 medium scallions, finely chopped

12 leaves red leaf lettuce

garnish (optional) toasted sesame seeds (see Tip, page 125)

tempeh with black bean–tomato sauce

When I have no time to shop and very little time to cook, this recipe serves as a pantry standby. All of the ingredients are staples that I'm likely to have on hand in the refrigerator or freezer. Rice, a green salad, and warmed flour tortillas will make the meal complete.

makes 4 servings

1 tablespoon olive oil

8 ounces tempeh, cut cross-wise into 12 even-size slices

For the Black Bean–Tomato Sauce

1 tablespoon olive oil

$1/2$ green bell pepper, coarsely chopped

$1/4$ cup coarsely chopped onion

One 15-ounce can black beans, drained and rinsed (see Tip)

One $14 1/2$-ounce can diced tomatoes, with juice (see Tip)

One 4-ounce can diced mild green chilies, drained

$1/2$ cup frozen corn, thawed

$1/2$ teaspoon freshly ground black pepper, or to taste

$1/2$ teaspoon ground cumin

2 tablespoons minced fresh cilantro, or to taste (do not use dried cilantro; if fresh is unavailable, substitute 2 tablespoons fresh or 1 teaspoon dried basil or oregano)

2 tablespoons freshly squeezed lime or lemon juice

Heat the olive oil in a large nonstick sauté pan over medium-high heat. Arrange the tempeh strips in a single layer; cook until lightly browned, 4 to 5 minutes per side. Transfer to a plate and cover to keep warm.

To prepare the sauce, heat the oil in the sauté pan over medium-high heat. Add the bell pepper and onion; cook, stirring occasionally, until crisp-tender, about 4 minutes. Stir in the beans, tomatoes with juice, green chilies, corn, pepper, cumin, and dried basil or oregano (if using).

Reduce the heat to medium and stir in the tempeh strips. Heat until warm, about 3 minutes. Stir in the lime or lemon juice and the fresh cilantro or the fresh basil or oregano (if using). Adjust the seasonings to taste.

Per serving: Cal 284/Pro 16.4g/Carb 26.9g/Fat 12.4g/Chol 0mg/Sod 1,093mg

ADVANCE PREPARATION Covered and refrigerated, the sauce will keep for up to 3 days. Reheat and combine with the warm tempeh strips just before serving.

VARIATIONS

❧ When stirring in the beans, add up to $1/2$ cup drained and coarsely chopped oil-packed sun-dried tomatoes.

❧ For a hotter flavor, when stirring in the beans, add minced jalapeño peppers, red pepper flakes, or a dash of hot pepper sauce.

tips

Black beans, also called turtle beans, are a member of the kidney bean family. Black on the outside, cream-colored within, they keep their shape and sweet, hearty flavor after cooking. Black beans contain high amounts of potassium, phosphorus, and fiber; they are also a good source of calcium and contain iron. Canned black beans are available in most supermarkets. The black bean is not the same as the Asian black bean, which is actually a type of soybean that is fermented with salt and used as a flavoring.

When buying canned tomatoes, read the labels. Some tomatoes are canned whole. Others are diced (recipe-ready tomatoes); select these for recipes calling for chopped canned tomatoes. Other canned tomatoes contain herbs and seasonings, such as stewed tomatoes and Italian style tomatoes (with Italian herbs). "Italian tomatoes" is the labeling for whole plum tomatoes. In cooked dishes canned tomatoes are usually preferable to fresh tomatoes of poor quality.

garnish *(optional)* freshly ground black pepper, sprigs of fresh cilantro, basil, or oregano

Stir-Fries

vegetable stir-fry with ginger sauce ✓

makes 4 servings

1 cup Ginger Sauce (page 26)

1 tablespoon safflower oil

2 carrots, cut diagonally into 1/8-inch-thick slices

1 small onion, thinly sliced (about 1/2 cup)

1 teaspoon minced garlic

4 ribs bok choy, cut diagonally into 1/2 inch thick slices; include green tops (see Tip, page 123)

1 1/2 cups sliced mushrooms

1 red bell pepper, cut into strips about 2 inches long by 1/4 inch wide

1/2 cup frozen baby peas, thawed (see Tip, page 107)

1 cup silken extra-firm tofu, cut into 1/2-inch cubes

garnish (optional) toasted sesame seeds (see Tip, page 125), raw cashews, sliced almonds, mandarin orange sections, scallion curls (see Tip)

Consider this your basic stir-fry recipe, and vary the vegetables to suit your taste or to use whatever you have on hand. When you prepare the recipe for entertaining and want to keep last-minute chores to a minimum, chop the vegetables and make the Ginger Sauce and rice accompaniment in advance.

Prepare the Ginger Sauce. Set aside and cover to keep warm.

Heat the oil in a large nonstick skillet over medium-high heat (see Tip). Add the carrots; stir-fry for about 2 minutes. Add the onion and garlic; continue to stir-fry for 2 minutes. Add the remaining ingredients except the tofu; stir-fry until the vegetables are crisp-tender, about 4 minutes. Reduce the heat to medium; gently stir in the tofu and heat until warm, about 1 minute.

To serve, spread beds of rice onto individual serving plates. Top with the stir-fried vegetables; drizzle with half of the Ginger Sauce. Top with garnishes and serve immediately; pass the remaining sauce.

Per serving: Cal 220/Pro 8.1g/Carb 35.4g/Fat 5.1g/Chol 0mg/Sod 379mg

ADVANCE PREPARATION Covered and refrigerated, the Ginger Sauce will keep for up to 2 days; reheat gently just before serving. The vegetables can be chopped in advance; stir-fry the vegetables and add the tofu and sauce just before serving.

VARIATIONS

❧ Substitute for the carrots, bok choy, mushrooms, or red bell pepper or add other vegetables (6 to 8 cups total) such as broccoli florets, baby corn ears, water chestnuts, bean sprouts, snow peas, shredded Chinese (Napa) cabbage, or sliced jícama, zucchini, celery, or tomato.

❧ For a firmer texture, substitute pressed tofu (see page xxxii).

tips

To make "scallion curls," slice the green parts of scallions very thinly lengthwise. Drop into a bowl of ice water; curls will form in 10 to 15 minutes.

Stir-frying over high or medium-high heat (depending on the stove and the pan) cooks food quickly as it is constantly and briskly stirred and tossed with a spatula or large spoon. Woks are the traditional pan used for this method; however, they are not necessarily the best choice for stovetop cooking. Horizontal pans with wide bottoms, such as a 12-inch skillet or sauté pan, are usually a better choice. For the best results, the food is never more than an inch deep as it cooks.

sweet bean stir-fry with hoisin-orange sauce

Orange juice, ginger, and hoisin sauce come together to add flavor intrigue to this vegetable stir-fry, which I like to serve over basmati rice, couscous, or Chinese wheat-flour noodles (see Tip, page 162). When making substitutions for the vegetables in this recipe, no need to limit yourself to typically Asian vegetables; nearly any vegetable can be used.

makes 4 servings

2 cups frozen sweet beans (see page xxvi)

For the Hoisin-Orange Sauce

1 tablespoon cold water

1 tablespoon cornstarch

1 cup freshly squeezed orange juice

1/4 cup hoisin sauce (see Tip, page 147)

1/4 cup low-sodium soy sauce

1 teaspoon minced gingerroot

1 teaspoon minced garlic

Dash of ground white pepper, or to taste

To complete the recipe

1 tablespoon roasted peanut oil (see Tip, page 149)

2 cups broccoli florets

1 meduim onion cut into 1/8-inch-thick slices and separated into rings (about 1 cup)

2 carrots, cut into 1/8-inch-thick slices

Put the sweet beans into a medium microwave-proof dish; add about 1/4 cup water. Cover and microwave on high until crisp-tender, about 6 to 8 minutes; drain well and set aside. (Or cook the sweet beans in a stovetop steamer.)

While the sweet beans are cooking, prepare the sauce. Stir together the water and cornstarch in a medium bowl until smooth. Whisk in the remaining sauce ingredients; set aside.

Heat the peanut oil in a large nonstick skillet over medium-high heat. Add the broccoli, onion, and carrots; stir-fry until the carrots are crisp-tender, about 4 minutes. Add the bok choy and bell pepper; continue to stir-fry until crisp-tender, about 3 minutes. Stir in the sweet beans and plum tomatoes; stir gently until heated through, about 2 minutes.

Reduce the heat to medium. Stir the sauce and pour it over the vegetables; stir until the sauce thickens slightly, about 1 minute. Adjust the seasoning to taste.

Spoon the vegetables over individual servings of rice, couscous, or noodles and drizzle with the sauce.

Per serving: Cal 273/Pro 13.3g/Carb 40g/Fat 6.7g/Chol 0mg/Sod 1,115mg

ADVANCE PREPARATION The vegetables can be chopped in advance; prepare the sauce and stir-fry the vegetables just before serving.

VARIATION

❧ Substitute for the broccoli, carrot, or red bell pepper or add other vegetables (6 to 8 cups total) such as snow peas or mushrooms.

tip

Bok choy, sometimes called mustard cabbage, pak choy, or pak choi, should have bright dark green, unwilted leaves attached to crisp lighter green unblemished stalks; both the leaves and stalks are edible cooked or raw. Store bok choy in a plastic bag in the refrigerator for up to 3 days.

3 ribs bok choy, cut into
   $1/4$-inch-thick slices;
   include green tops
   (see Tip)

1 red bell pepper, cut into
   $1/2$-inch squares

2 plum tomatoes (at room
   temperature), halved
   lengthwise and cut into
   $1/4$-inch-thick slices

garnish (optional) ↗ chopped
unsalted dry-roasted peanuts

sweet-and-sour tofu

The art to a Chinese sweet-and-sour sauce is a combination of flavors that balances the sweet and tart elements so that one does not overpower the other yet both can be detected. Serve this over brown rice, couscous, or buckwheat noodles.

makes 4 servings

For the sweet-and-sour sauce
2 tablespoons cold water

2 tablespoons cornstarch

1 cup pineapple juice

1/3 cup white rice vinegar

2 tablespoons low-sodium soy sauce

3 tablespoons tomato paste (see Tip, page 4)

2 tablespoons honey

1 tablespoon minced gingerroot

Dash of ground white pepper

To complete the recipe
1 tablespoon safflower oil

2 carrots, thinly sliced

1 green bell pepper, cut into 1/4-inch-wide strips

1 red bell pepper, cut into 1/4-inch-wide strips

1 medium onion, cut into 1/4-inch-thick slices

2 teaspoons minced garlic

12 ounces silken extra-firm tofu cut into 1/2-inch cubes (about 2 cups)

1 large tomato (at room temperature), cut into 16 wedges

One 8-ounce can pineapple chunks, drained

Stir together the water and cornstarch in a medium bowl until smooth. Whisk in the remaining sauce ingredients; set aside.

Heat the oil in a large nonstick skillet over medium-high heat. Add the carrots, bell peppers, onion, and garlic; cook, stirring constantly, until the carrots are crisp-tender, about 5 minutes.

Reduce the heat to medium. Stir the sweet-and-sour sauce; pour it over the vegetables. Stir constantly until the sauce thickens slightly, about 1 minute. Gently stir in the tofu, tomato wedges, and pineapple chunks; heat until warm, about 1 minute.

Per serving: Cal 261/Pro 10g/Carb 41.9g/Fat 5.9g/Chol 0mg/Sod 388mg

ADVANCE PREPARATION The vegetables can be chopped in advance; prepare the sauce and cook the dish just before serving.

VARIATION

❧ Substitute for the carrots or bell peppers or add other vegetables (up to 3 cups total) such as broccoli florets, cut asparagus, or sliced mushrooms.

tips

Sesame seeds are sold with or without their brownish-gray hulls; they are more nutritious if hulled. Because they contain oil, sesame seeds become rancid at room temperature; in an airtight container, store them in the refrigerator for up to 6 months or in the freezer for up to a year.

To toast sesame seeds, place them in a dry nonstick skillet over medium-high heat for 3 to 5 minutes. Toss constantly and watch closely; immediately remove the seeds from the pan when they become lightly browned. As an alternative, spread the seeds on an ungreased baking sheet and bake in a 350°F oven. Shake the pan or stir occasionally until the seeds are lightly browned, about 10 minutes. Either method will give the seeds a nutty flavor and a slightly crispy texture. It takes the same amount of time to toast 1 tablespoon or $^1/2$ cup—so toast extra seeds, store them in an airtight container, and refrigerate or freeze.

garnish *(optional)* toasted sesame seeds (see Tips), scallion curls (see Tip, page 125)

spicy cashew stir-fry

Make this dish spicy or keep it mild by adjusting the amount of red pepper flakes in the sauce. I like to serve this stir-fry over brown rice or couscous; either accompaniment will tone down the heat.

makes 4 servings

For the spicy sauce

1 tablespoon cold water

1 tablespoon cornstarch

1 1/4 cups vegetable stock (see page 34)

2 tablespoons low-sodium soy sauce

2 teaspoons minced garlic

1/2 teaspoon red pepper flakes, or to taste

1/2 teaspoon turmeric

Dash of ground white pepper, or to taste

To complete the recipe

2 tablespoons safflower oil

3 cups broccoli florets

2 ribs bok choy, chopped; also coarsely chop leaves (see Tip, page 123)

1 red bell pepper, cut into strips about 2 inches long by 1/4 inch wide

3 medium scallions, coarsely chopped

12 ounces silken extra-firm tofu, cut into 2 × 1/2 × 3/8- inch strips (about 2 cups)

1/2 cup whole raw cashews (see Tip)

To prepare the sauce, stir together the water and cornstarch in a medium bowl until smooth. Whisk in the remaining sauce ingredients; set aside.

Heat the safflower oil in a large nonstick skillet over medium-high heat. Add the broccoli; stir-fry for about 3 minutes. Add the bok choy, bell pepper, and scallions; continue to stir-fry until the broccoli and red pepper are crisp-tender, about 3 minutes.

Reduce the heat to medium. Stir the sauce and pour it over the vegetables; stir until the sauce thickens, about 1 minute. Gently stir in the tofu and cashews; heat until warm, about 1 minute. Adjust the seasonings to taste.

Per serving: Cal 242/Pro 13.1g/Carb 16.6g/Fat 13.7g/Chol 0mg/Sod 365mg

ADVANCE PREPARATION The vegetables can be chopped in advance; prepare the sauce and cook the dish just before serving.

VARIATIONS

❧ Substitute for the broccoli, bok choy, or red bell pepper or add other vegetables (up to 5 cups total) such as cut asparagus, sliced celery, julienned carrots, or snow peas.

❧ For a firmer texture, substitute pressed tofu (see page xxxii).

❧ Substitute pine nuts (see Tip, page 75) for the cashews.

tip

For cooking, raw cashews are preferable to roasted and salted cashews. Because they have no added salt or fat, they will absorb the other flavors in your recipe and soften and plump up to a pleasing consistency.

Rice Dishes

tempeh paella

Paella, a Spanish classic, traditionally includes seafood and chicken. This vegetarian version featuring tempeh captures the spirit of the dish in a minimum of time but with a maximum of flourish.

Combine the vegetable stock and saffron in a medium saucepan; stir in the rice. Bring the liquid to a boil over high heat. Reduce the heat to medium-low; cover tightly and simmer until the liquid is completely absorbed, about 15 minutes.

While the rice is cooking, heat the oil in a medium nonstick skillet over medium-high heat. Add the tempeh, onion, and garlic; cook, turning the tempeh strips occasionally, until lightly browned, about 5 minutes.

When the rice is done, fluff it with a fork. Reduce the heat to low. Stir in the tomatoes and juice, artichoke hearts, peas, sundried tomatoes, red pepper flakes, black pepper, and salt; cover until heated through, about 3 minutes. Adjust the seasonings to taste.

To serve, spread the rice-vegetable mixture on a large serving plate; top with the tempeh strips and garnish.

Per serving: Cal 446/Pro 21.4g/Carb 70.2g/Fat 8.8g/Chol 0mg/Sod 301mg

tip

Saffron, derived from a small purple crocus, is the world's most expensive spice. Fortunately, it is pungent and aromatic, so a little goes a long way. Saffron can be purchased in threads (which should be crushed just before using) or in powdered form. Store saffron in an airtight container in a cool, dark place for up to 6 months. Turmeric will impart a similar yellow color to food, but there is no substitute for saffron's exquisite flavor and earthy aroma.

makes 4 servings

1 1/2 cups vegetable stock
(see page 34)

1/4 teaspoon powdered saffron
(see Tip)

1 cup uncooked basmati rice

1 tablespoon olive oil

8 ounces tempeh, cut into
strips about 3 inches long
by 1/2 inch wide

1/4 cup coarsely chopped onion

2 teaspoons minced garlic

One 14 1/2-ounce can diced
tomatoes, with juice

One 14-ounce can artichoke
hearts packed in water,
drained and quartered

1/2 cup frozen peas, thawed

1/4 cup drained and coarsely
chopped oil-packed sun-
dried tomatoes

1/4 teaspoon red pepper flakes,
or to taste

1/4 teaspoon freshly ground
black pepper, or to taste

Dash of salt, or to taste

garnish *(optional)* sprigs of
fresh flat-leaf parsley

italian tempeh, vegetable, and rice skillet

This versatile entrée can be varied by substituting or adding other vegetables (about 4 cups total) such as green beans or asparagus spears. For a zestier flavor, add more red pepper flakes.

makes 6 servings

2 tablespoons olive oil

3 cups small broccoli florets and chopped stems (see Tip)

8 ounces tempeh, cut into 1/2-inch cubes

1 red bell pepper, coarsely chopped

1/4 cup coarsely chopped shallots

3 cups cooked brown or white rice

One 15-ounce can diced tomatoes, with juice

1/2 cup freshly grated Parmesan cheese

2 tablespoons minced fresh basil (or 1 teaspoon dried)

1/2 teaspoon freshly ground black pepper, or to taste

Pinch red pepper flakes, or to taste

garnish *(optional)* chèvre (goat cheese), freshly grated Parmesan cheese

Heat the oil in a large nonstick sauté pan over medium-high heat. Add the broccoli, tempeh, and bell pepper. Cook, stirring occasionally, until the vegetables are tender and the tempeh is lightly browned, about 8 minutes. Add the shallots during the last 2 minutes.

Reduce the heat to medium-low; add the remaining ingredients. Stir gently until the mixture is heated through and the cheese is melted. Adjust the seasonings to taste.

Per serving: Cal 291/Pro 15.6g/Carb 32.1g/Fat 11.1g/Chol 7mg/Sod 173mg

ADVANCE PREPARATION This dish can be prepared, omitting the Parmesan cheese and fresh basil (if using), up to 1 day in advance; cover and refrigerate. Reheat over medium-low heat; since some of the liquid becomes absorbed into the rice while standing, stir in tomato juice or water as needed. Just before serving, add the fresh basil (if using) and the cheese; stir gently until the cheese is melted.

tip

When buying broccoli, look for tight, dark green heads on firm but pliable stalks; slender stalks will be more tender for eating. (If the stalks are coarse, peel the outer coverings and use the tender interiors for cooking.) Many markets also sell the florets separately. Store unwashed broccoli in an open plastic bag, or wrap in damp paper towels and store in the crisper drawer of your refrigerator; it will keep for up to 4 days.

tofu fried rice

With the addition of tofu and vegetables, stir-fried rice is transformed from a simple side dish to become a satisfying entrée. This is a vegetarian version of one of my favorite recipes in The 15-Minute Chicken Gourmet (Macmillan, 1997).

Heat the oil in a large nonstick skillet over medium-high heat. Add the bell pepper, carrot, and celery; stir-fry until the vegetables are nearly tender, about 3 minutes. Add the mushrooms, scallions, and garlic; stir-fry until the vegetables are tender, about 2 minutes. Add the rice; stir-fry for about 3 minutes.

Reduce the heat to medium; stir in the soy sauce and white pepper. Gently stir in the tofu and peas; heat until the tofu is warm, about 2 minutes. Adjust the seasonings to taste.

Per serving: Cal 249/Pro 9.6g/Carb 40.3g/Fat 5.5g/Chol 0mg/Sod 308mg

ADVANCE PREPARATION This dish is best when prepared just before serving, but it will keep, covered and refrigerated, for up to 2 days. Stir in water as needed when reheating.

VARIATIONS

❧ Substitute for the bell pepper, carrot, celery, or mushrooms or add other vegetables (up to 4 cups total) such as cut asparagus, cauliflower florets, bok choy, jícama, or water chestnuts.

❧ In a separate skillet, scramble 2 eggs or 1/2 cup cholesterol-free egg substitute; stir in with the tofu and peas.

tips

The shelf life of white rice is a year or longer; keep it in a container with a tight-fitting lid in a dark, dry place. Brown rice will keep for several months if stored in the refrigerator.

One cup of uncooked rice yields about 3 cups of cooked rice.

makes 4 servings

2 teaspoons safflower oil

1/2 cup diced red bell pepper

1 carrot, diced

1 rib celery, diced

1 cup sliced mushrooms

2 medium scallions, finely chopped

1 teaspoon minced garlic

3 cups cooked brown rice (see Tip)

2 tablespoons low-sodium soy sauce

Dash of ground white pepper, or to taste

1 cup silken extra-firm tofu in 1/2-inch cubes

1/4 cup frozen baby peas, thawed (see Tip, page 107)

garnish *(optional)* red bell pepper strips

soybean-mushroom risotto

makes 4 servings

5 cups vegetable stock
(see page 34)

2 tablespoons olive oil

1 cup sliced cremini mushrooms
(see Tip, page 3)

2 tablespoons minced shallot

1 cup Arborio rice (see Tip)

1 cup cooked soybeans

1/2 cup freshly grated
Parmesan cheese

1/4 cup minced fresh flat-leaf
parsley

1/2 teaspoon freshly ground
black pepper, or to taste

garnish *(optional)* freshly
ground black pepper, sprigs of
fresh flat-leaf parsley

Arborio rice is a must for preparing risotto. In the Italian method of cooking, each grain remains separate and slightly al dente—totally different from the rice dishes of other countries. To achieve the creaminess that gives risotto its distinctive personality, first the rice must be sautéed. Then hot liquid is added gradually, stirring continually while it cooks; more liquid is added when each addition of liquid has been absorbed.

Bring the vegetable stock to a boil in a small saucepan over high heat. Cover and reduce the heat to medium.

Meanwhile, heat 1 tablespoon of the oil in a small nonstick skillet over medium-high heat. Add the mushrooms and shallot; cook, stirring occasionally, until tender, about 5 minutes. Remove the pan from the heat; cover and set aside.

While the mushrooms and shallot are cooking, heat the remaining 1 tablespoon of oil in a large nonstick skillet over medium-high heat. Add the rice; stir until each grain is coated with oil, about 2 minutes. Pour 1 cup of the hot vegetable stock into the skillet; cook, stirring constantly, until the liquid is absorbed, about 3 minutes. (During the period the liquid is being added, it should remain bubbly, so it may be necessary to alternate the heat between medium-high and medium settings.)

Stir the mushroom-shallot mixture into the rice and continue adding the hot vegetable stock, 1 cup at a time. Pour it in slowly, adding more only when the previous liquid has been absorbed. (The exact amount necessary varies with different rices; add the liquid only until the rice is tender but still firm to the bite. This process will take about 10 to 15 minutes.)

Remove the pan from the heat; add the soybeans, Parmesan cheese, parsley, and pepper. Stir until the soybeans are warm and the cheese is melted into the rice. Adjust the seasoning to taste.

Per serving: Cal 568/Pro 22.8g/Carb 76.2g/Fat 19.1g/Chol 16mg/Sod 2,270mg

ADVANCE PREPARATION Risotto is best when prepared just before serving. Leftovers can be refrigerated and served the next day. To reheat, add a little water and cook over low heat, stirring constantly; or microwave at the medium setting for about 1 or 2 minutes.

VARIATIONS

❧ Substitute white mushrooms for the cremini mushrooms.

❧ Substitute white wine for part of the liquid, such as 4 cups stock and 1 cup wine.

❧ Add up to 1 cup other vegetables, such as red bell pepper strips or cut asparagus; cook with the mushrooms.

❧ When adding the soybeans and Parmesan cheese, stir in 1 tablespoon minced fresh basil or rosemary (or 1 teaspoon dried) or add up to 2 tablespoons Tofu-Basil Pesto (page 6). You may also stir in up to $1/2$ cup drained and coarsely chopped oil-packed sun-dried tomatoes.

tip

Arborio rice is an Italian short-grain rice that can be found in the rice section or among the ethnic foods in most supermarkets and specialty stores. It is the ideal rice for risotto, Spanish paella, and rice puddings because the high starch in its grains imparts a creamy texture when cooked.

chili-rice skillet

This recipe couldn't be quicker to assemble. Serve this spicy dish accompanied by romaine lettuce tossed with Parmesan Vinaigrette (page 156).

makes 6 servings

1¹/4 cups texturized vegetable protein (TVP)

1 cup hot water

1 tablespoon olive oil

1 cup coarsely chopped onion

¹/2 green bell pepper, coarsely chopped

1 teaspoon minced garlic

One 15-ounce can diced tomatoes, with juice

One 15-ounce can kidney beans, drained and rinsed

1 cup cooked white or brown rice

¹/2 cup drained and coarsely chopped oil-packed sun-dried tomatoes (see Tip)

2 teaspoons minced jalapeño pepper, or to taste

1 teaspoon sugar

2 teaspoons minced fresh basil (or ¹/2 teaspoon dried)

2 teaspoons minced fresh oregano (or ¹/2 teaspoon dried)

¹/4 teaspoon red pepper flakes, or to taste

¹/4 teaspoon freshly ground black pepper, or to taste

garnish *(optional)* shredded cheddar cheese

Stir together the texturized vegetable protein and hot water in a medium bowl; allow to stand until the water is absorbed and the TVP is softened, about 5 minutes.

Meanwhile, heat the oil in a large nonstick sauté pan over medium-high heat. Add the onion and bell pepper; cook until the bell pepper is crisp-tender, about 5 minutes. Add the garlic during the last minute.

Reduce the heat to medium. Add the softened TVP and the remaining ingredients; continue to cook, stirring occasionally, until the bell pepper is tender, about 5 minutes. Adjust the seasonings to taste.

Per serving: Cal 284/Pro 18g/Carb 46.5g/Fat 2.9g/Chol 0mg/Sod 387mg

ADVANCE PREPARATION Covered and refrigerated, this dish will keep for up to 3 days. Since the mixture thickens while standing, stir in tomato juice or water as needed when reheating.

tip

Dried tomatoes, which will keep in an airtight container for several months, must be rehydrated before using in many recipes. Cover them with boiling water and allow to soak for about 10 to 15 minutes, depending on how soft you want them; then drain off the water. Use immediately or marinate in olive oil (be sure to refrigerate) for use later. Because of their superior flavor and ease of use, I prefer to purchase the jars of sun-dried tomatoes that have been rehydrated and packed in an olive oil marinade; these, too, must be refrigerated after opening. Drain off the excess oil before using. In both the dried and oil-packed forms, the tomatoes are packaged whole, halved, or already chopped; to chop them yourself, the easiest method is to use kitchen shears.

Stovetop Pasta Dishes

penne with cremini mushrooms and tomato-tofu pesto ✓

Cremini mushrooms are simply immature portobello mushrooms; they have a fuller flavor than ordinary white mushrooms. In this recipe you can substitute white mushrooms or use a combination of both white and cremini mushrooms.

Bring a large pot of water to a boil over high heat; add the penne. When the water returns to a boil, stir once to separate the pasta. Reduce the heat to medium-high and cook until *al dente*, about 10 to 12 minutes.

Meanwhile, heat the oil in a small nonstick skillet over medium heat. Add the mushrooms and shallot; cook, stirring occasionally, until they are tender but not browned, about 4 minutes. Remove from the heat and set aside.

To prepare the pesto, put the stewed tomatoes, tofu, sun-dried tomatoes, and pepper into a food processor; process until the mixture is smooth. Stir in the basil.

When the pasta is done, drain well; return it to the pot. Add the mushrooms and shallots; toss. Add the pesto; toss until well combined. Adjust the seasoning to taste.

Per serving: Cal 273/Pro 9.9g/Carb 38.4g/Fat 8.9g/Chol 29mg/Sod 180mg

ADVANCE PREPARATION Covered and refrigerated, the pesto will keep for up to 2 days. Since it thickens while standing, stir in tomato juice or water as needed. If possible, bring the pesto to room temperature before tossing with freshly cooked hot pasta and mushrooms.

makes 4 servings

12 ounces penne pasta
(about 4^1/2 cups)

2 tablespoons olive oil

3 cups sliced cremini mushrooms
(see Tip, page 3)

1 tablespoon minced shallot

For the Tomato-Tofu Pesto

One 8-ounce can stewed
tomatoes (see Tip,
page 119)

^{1}/2 cup mashed silken firm tofu
(at room temperature)

^{1}/4 cup drained and coarsely
chopped oil-packed sun-
dried tomatoes

^{1}/4 teaspoon freshly ground
black pepper, or to taste

2 tablespoons chopped fresh
basil (fresh is essential!)

garnish *(optional)* freshly
ground black pepper, freshly
grated Parmesan cheese,
Tofu Chèvre Spread (page 5),
toasted pine nuts (see Tip,
page 75)

udon noodles with tempeh and hijiki

makes 6 servings

1/2 cup dried hijiki (see Tip)

8 ounces udon noodles (see Tip)

2 tablespoons safflower oil

1 cup sliced mushrooms

2 medium scallions, finely chopped

8 ounces tempeh, cut into strips about 2 inches long by 1/4 inch wide

1/4 cup pine nuts

1 teaspoon minced garlic

1 teaspoon minced gingerroot

2 tablespoons low-sodium soy sauce

2 teaspoons dark sesame oil

1/4 teaspoon red pepper flakes, or to taste

Although some of the ingredients for this recipe may require special a trip to an Asian market, the results will make your efforts worthwhile. If you have never tasted sea vegetables such as hijiki, you are in for a pleasant surprise. I like this best served warm, but the leftovers are always a special treat the next day as a chilled salad.

Put the hijiki into a medium bowl and cover with warm water; allow to stand until the hijiki begins to soften, about 15 minutes. Drain in a colander and rinse well. Transfer the hijiki to a small saucepan; cover with water. Bring the water to a boil over medium-high heat. Reduce the heat to medium and simmer until the hijiki is softened, about 15 to 20 minutes; drain well.

Meanwhile, bring a large saucepan of water to a boil over high heat; add the udon noodles. When the water returns to a boil, stir once to separate the noodles. Reduce the heat to medium-high and cook until the noodles are tender, about 8 to 10 minutes (see Tip). Drain well.

While the noodles are cooking, heat the oil in a large non-stick skillet over medium-high heat. Add the mushrooms, scallions, tempeh, and pine nuts. Cook, stirring occasionally, until the mushrooms and scallions are tender and the tempeh and pine nuts are lightly browned, about 10 minutes. Add the garlic and gingerroot; continue to cook for about 2 minutes, stirring constantly.

Transfer the noodles to a large bowl and add the soy sauce, sesame oil, and red pepper flakes; toss to combine. Add the hijiki and tempeh mixture; toss again. Adjust the seasoning to taste.

Per serving: Cal 204/Pro 10.1g/Carb 11.2g/Fat 13.2g/Chol 0mg/Sod 260mg

ADVANCE PREPARATION Covered and refrigerated, this dish will keep for up to 2 days.

VARIATION

❧ For the udon noodles, substitute soba (buckwheat) noodles (see Tip); cook the noodles until tender, about 4 to 6 minutes.

tips

Hijiki (sometimes spelled "hiziki") is a dried black seaweed, or sea vegetable, with a slight anise flavor and high calcium content; it must be hydrated before using. This product is found in Asian markets and with the Asian foods some supermarkets.

Udon noodles are made from wheat flour and water; they are round, square, or flat in shape. The diameter can vary, so check the packaging for recommended cooking times. Udon is available with the Oriental foods in some supermarkets and in Asian markets, where it is often found in both fresh and dried forms; the fresh noodles will cook more quickly.

Soba are long, flat Japanese noodles made from buckwheat and wheat flours, giving them a brownish color and a nutty flavor.

spaghetti with tempeh in mexican chili sauce

makes 4 servings

12 ounces spaghetti

For the Mexican Chili Sauce

2 tablespoons olive oil

8 ounces tempeh, cut into
1/2-inch cubes

2 cups sliced mushrooms

1 green bell pepper, coarsely
chopped

1/2 cup coarsely chopped onion

2 ribs celery, coarsely chopped

2 teaspoons minced jalapeño
pepper, or to taste (see
Tips)

1 teaspoon minced garlic

One 6-ounce can tomato paste

1/4 cup water

One 141/2-ounce can diced
tomatoes, with juice

2 teaspoons chili powder,
or to taste

2 teaspoons minced fresh
oregano (or 1/2 teaspoon
dried)

1/4 teaspoon ground cumin

1/4 teaspoon freshly ground
black pepper, or to taste

Once thought of as being strictly Italian, pasta has broken out of the stereotype as it has become prevalent in "fusion cooking," combining the elements of various cuisines in non-traditional ways. This richly flavored sauce contains herbs, flavorings, and ingredients in a distinctly Mexican combination. Although the list of ingredients is long, this sauce can be prepared quickly and simply.

Bring a large pot of water to a boil over high heat; add the spaghetti. When the water returns to a boil, stir once to separate the spaghetti. Reduce the heat to medium-high and cook until *al dente*, about 8 to 10 minutes.

Meanwhile, heat the oil in a large nonstick skillet over medium-high heat. Add the tempeh; cook, stirring gently, until it is lightly browned, about 5 minutes. Add the mushrooms, bell pepper, onion, celery, jalapeño pepper, and garlic. Cook, stirring occasionally, until the vegetables are tender, about 8 minutes. Reduce the heat to medium.

Combine the tomato paste and water in a small bowl; add to the skillet. Stir in the remaining ingredients except the cilantro. Stir gently until warmed through, about 5 minutes. Stir in the cilantro. Adjust the seasonings to taste.

When the pasta is done, drain well.

To serve, place a mound of spaghetti on each serving plate; top with the sauce and garnish.

Per serving: Cal 380/Pro 20.1g/Carb 46.1g/Fat 12.8g/Chol 28mg/Sod 331mg

ADVANCE PREPARATION Covered and refrigerated, the sauce will keep for up to 2 days; it reheats well. Serve the warmed sauce over freshly cooked hot pasta.

VARIATION

❧ Serve the sauce over rice rather than spaghetti.

tips

Jalapeños, one of the most familiar chili peppers, are small, smooth-skinned green peppers (scarlet when ripe) about 2 inches in length. They are readily available in most markets, both fresh and canned. Those in cans or jars are milder than fresh because they are peeled, seeded, and packed in liquid. Store fresh peppers in a plastic bag in your refrigerator, where they will keep for 1 to 3 weeks.

Just how hot a pepper is depends on the amount of a substance called capsaicin (kap-SAY-ih-sihn), found mainly in the veins near the seeds. Unaffected by heat or cold, capsaicin retains its potency despite time, cooking, or freezing, so removing the membranes and seeds before using peppers is the only way to reduce the heat. Small peppers have more membranes and seeds than large peppers, so generally they are hotter.

To avoid irritation from the caustic oils in fresh or dried chili peppers, do not touch your eyes, nose, or lips while handling them. Many cooks wear disposable plastic gloves when working with hot chilies. Afterward, wash your hands, knife, and cutting board in hot, soapy water.

1/4 teaspoon hot pepper sauce, or to taste

1/4 cup coarsely chopped fresh cilantro (do not substitute dried cilantro—if fresh is unavailable, substitute fresh flat-leaf parsley)

garnish *(optional)* ↗ freshly ground black pepper, shredded mozzarella cheese or cheddar cheese, sprigs of fresh cilantro or flat-leaf parsley

spicy asian peanut pasta

I like this best served warm, but it is also delicious chilled. To serve as a chilled pasta salad, toss the freshly cooked fusilli and vegetables with about half of the peanut sauce; cover and refrigerate for up to 2 days. Add the remaining sauce just before serving.

makes 4 servings

8 ounces short fusilli pasta (about 3 cups) (see Tip)

2 cups broccoli florets

1 carrot, cut into strips about 2 inches long by $1/4$ inch wide

$3/4$ cup Hoisin Peanut Sauce (page 9)

1 red bell pepper, cut into strips about 2 inches long by $1/4$ inch wide

$1/2$ cup sliced scallions (both green and white parts)

garnish *(optional)* chopped unsalted dry-roasted peanuts or toasted sesame seeds (see Tip, page 125)

Bring a medium pot of water to a boil over high heat; add the fusilli. When the water returns to a boil, stir once to separate the pasta. Reduce the heat to medium-high and cook until *al dente*, about 6 to 8 minutes.

Meanwhile, put the broccoli and carrot into a medium microwave-proof dish; add about $1/4$ cup water. Cover and microwave on high until crisp-tender, about 4 to 6 minutes. (Or cook the broccoli and carrot in a stovetop steamer.)

While the pasta and vegetables are cooking, prepare the peanut sauce. Set aside.

When the pasta and vegetables are done, drain well. Transfer to a medium bowl. Toss in the bell pepper and scallions. Add the peanut sauce; toss again.

Per serving: Cal 229/Pro 9.7g/Carb 35.7g/Fat 5.3g/Chol 0mg/Sod 558mg

ADVANCE PREPARATION Covered and refrigerated, the sauce will keep for up to 2 days. For serving this dish warm, bring the chilled sauce to room temperature or heat gently before tossing with freshly cooked hot pasta and vegetables.

tip

Fusilli is a spiral-shaped spaghetti that can range from $1^1/2$ to 12 inches long.

mostaccioli and plum tomatoes with tofu-basil pesto

This pasta dish is one of the quickest to prepare. In the time it takes to cook the pasta, you can make the pesto and chop the tomatoes. Then toss the mixture together, and it's ready to serve.

Bring a large pot of water to a boil over high heat; add the mostaccioli. When the water returns to a boil, stir once to separate the pasta. Reduce the heat to medium-high and cook until *al dente*, about 10 to 12 minutes.

Meanwhile, prepare the Tofu-Basil Pesto.

When the pasta is done, drain well; return it to the pot. Add the pesto; toss until the mixture is evenly combined. Add the tomato cubes and toss again. Adjust the seasonings to taste.

Per serving: Cal 266/Pro 12.1g/Carb 28.4g/Fat 11.6g/Chol 33mg/Sod 154mg

ADVANCE PREPARATION Covered and refrigerated, the pesto will keep for up to 4 days. Bring to room temperature before tossing with freshly cooked hot pasta and cubed tomatoes.

VARIATION

❧ For the plum tomatoes, substitute 1 red bell pepper cut into strips about 2 inches long by 1/4 inch wide and sautéed in 1 tablespoon olive oil.

tips

Mostaccioli is 2-inch-long macaroni tubes cut on the diagonal. The surface is either plain or ridged, "rigate."

Rigate means that the pasta is shaped with ridges that help the sauce adhere to the surface of the noodle.

makes 4 servings

12 ounces mostaccioli pasta (about 4 cups) (see Tip)

1 cup Tofu-Basil Pesto (page 6)

4 plum tomatoes (at room temperature), cut into 1/2-inch cubes (see Tip, page 163)

garnish *(optional)* freshly ground black pepper, freshly grated Parmesan cheese, toasted pine nuts (see Tip, page 75)

penne rigate with parmesan-peppercorn sauce

When warmed, Parmesan-Peppercorn Dip can serve as an Alfredo-type sauce on pasta. This is definitely lower in fat than the original butter and heavy cream dish.

makes 4 servings

8 ounces penne rigate pasta (about 3 cups) (see Tip, page 139)

1 cup Parmesan-Peppercorn Dip (page 10)

3 cups broccoli florets

1 tablespoon olive oil

1/2 red bell pepper, finely chopped

1/4 cup minced shallots

garnish *(optional)* freshly ground black pepper, freshly grated Parmesan cheese

Bring a large pot of water to a boil over high heat; add the penne. When the water returns to a boil, stir once to separate the pasta. Reduce the heat to medium-high and cook until *al dente*, about 12 to 14 minutes.

Meanwhile, prepare the Parmesan-Peppercorn Dip. Pour it into a small nonstick saucepan; set aside.

Put the broccoli into a medium microwave-proof dish; add about 1/4 cup water. Cover and cook in the microwave on high until crisp-tender, about 4 to 6 minutes; drain well. (Or cook the broccoli in a stovetop steamer.)

Heat the oil in a small nonstick skillet over medium-high heat. Add the bell pepper and shallots; cook, stirring constantly, until tender, about 4 minutes.

Warm the Parmesan-Peppercorn Dip over medium heat, stirring constantly.

When the pasta is done, drain well; return it to the pot. Add the broccoli, bell pepper, and shallots; toss. Add the warmed dip; toss again.

Per serving: Cal 237/Pro 14.6g/Carb 22.9g/Fat 9.7g/Chol 29mg/Sod 276mg

ADVANCE PREPARATION The sauce will keep for up to 2 days in a tightly closed container in the refrigerator. Warm the sauce gently and toss with freshly cooked hot pasta and vegetables just before serving.

VARIATION

❧ Substitute asparagus cut in 2-inch lengths for the broccoli.

rotini with parsley-nut pesto

*Here's a good choice for a simple but elegant entrée to serve
to company. The uncooked sauce can be prepared in advance
or while the pasta cooks. To combine properly, it is important
that the pesto be tossed with the pasta while it is hot.*

Bring a large pot of water to a boil over high heat; add the
rotini. When the water returns to a boil, stir once to separate the
pasta. Reduce the heat to medium-high and cook until *al dente,*
about 8 to 10 minutes.

Meanwhile, to make the pesto, put the pecans, walnuts, pistachios, olive oil, lemon juice, garlic, and pepper into a food
processor; process until the nuts are finely chopped but the mixture is still slightly chunky. Add the parsley; process only until it is
combined with the other ingredients.

When the pasta is done, drain well; return it to the pot. Add
the pesto; toss. Add the soybeans and toss again. Garnish and serve
immediately.

Per serving: Cal 293/Pro 11.5g/Carb 22.5g/Fat 17.4g/Chol 19mg/Sod 10mg

ADVANCE PREPARATION Covered and refrigerated, the pesto
will keep for up to 2 days. Bring to room temperature before tossing with freshly cooked hot pasta just before serving.

tip

*Commercially packaged grated Parmesan cheese, which is loaded with
preservatives, has the consistency of sawdust and very little flavor.
Always buy freshly grated Parmesan or, better yet, grate your own from
a block of Parmesan using a hand grater or a food processor. Sealed in
a tightly closed container, freshly grated Parmesan will keep in the
refrigerator for up to a week; it can be frozen, although the flavor and
texture will deteriorate. Wrapped tightly in plastic wrap and refrigerated, a block of Parmesan will keep for up to 4 weeks.*

makes 4 servings

8 ounces rotini pasta
   (about 3 cups)

For the Parsley-Nut Pesto

2 tablespoons coarsely
   chopped pecans

2 tablespoons coarsely
   chopped walnuts

2 tablespoons coarsely
   chopped pistachios

2 tablespoons extra-virgin
   olive oil (see page xlv)

2 tablespoons freshly
   squeezed lemon juice

1 teaspoon minced garlic

1/2 teaspoon freshly ground
   black pepper

1 cup coarsely chopped fresh
   flat-leaf parsley

To complete the recipe

1 cup cooked soybeans
   (at room temperature)

garnish *(optional)* freshly
ground black pepper, freshly
grated Parmesan cheese
(see Tip), thin tomato slices,
sprigs of fresh flat-leaf parsley

bell pepper–soybean toss with pasta

Penne is my favorite pasta for this colorful dish. But sometimes, for variety, I cut the bell pepper strips longer and thinner and serve the mixture atop angel hair pasta or spaghetti.

makes 4 servings

8 ounces penne pasta (about 3 cups)

2 tablespoons olive oil

1 red bell pepper, cut into strips about 2 inches long by 1/4 inch wide

1 green bell pepper, cut into strips about 2 inches long by 1/4 inch wide

1 medium onion, cut into strips about 2 inches long by 1/4 inch wide (about 1 cup) (see Tip)

1 teaspoon minced garlic

1 1/2 cups cooked soybeans (one 15-ounce can, drained and rinsed)

2 plum tomatoes (at room temperature), halved lengthwise and cut into 1/4-inch-thick slices

1/2 cup drained and coarsely chopped oil-packed sun-dried tomatoes

2 tablespoons minced fresh basil (or 1 teaspoon dried)

1/2 teaspoon freshly ground black pepper, or to taste

Dash of salt, or to taste

Bring a large pot of water to a boil over high heat; add the penne. When the water returns to a boil, stir once to separate the pasta. Reduce the heat to medium-high and cook until *al dente*, about 10 to 12 minutes.

Meanwhile, heat 1 tablespoon of the oil in a large nonstick skillet over medium-high heat. Add the bell pepper strips, onion, and garlic. Cook, stirring occasionally, until the vegetables are tender but not browned, about 5 minutes. Stir in the soybeans, plum tomatoes, sun-dried tomatoes, and dried basil (if using). Cook, stirring occasionally, until the tomatoes are softened and the soybeans are heated through, about 3 minutes. Stir in the fresh basil (if using), pepper, and salt. Adjust the seasonings to taste. Remove from the heat and cover to keep warm.

When the pasta is done, drain well; return it to the pot. Toss with the remaining 1 tablespoon olive oil.

To serve, spoon the penne into 4 pasta bowls. Top with the bell pepper–soybean mixture and garnish.

Per serving: Cal 385/Pro 18.8g/Carb 46.2g/Fat 13.9g/Chol 19mg/Sod 75mg

ADVANCE PREPARATION The bell pepper–soybean mixture can be cooked early the day it is to be served; cover and refrigerate. Reheat, stirring gently, over medium-low heat; serve over freshly cooked hot pasta.

VARIATION

❧ Use 2 red bell peppers rather than 1 red and 1 green, or substitute others such as orange, golden, or purple (see Tip, page 195).

tip

Choose onions that are heavy for their size, with dry skins and no soft spots. Yellow, or Spanish, onions usually have a sweeter flavor than white onions. Stored in a cool, dry place with good air circulation, onions will keep for up to 2 months. They can be refrigerated for up to a week; because of the humidity, longer refrigeration will cause spoilage.

garnish *(optional)* ↗ freshly ground black pepper, freshly grated Parmesan cheese, Tofu-Chèvre Spread (page 5), or Parmesan Cream (page 49)

cabbage and noodles with tofu

This deceptively rich-tasting but low-fat skillet dish is a good choice for preparing tofu that has been frozen and thawed (see page xxx).

makes 6 servings

8 ounces medium-wide egg noodles

2 tablespoons safflower oil

1/4 cup finely chopped onion

1/2 green bell pepper, finely chopped

1/2 red bell pepper, finely chopped

2 cups finely shredded white or green head cabbage (see Tip)

1 teaspoon minced garlic

12 ounces silken extra-firm tofu, frozen, thawed, squeezed, and crumbled (see page xxx)

1/4 cup vegetable stock (see page 34)

2 teaspoons sweet Hungarian paprika (see Tip, page 213)

1 teaspoon minced fresh thyme (or 1/4 teaspoon dried)

One 15-ounce can chopped tomatoes

Dash of salt, or to taste

Dash of freshly ground black pepper, or to taste

1 cup nonfat sour cream (at room temperature)

Bring a large pot of water to a boil over high heat; add the noodles. When the water returns to a boil, stir once to separate the noodles. Reduce the heat to medium-high and cook until *al dente*, about 5 to 7 minutes. Drain well.

While the noodles are cooking, heat the oil in a large non-stick sauté pan over medium-high heat. Add the onion and bell peppers; cook, stirring occasionally, until softened, about 5 minutes.

Add the cabbage and garlic; cook, stirring frequently, until the cabbage is softened and tender, about 2 minutes. Stir in the tofu, vegetable stock, paprika, and the dried or fresh thyme. Reduce the heat to medium.

Stir the noodles, tomatoes, salt, and pepper into the saucepan. Reduce the heat to low. Gently stir in the sour cream and adjust the seasonings to taste just before serving.

Per serving: Cal 184/Pro 10.3g/Carb 20.6g/Fat 6.7g/Chol 12mg/Sod 261mg

ADVANCE PREPARATION This dish is best when prepared just before serving. Covered and refrigerated, it will keep for up to 2 days; reheat, stirring gently, over medium-low heat to prevent the sour cream from curdling. It's best to stir in the sour cream just before serving.

tip

Head cabbage comes in many colors, ranging from white to green to red. Choose heads with waxy, tightly wrapped leaves; the head should be heavy for its size. Tightly wrapped, it can be refrigerated for about a week.

Stovetop Dishes

curried acorn squash ragout

A ragout is a thick, rich, and well-seasoned stew of meat, poultry, or fish; this vegetable and tofu version is one of my favorite fall and winter entrées. It's especially delicious served over couscous; prepare the couscous while the curry mixture simmers.

Heat the oil in a large nonstick sauté pan over medium-high heat. Add the bell pepper, carrot, onion, and garlic; cook, stirring occasionally, until the vegetables are tender but not browned, about 6 minutes. Add the curry powder; stir for about 30 seconds.

Stir in the stock, squash, pepper, and salt. When the liquid comes to a boil, reduce the heat to medium-low. Cover and cook until the squash chunks are tender, about 15 minutes. Gently stir in the tofu; heat until warm, about 3 minutes. Adjust the seasonings to taste.

Per serving: Cal 309/Pro 10.3g/Carb 52.2g/Fat 6.6g/Chol 0mg/Sod 83mg

VARIATION

❯ Substitute butternut squash for the acorn squash.

tip

Studies have proven that color affects appetite. Bright colors like orange, red, and yellow stimulate hunger. Cool pastels or dreary blacks and browns tend to squelch appetites. Everything, from dishes, tablecloths, and walls, to foods themselves, can send color cues that influence the appetite.

makes 4 servings

1 tablespoon olive oil

1 red bell pepper, coarsely chopped

1/2 cup coarsely chopped carrot

1/2 cup coarsely chopped onion

1 teaspoon minced garlic

1 tablespoon curry powder

1 1/2 cups vegetable stock (see page 34)

2 medium acorn squash, peeled, halved, seeded, and cut into 1-inch chunks (about 6 cups)

1/4 teaspoon freshly ground black pepper, or to taste

Dash of salt, or to taste

12 ounces silken firm tofu, cut into 1-inch cubes (about 2 cups)

garnish *(optional)* ↗ toasted chopped walnuts (see Tip, page 50), chopped fresh flat-leaf parsley

mu shu tofu V

makes 4 servings

1/2 cup vegetable stock
   (see page 34)

1/4 cup dry sherry (see Tip,
   page 159)

1/4 cup low-sodium soy sauce

2 teaspoons cornstarch

2 tablespoons roasted peanut
   oil (see Tip, page 149)

6 cups broccoli-coleslaw mix
   (julienned vegetables)

1 cup sliced mushrooms

1/2 cup coarsely chopped
   scallions (both green and
   white parts)

2 teaspoons minced garlic

12 ounces silken extra-firm
   tofu, cut into 1/2-inch
   cubes (about 2 cups)

Eight 6- or 7-inch flour tortillas

1/2 cup hoisin sauce (see Tip)

Using preshredded broccoli-coleslaw mix (which usually also contains some julienned carrots and shredded red cabbage) and sliced mushrooms—both available in the supermarket's produce department—will speed you through the preparation for this dish. As an accompaniment, authentic Mu Shu pancakes are available in many Asian markets; flour tortillas, which are found in the dairy case at most supermarkets, work wonderfully too.

Combine the vegetable stock, sherry, soy sauce, and cornstarch in a small bowl or 2-cup measure; stir until smooth. Set aside.

Heat the oil in a large nonstick skillet over medium-high heat. Add the broccoli-coleslaw mix; stir-fry until the vegetables just begin to soften, about 5 minutes. Add the mushrooms, scallions, and garlic; continue to stir-fry until all of the vegetables are lightly cooked, about 3 minutes.

Reduce the heat to medium. Stir the sherry mixture and add all at once to the vegetables. Stir constantly as the sauce thickens, about 1 minute. Add the tofu and stir gently until heated through.

Place the tortillas between 2 double layers of moistened paper towels; microwave until softened and warm, about 45 to 60 seconds. (Or wrap the tortillas in aluminum foil and heat in a 325°F oven for about 10 minutes.)

To serve, put the warm tortillas in a covered basket and the hoisin sauce into a bowl. Spoon servings of the Mu Shu Tofu onto individual plates. As you eat, spread about 1 tablespoon hoisin sauce on each tortilla and top with about 1/2 cup of the stir-fried vegetables. Roll each tortilla, burrito style, and enjoy.

Per serving: Cal 482/Pro 20.1g/Carb 69.1g/Fat 13.9g/Chol 0mg/Sod 1,655mg

ADVANCE PREPARATION The vegetables can be chopped in advance; mix the sauce, stir-fry the vegetables, and heat the tortillas just before serving.

VARIATIONS

❯ Substitute cauliflower-coleslaw mix for the broccoli-coleslaw mix.

❯ Shred broccoli stalks in your food processor; substitute for the broccoli-coleslaw mix.

❯ For a sweeter, less salty flavor, substitute Chinese plum sauce (see Tip, page 97) for the hoisin sauce.

❯ Stir about 2 tablespoons hoisin sauce into the cooked vegetables when adding the sherry sauce; omit the tortillas and serve the dish over rice.

❯ Rather than rolling the tortillas like burritos, fold them envelope-style: spoon the hoisin sauce and a mound of the stir-fried mixture into the center of each tortilla, fold the bottoms of the tortillas up over the filling, and fold the sides of the tortillas to the center, overlapping slightly.

tip

Hoisin sauce is a thick, sweet, reddish brown sauce made from soybeans, sugar, chilies, spices, and garlic. It is sold in specialty Asian markets and in many supermarkets. Tightly sealed and refrigerated, it will keep almost indefinitely. There is no substitute.

romaine spring rolls with five-spice soybeans

makes 4 servings

1/3 cup Chinese plum sauce
(see Tip, page 97)

1 tablespoon water, or as
needed

12 large romaine leaves

1 tablespoon roasted peanut
oil (see Tip)

4 ribs bok choy, cut into
1/4-inch-thick slices;
also coarsely chop leaves
(see Tip, page 123)

4 medium scallions, finely
chopped

1 red bell pepper, diced

2 teaspoons minced garlic

1 cup cooked soybeans

1 teaspoon Chinese five-spice
powder (see Tip)

Dash of ground white pepper,
or to taste

Dash of salt, or to taste

garnish (optional) toasted
pine nuts (see Tip, page 75)

One romantic evening in southern California, a special friend and I lingered in a nouvelle Asian restaurant, savoring taste after taste. A shrimp appetizer we enjoyed there provided inspiration for this recipe. The Chinese plum sauce and five-spice powder are the secrets to the extraordinary mix of flavors.

Combine the Chinese plum sauce and water in a small bowl. (Depending upon the thickness, a little more or less water may be necessary to bring the sauce to maple syrup consistency.) Set aside.

Arrange the romaine leaves on a serving plate; set aside.

Heat the peanut oil in a large nonstick skillet over medium-high heat. Add the bok choy, scallions, and bell pepper; cook, stirring occasionally, until crisp-tender, about 3 minutes. Add the garlic during the last minute. Add the remaining ingredients; stir occasionally until the soybeans are warmed through. Adjust the seasonings to taste. Spoon into a serving bowl.

Assemble the rolls at the table. Spoon the warm five-spice soybean mixture onto a romaine leaf; drizzle with the plum sauce. Roll up the sides of the leaf and enjoy!

Per serving: Cal 177/Pro 7.4g/Carb 21.2g/Fat 6.9g/Chol 0mg/Sod 27mg

ADVANCE PREPARATION The five-spice soybean mixture can be made in advance, chilled, and served as a salad mounded on romaine leaves.

VARIATIONS

Substitute for the bok choy or red bell pepper or add other vegetables (up to 3 cups total) such as shredded carrot, sliced mushrooms, or bean sprouts.

➤ Serve the five-spice soybean mixture (warm, room temperature, or chilled) in pita bread pockets.

tips

Roasted peanut oil is made from peanuts that are dry-roasted prior to pressing; the aroma and flavor are far superior to those of other peanut oils. Roasted peanut oil is available in some supermarkets and gourmet shops; my favorite is from Loriva Supreme Foods, Inc. Call 1-800-94LORIV (1-800-945-6748) for information.

Chinese five-spice powder, sometimes called five-fragrance powder, is a sweet and pungent mixture of five ground spices, including fennel, star anise, Szechuan peppercorns, cinnamon, and cloves. A licorice flavor predominates, thanks to the fennel seeds. Some brands also contain ginger and licorice root.

garden frittata

Frittatas are to the Italians what omelettes are to the French. The difference is that an omelette encloses its filling, while a frittata incorporates it evenly throughout. Also, omelettes must be served warm, but frittatas are delicious hot, cold, or at room temperature. For a special presentation, top the servings of frittata with warmed Roasted Sweet Red Pepper Dressing (page 92).

makes 4 servings

1 cup mashed silken firm tofu

3 large eggs (at room temperature)

3 tablespoons cold water

1/2 cup freshly grated Parmesan cheese

1/4 teaspoon freshly ground black pepper

3 tablespoons coarsely chopped fresh basil (or 1 teaspoon dried)

1 tablespoon olive oil

1/2 red bell pepper, cut into strips about 2 inches long by 1/4 inch wide

1 cup sliced fresh mushrooms (see Tip)

1 small zucchini, cut into 1/4-inch-thick slices (about 1 cup)

1 medium scallion, finely chopped

1 teaspoon minced garlic

garnish *(optional)* paprika or freshly ground black pepper, sprigs of fresh basil

Put the tofu, eggs, water, 1/4 cup of the Parmesan cheese, and pepper into a food processor; process until the mixture is smooth. Stir in the fresh or dried basil; set aside.

Heat the oil in a large nonstick skillet over medium-high heat. Add the bell pepper; cook, stirring occasionally, until crisp-tender, about 3 minutes. Add the mushrooms, zucchini, scallion, and garlic; continue to cook, stirring occasionally, until the vegetables are tender, about 3 minutes.

Reduce the heat to medium; pour the tofu-egg mixture evenly over the cooked vegetables. Once the bottom is firm, about 2 minutes, use a spatula to create openings in the frittata so that the uncooked egg mixture runs underneath. Cover and cook until the egg mixture is thoroughly cooked, about 2 to 3 minutes (see Tip, page 64).

To serve, loosen the edges of the frittata with a spatula and cut into 4 wedges. Sprinkle the servings with the remaining Parmesan cheese; garnish and serve.

Per serving: Cal 196/Pro 15g/Carb 5.5g/Fat 12.7g/Chol 170mg/Sod 304mg

VARIATIONS

❧ Substitute for the bell pepper, mushrooms, or zucchini or add other vegetables (up to 3 cups total) such as shredded carrots, cut asparagus, thinly sliced new potatoes, small broccoli florets, peas, sliced plum tomatoes, or drained and chopped oil-packed sun-dried tomatoes.

❧ Substitute 3/4 cup cholesterol-free egg substitute for the eggs.

tip

Refrigerate mushrooms for up to 4 days in a paper bag, an open plastic bag, or in a basket so air can circulate around them. Do not wash prior to storage; before using, simply brush with a mushroom brush or wipe with a moist paper towel. If it is necessary to rinse them, do so quickly; because mushrooms are very absorbent, they should not be allowed to soak in water. Before using, cut off any woody stems and trim the bottoms off tender stems. Mushrooms must be cooked quickly; they are 90 percent water, and overcooking results in a mushy texture.

huevos rancheros

This classic Mexican egg dish—with the nontraditional addition of Parmesan cheese—is equally satisfying at break- fast, lunch, or dinner. Make it spicy or keep it mild by selecting your favorite bottled salsa or taco sauce.

makes 4 servings

2 tablespoons olive oil

1 red bell pepper, coarsely chopped

1/4 cup coarsely chopped onion

1 teaspoon minced garlic

3 plum tomatoes, cut into 1/2-inch cubes (about 1 cup)

One 4-ounce can diced mild green chilies, drained

1/2 teaspoon chili powder, or to taste

2 teaspoons minced fresh oregano (or 1/2 teaspoon dried)

Dash of ground cumin

Dash of freshly ground black pepper, or to taste

Four 6- or 7-inch flour tortillas (at room temperature)

1 cup bottled salsa or taco sauce (at room temperature)

11/2 cups cooked soybeans (one 15-ounce can, drained and rinsed)

1/4 cup freshly grated Parmesan cheese

4 large eggs (see Tips)

2 tablespoons cold water

Dash of salt, or to taste

Dash of freshly ground black pepper, or to taste

Adjust the oven broiler rack to 4 to 5 inches from the heating element; preheat the broiler.

Heat 1 tablespoon of the oil in a large nonstick skillet over medium-high heat. Add the bell pepper, onion, and garlic; cook, stirring occasionally, until the vegetables are crisp-tender, about 5 minutes. Reduce the heat to medium; stir in the tomatoes, green chilies, chili powder, fresh or dried oregano, cumin, and pepper. Cook, uncovered, stirring occasionally, until the vegetables are tender, about 3 minutes. Adjust the seasoning to taste. Remove from the heat; cover to keep warm.

Arrange the tortillas in a single layer on a baking sheet; spread the top of each tortilla with about 2 tablespoons of the salsa or taco sauce.

Put the soybeans and the remaining 1/2 cup salsa into a food processor; process until smooth. Spread the mixture on the tortillas and sprinkle each with 1 tablespoon Parmesan cheese. Set aside.

Lightly whisk the eggs in a small bowl. Whisk in the water, salt, and pepper. Heat the remaining 1 tablespoon oil in a small nonstick skillet over medium heat; add the eggs. Cook, stirring constantly, until the eggs are set but still soft, about 2 minutes. Remove from the heat; cover to keep warm.

Put the cheese-topped tortillas under the broiler until the cheese melts, about 2 minutes.

To assemble the servings, transfer the tortillas to 4 plates. Divide the cooked vegetables among the tortillas; top with the eggs. Garnish and serve immediately.

Per serving: Cal 428/Pro 23.9g/Carb 33.4g/Fat 22.1g/Chol 218mg/Sod 845mg

ADVANCE PREPARATION The tomato–bell pepper and soybean-salsa mixtures can be prepared in advance; cover and refrigerate for up to 2 days. Bring to room temperature before assembling with the tortillas and freshly cooked eggs.

VARIATION

> Substitute 1 cup cholesterol-free egg substitute for the eggs.

tips

With proper care and handling, eggs pose no greater health risk than other perishable foods. Since salmonella bacteria are found in some eggs, it is wise to take the following precautions:

Buy only clean, uncracked eggs that have been refrigerated.

Do not leave eggs in any form at room temperature for more than 2 hours.

Cook eggs until no visible liquid remains.

Do not taste mixtures or batters containing raw egg.

Use only pasteurized eggs or an egg substitute when preparing recipes calling for raw eggs that will not be cooked before they are consumed.

Although eggs will keep for up to 1 month in the refrigerator, they lose their fresh flavor after 1 week. Store them with the large end up in the coldest part of your refrigerator. (The molded door rack is not the best place to store eggs, since they are exposed to warm air every time the door is opened.) Since eggs can absorb odors through their porous shells, storing eggs in the carton helps protect them from the aromas of other foods.

Cholesterol-free egg substitutes are made from real egg whites. The flavor is enhanced by the addition of a small amount of corn oil, and some yellow coloring is added to give the appearance of whole eggs. Reduced-cholesterol egg products are made from whole eggs from which nearly all of the cholesterol has been removed. These egg substitutes are found both in the freezer and in the refrigerated sections of most supermarkets.

garnish *(optional)* nonfat sour cream or plain yogurt, sprigs of fresh cilantro or flat-leaf parsley

scrambled tofu

As an alternative to scrambled eggs, this recipe can steal the show at brunch, lunch, or even dinner. For variety, stuff it into warmed pita bread pockets or roll in warmed flour tortillas.

makes 4 servings

1 tablespoon olive oil

1 cup sliced mushrooms

1/2 cup finely chopped green bell pepper

2 medium scallions, finely chopped

1 teaspoon minced garlic

1 1/2 cups mashed silken firm tofu (12 ounces)

3 plum tomatoes, cut into 1/2-inch cubes (about 1 cup)

2 tablespoons low-sodium soy sauce

1 tablespoon minced fresh flat-leaf parsley

1 tablespoon minced fresh basil (or 1/2 teaspoon dried)

1 tablespoon minced fresh oregano (or 1/2 teaspoon dried)

1/2 teaspoon freshly ground black pepper, or to taste

garnish *(optional)* freshly grated Parmesan cheese, sprigs of fresh flat-leaf parsley or basil

Heat the oil in a medium nonstick skillet over medium heat. Add the mushrooms, bell pepper, scallions, and garlic. Cook, stirring occasionally, until the vegetables are tender, about 4 minutes.

Stir in the tofu, tomatoes, soy sauce, parsley, fresh or dried basil and oregano, and pepper. Heat until warmed through, about 3 minutes. Adjust the seasoning to taste.

Per serving: Cal 119/Pro 8g/Carb 7.8g/Fat 6.2g/Chol 0mg/Sod 316mg

VARIATIONS

❯ Substitute for the mushrooms or green bell pepper or add other vegetables (up to 2 cups total) such as shredded carrots, small broccoli florets, chopped red bell pepper, or sliced zucchini.

❯ For the mashed fresh tofu, substitute 18 ounces silken extra-firm tofu that has been frozen, thawed, squeezed, and crumbled (see page xxx).

❯ In addition to the tofu, use 1 lightly beaten egg, 2 lightly beaten egg whites, or 1/4 cup cholesterol-free egg substitute. Scramble the eggs first until no visible liquid remains (see Tip, page 153); remove from the pan, set aside, and cover to keep warm. Stir in when adding the tofu.

❯ For the basil and oregano, substitute other herbs such as rosemary, thyme, or dill, or add chili powder or curry powder to taste.

tofu tacos

Many cooking class students have told me that this has become their favorite weeknight family dinner. The filling can be varied to use the vegetables you have on hand; broccoli florets are one of my favorite additions.

Preheat the oven to 350°F.

Heat the olive oil in a large nonstick skillet over medium-high heat. Add the zucchini, mushrooms, carrots, onion, and garlic. Cook, stirring occasionally, until the vegetables are tender but not browned, about 5 minutes.

Meanwhile, combine the tomato paste, water, chili powder, hot pepper sauce, cumin, and pepper in a small bowl; add the mixture to the skillet. Gently stir in the tofu cubes and plum tomatoes. Reduce the heat to low; cover and heat through, about 5 minutes.

Meanwhile, place the taco shells on a baking sheet. Heat in the preheated oven until warm, about 5 minutes.

To serve, spoon about $1/2$ cup of the vegetable-tofu mixture into each of the taco shells.

Per serving (2 filled tacos): Cal 249/Pro 9.4g/Carb 28.8g/Fat 10.7g/Chol 0mg/Sod 136mg

ADVANCE PREPARATION The filling can be prepared up to 1 day in advance; cover and refrigerate. Reheat, stirring gently. Assemble the tacos just before serving.

VARIATIONS

➤ In addition to the taco filling, stuff the tacos with shredded lettuce and shredded cheddar cheese.

➤ In place of the taco shells, toast 4 flour tortillas: Lightly brush both sides of each tortilla with olive oil and prick the surfaces several places with a fork. Place the tortillas directly on the oven rack in a preheated 400°F oven; toast until crispy, about 3 minutes on each side. To serve, top the tortillas with layers of lettuce and warm taco filling; sprinkle with shredded cheese.

makes 12 tacos (6 servings)

2 tablespoons olive oil

2 small zucchini, halved lengthwise and cut into $1/4$-inch-thick slices (about 2 cups)

2 cups sliced mushrooms

2 carrots, coarsely shredded

1 small onion, cut into strips about $1/4$ inch wide

1 teaspoon minced garlic

One 6-ounce can tomato paste

$3/4$ cup water

2 teaspoons chili powder, or to taste

$1/2$ teaspoon hot pepper sauce, or to taste

$1/4$ teaspoon ground cumin

$1/4$ teaspoon freshly ground black pepper, or to taste

12 ounces silken extra-firm tofu, cut into $1/2$-inch cubes (about 2 cups)

3 plum tomatoes, cut into $1/2$-inch cubes (about 1 cup)

12 taco shells

garnish *(optional)* orange slices

grilled tofu-vegetable towers
with parmesan vinaigrette

Get ready for raves—these towers are a showstopper. Another beautiful feature: You can make them up to 8 hours ahead. Serve with warm, crusty Italian rolls. For convenience, I usually grill the vegetables and tofu on a stovetop grill pan (see Tip), one of my frequently used pieces of cookware. If you prefer, the ingredients can be grilled on an outdoor barbecue.

makes 4 servings

For the Parmesan Vinaigrette

1/4 cup extra-virgin olive oil

2 tablespoons red wine vinegar

2 tablespoons freshly squeezed lemon juice

2 tablespoons freshly grated Parmesan cheese

1 teaspoon Dijon mustard

1/2 teaspoon minced garlic

1 teaspoon minced fresh oregano (or 1/4 teaspoon dried)

1/4 teaspoon freshly ground black pepper, or to taste

Dash of salt, or to taste

To complete the recipe

2 tablespoons olive oil

1/2 medium eggplant, peeled and cut lengthwise into four 1/2-inch-thick slices (see Tip)

1 medium yellow summer squash, cut lengthwise into four 1/2-inch-thick slices

1/2 teaspoon freshly ground black pepper, or to taste

Four 1/4-inch-thick slices red onion

Whisk together the vinaigrette ingredients in a small bowl. Adjust the seasonings to taste. Set aside.

Heat a stovetop grill over high heat. Lightly brush one side of the slices of eggplant and squash with olive oil. Reduce the heat to medium-high and arrange the slices on the grill, oiled sides down; cook until the vegetables are lightly browned, about 3 minutes. Brush the top surfaces with oil; turn and cook until the eggplant and squash slices are lightly browned and cooked through, about 2 minutes. Arrange the eggplant slices in a single layer in a 9-inch square glass baking dish. Top each eggplant slice with a squash slice; sprinkle lightly with pepper.

Brush one side of the onion and tofu slices with oil. Arrange the slices, oiled sides down, on the stovetop grill over medium-high heat; cook until lightly browned, about 2 minutes. Brush the top surfaces with the remaining oil; turn and cook until the onion is tender and the tofu is lightly browned, about 2 minutes. Transfer to the baking dish; layer the onion and tofu slices atop the squash.

Top each stack with a layer of tomato slices. Surround the "towers" with the mushroom slices.

Whisk the vinaigrette and pour it over the layered ingredients and mushrooms. Cover and refrigerate for at least 1 hour or up to 8 hours.

When ready to serve, arrange 3 arugula leaves on each of 4 serving plates. Using a slotted spatula, place the stacks of layered vegetables atop the arugula. Use a slotted spoon to transfer mushroom slices to surround each stack; garnish. Discard the remaining vinaigrette.

Per serving: Cal 243/Pro 9.9g/Carb 13.4g/Fat 16.6g/Chol 1mg/Sod 125mg

ADVANCE PREPARATION The vinaigrette will keep for up to 2 days in a tightly closed container in the refrigerator. The vegetable stacks with vinaigrette should be refrigerated for at least 1 hour or up to 8 hours before serving. Assemble the plates with the arugula just before serving.

VARIATIONS

❧ For a firmer texture, substitute pressed tofu (see page xxxii).

❧ Add 1/4-inch-thick slices of fresh mozzarella cheese or tofu mozzarella (see page xl) between the onion and tofu slices.

❧ Substitute white mushrooms for the cremini mushrooms.

tips

Eggplant does not necessarily need to be sliced, salted, and weighted to squeeze out the juice, as some cookbooks recommend. Only overripe fruit is tough and bitter, so select young, smaller eggplants. Store them in a plastic bag in the refrigerator for up to 2 weeks. The peel is edible, so it is not necessary to remove it unless you choose to peel it for the sake of appearance or texture. In some recipes, leaving the skin on is actually an advantage, since it not only adds color but also helps cut-up pieces hold their shape. Eggplant is very porous and soaks up oil like a sponge; keep fat to a minimum by using a nonstick pan, making sure the pan is very hot before adding the eggplant, and tossing and turning the eggplant as it cooks to coat all pieces evenly with the oil.

Stovetop grill pans are available in a variety of materials and in a range of shapes, sizes, and prices. Not only does this type of pan grill ingredients quickly, but it also achieves a smoky, grilled flavor along with those visually appealing grill lines.

12 ounces silken extra-firm tofu, cut into four 3-inch by 1/4-inch slices

1 large tomato, cut into 1/2-inch-thick slices

1 cup sliced cremini mushrooms

12 arugula leaves

garnish *(optional)* freshly ground black pepper, sprigs of fresh oregano or flat-leaf parsley

sherried tofu steaks

makes 4 servings

12 ounces silken extra-firm tofu

1/2 cup dry sherry (see Tip, page 159)

1/4 cup low-sodium soy sauce

1 tablespoon minced fresh thyme (or 1 teaspoon dried)

1 tablespoon olive oil

1 medium onion, cut into 1/4-inch-thick slices (about 1 cup)

1 teaspoon minced garlic

garnish *(optional)* sprigs of fresh flat-leaf parsley

For "tofu steaks," freeze the tofu in advance, then thaw and cook. Serve the tasty steaks and sauce with rice and a steamed green vegetable, such as asparagus or broccoli. For an interesting presentation, the tofu steaks can be placed on serving plates atop beds of wilted spinach (see Variation), or use them as in an ingredient in Sherried Tofu–Roasted Eggplant Sandwiches (page 164).

At least 4 hours in advance, cut the block of tofu horizontally into 4 even slices. Arrange the slices in a single layer on a nonstick baking sheet; cover with plastic wrap and freeze. Before cooking, thaw the frozen slices; then press them and drain the liquid (see page xxxii). Dry the slices by blotting them with paper towels before cooking.

Just before cooking, stir together the sherry, soy sauce, and fresh or dried thyme in a small bowl or measuring cup; set aside.

Heat the oil in a large nonstick skillet over medium heat. Add the onion and garlic; cook, stirring constantly, until the onion softens, about 3 minutes. Place the tofu slices in the skillet in a single layer on top of the onion-garlic mixture. Cook until lightly browned, about 4 minutes per side. Pour the sherry mixture over the tofu. Cover and cook for about 2 minutes per side, or until the tofu absorbs some of the sauce and the remaining sauce is bubbly.

Use a slotted spatula to transfer the tofu steaks to serving plates. Top with the onions and garlic, drizzle with the sauce, and garnish.

Per serving: Cal 115/Pro 8.9g/Carb 7.7g/Fat 5.4g/Chol 0mg/Sod 618mg

ADVANCE PREPARATION Freeze the tofu in advance (for at least 4 hours or for up to 3 months) and thaw the slices thoroughly before preparing this recipe (see page xxx).

❧ Rather than freezing the tofu slices, use pressed tofu (see page xxxii).

❧ Serve each tofu steak on a bed of wilted spinach: Begin with 8 cups loosely packed fresh spinach leaves, stems removed (preferably tender salad spinach leaves). Rinse them in cool water; do not dry (the spinach will steam in the water that clings). Drop the leaves into a medium saucepan; cover and cook over medium heat until the leaves are wilted, 3 to 4 minutes. Remove the pan from the heat; keep covered until ready to serve. Allow any excess water to drain off by using tongs to transfer the warm, wilted leaves to plates. (The 8 cups fresh spinach leaves will yield 4 cups after steaming.)

tip

Sherry is wine to which brandy has been added to increase the flavor and alcohol content. Sherries vary in color, flavor, and sweetness. Finos are dry and light; manzanillas are very dry, delicate finos with a hint of saltiness. Olorosos, often labeled cream or golden sherry, are darker in color and sweet.

tofu teriyaki

These versatile, slightly sweet tofu triangles can be served in a variety of ways. For casual dinners I serve Tofu Teriyaki sandwiches, assembled by placing the lightly browned tofu, thin slices of tomato, and shredded mozzarella cheese between slices of toasted whole wheat buns. For more elegant dining, I serve the triangles accompanied by steamed asparagus spears atop warm brown rice or Chinese Wheat-Flour Noodles with Sesame-Pepper Dressing (page 162). Tofu Teriyaki is also a component of Thai Noodle Salad (page 72).

makes 4 servings

For the Teriyaki Marinade

3 tablespoons low-sodium soy sauce

2 tablespoons freshly squeezed lemon juice

2 tablespoons honey

1 tablespoon dark sesame oil

2 teaspoons minced garlic

2 teaspoons minced gingerroot (see Tip)

To complete the dish

12 ounces silken extra-firm tofu

2 tablespoons safflower oil

Combine the marinade ingredients in a small bowl.

Slice the block of tofu into 4 even horizontal slices; keep the slices in an even stack. Then cut the entire block of tofu into quarters, slicing diagonally from corner to corner to form 16 triangles.

Pour half of the marinade into a 9-inch square glass baking dish or flat refrigerator container. Arrange the tofu triangles in the marinade; cover with the remaining marinade. Cover and set aside at room temperature for about 1 hour or refrigerate for up to 8 hours.

When ready to cook, heat the safflower oil in a nonstick skillet over medium-high heat. Use a slotted spatula to transfer the tofu to the skillet; cook until lightly browned, 3 to 4 minutes per side. Discard the remaining marinade.

Per serving: Cal 113/Pro 7.5g/Carb 5.8g/Fat 6.6g/Chol 0mg/Sod 193mg

ADVANCE PREPARATION The tofu should be marinated for at least 1 hour or up to 8 hours. It can be cooked in advance; cover and refrigerate. Serve within a day, chilled or at room temperature.

VARIATIONS

❧ For a firmer texture, substitute pressed tofu (see page xxxii).

❧ At least 4 hours in advance, arrange the tofu triangles in a single layer on a nonstick baking sheet; cover with plastic wrap and freeze. Thaw, drain off the liquid, and blot with paper towels before marinating (see page xxx for information on longer storage). This method also will result in a firmer texture.

tip

When buying fresh ginger, look for a piece that is firm, with smooth brown skin and no soft spots. Store at room temperature and use within a few days. Before adding to recipes, finely mince the ginger so the flavor will be distributed evenly in the dish. What remains can be preserved in two ways: Peel the fresh ginger and cut it into chunks, place in a jar and add sherry to cover. Cap the jar and refrigerate for up to 2 months. (The ginger won't absorb the flavor of the sherry.) For even longer storage, wrap the ginger tightly in aluminum foil or seal in a small zip-top plastic bag and freeze. When you need ginger, without thawing, use a fine grater to grate off the amount needed. Rewrap and replace immediately in the freezer. Frozen ginger will keep for up to 3 months. Jars of preminced ginger are available in most produce departments; check the labels, as some products also contain garlic and sweeteners.

chinese wheat-flour noodles with sesame-pepper dressing

This spicy noodle side dish is equally intriguing served warm, chilled, or at room temperature. Partner it with Tofu Teriyaki (pages 160–161) or tempeh marinated in Sesame-Soy marinade (page 80).

makes 4 servings

4 ounces Chinese wheat-flour noodles (see Tip)

For the Sesame-Pepper Dressing

2 tablespoons low-sodium soy sauce

2 tablespoons white rice vinegar

1 tablespoon dark sesame oil

1/4 teaspoon red pepper flakes

1/8 teaspoon freshly ground black pepper, or to taste

Bring a large saucepan of water to a boil over high heat; add the noodles. Reduce the heat to medium-high and cook until tender, about 3 minutes.

Meanwhile, whisk together the dressing ingredients in a small bowl or measuring cup; set aside.

When the noodles are done, drain well; return to the pan. Whisk the dressing again, add it to the noodles, and toss. Adjust the seasonings to taste.

Per serving: Cal 139/Pro 3.3g/Carb 23.8g/Fat 3.4g/Chol 0mg/Sod 280mg

ADVANCE PREPARATION The dressing will keep for up to 1 week in a tightly closed container in the refrigerator. Covered and refrigerated, the completed dish will keep for up to 2 days.

VARIATION

➤ Add vegetables (up to 1 cup) such as shredded carrot, diced cucumber, or diced red bell pepper.

tip

Chinese wheat-flour noodles are made of wheat flour, cornstarch, salt, and sugar, giving them a consistency and flavor different from Italian pastas. They vary in thickness and may be round or flat; for packaging, the noodles are compacted into blocks. To cook, break off the portion you need and drop it into boiling water; cook for about 3 minutes, then drain well. The noodles can be served immediately after draining, or they can be patted dry and sautéed in oil until lightly browned.

Sandwiches

bruschetta

Bruschetta, borrowed from the Italians, has taken the country by storm. The addition of beans turns these tasty little toasts into a warm open-faced sandwich perfect for a light lunch. For appetizer servings, mound the topping on 16 slices of French baguette.

makes 8 slices (4 servings)

4 plum tomatoes (at room temperature), cut into $1/4$-inch cubes (about $1 1/2$ cups) (see Tip)

$2/3$ cup cooked soybeans

$1/4$ cup chopped fresh basil (fresh is essential)

1 tablespoon extra-virgin olive oil

1 teaspoon minced garlic

$1/2$ teaspoon freshly ground black pepper, or to taste

Eight $3/4$-inch-thick slices Italian bread (see Tip)

$1/4$ cup freshly grated Parmesan cheese

Adjust the oven broiler rack to 4 to 5 inches from the heating element; preheat the broiler.

Combine the tomatoes, soybeans, basil, olive oil, garlic, and pepper in a medium bowl.

Place the bread slices in a single layer on a baking sheet. Broil until lightly toasted, about 1 minute.

Mound the tomato-soybean mixture on the toasted bread slices; sprinkle with the Parmesan cheese.

Broil until the cheese is melted, about $1 1/2$ to 2 minutes. Watch closely! Serve warm.

Per serving (2 slices): Cal 286/Pro 13.5g/Carb 40.5/ Fat 7.7g/Chol 5mg/Sod 428mg

VARIATION

➤ Substitute dollops of goat cheese (chèvre) for the Parmesan; increase the broiling time to heat and lightly brown the goat cheese.

tip

For the cleanest cuts, use a serrated knife for slicing bread.

Plum tomatoes, often called Italian or Roma tomatoes, have thick, meaty walls, small seeds, little juice, and a rich, sweet flavor. They are the best choice for salads or other recipes that benefit from less juicy tomatoes that retain their shape after being chopped or sliced.

sherried tofu–roasted eggplant sandwiches

By making Roasted Red Pepper Hummus in advance, these impressive sandwich stacks can be prepared quickly. They're certain to add an elegant flair to a casual occasion.

makes 4 servings

1 tablespoon olive oil

Four 1/2-inch-thick slices eggplant (cut crosswise) (see Tip, page 157)

1 tablespoon low-sodium soy sauce

4 cooked Sherried Tofu Steaks (page 158)

4 large Italian rolls, halved lengthwise

1/2 cup Roasted Red Pepper Hummus (page 17)

1 medium tomato, cut crosswise into eight 1/4-inch-thick slices

1/4 cup freshly grated Parmesan cheese

4 dashes of freshly ground black pepper, or to taste

Preheat the oven to 350°F.

To pan-roast the eggplant, heat the oil in a large nonstick skillet over medium-high heat. Add the eggplant slices in a single layer; cover and cook until they are tender and lightly browned, about 4 minutes per side. Remove the pan from the heat; drizzle the cooked eggplant with the soy sauce and cover to keep warm.

Cook the Sherried Tofu Steaks. Remove the pan from the heat; cover and set aside.

Place the Italian rolls on a baking sheet, cut sides up. Heat in the preheated oven until warm and crusty.

To assemble the sandwiches, spread each cut side of the rolls with about 1 tablespoon of the Roasted Red Pepper Hummus. Layer the remaining ingredients atop the hummus on the bottom halves of the rolls in the following order: 1 tofu steak (topped with onions, garlic, and sauce), 1 eggplant slice, and 2 tomato slices. Sprinkle each with 1 tablespoon of the Parmesan cheese and a dash of pepper.

Place the warm open-faced sandwiches on serving plates and serve immediately.

Per serving: Cal 421/Pro 21.4g/Carb 53.8g/Fat 13.3g/Chol 5mg/Sod 1,217mg

ADVANCE PREPARATION The tofu for the Tofu Steaks must be frozen and thawed (or pressed, if fresh) before cooking. Covered and refrigerated, the hummus will keep for up to 2 days. Cook the tofu, prepare the remaining ingredients, and assemble the sandwiches just before serving.

VARIATION

❧ Add a layer of wilted spinach (see Variation, page 159) atop the Roasted Red Pepper Hummus.

tip

When buying fresh spinach, look for springy, bright leaves and short stems. In general, the smaller the spinach leaves, the more tender and more delicately flavored the vegetable will be. Salad spinach, sold in most supermarkets, is tender spinach leaves that have been prewashed before packaging and are ready to use uncooked. For cooking, the larger, thicker, more mature leaves are the better choice. Before using the more mature leaves, be sure to rinse under cold running water to remove any sand, then dry. Remove the stems before using all spinach. Spinach will keep for only 2 to 4 days, so store it in a sealed plastic bag in the vegetable crisper, and use it soon. If it seems wilted, wrap the leaves in moist paper towels and refrigerate to revive.

roasted vegetable pitas

Roasting concentrates flavors without adding fat and lends a buttery-soft texture.

makes 4 servings

2 roasted red bell peppers
(see Tip, page 92)

1 medium eggplant (about
1 1/2 pounds) (see Tip,
page 157)

2 tablespoons freshly squeezed
lemon juice

1 tablespoon olive oil

1/2 teaspoon minced garlic

1/4 teaspoon salt, or to taste

1/4 teaspoon freshly ground
black pepper, or to taste

2 tablespoons chopped
fresh cilantro (do not use
dried cilantro; if fresh is
unavailable, substitute
fresh basil or flat-leaf
parsley)

1 1/2 cups cooked soybeans
(one 15-ounce can, drained
and rinsed)

1 teaspoon ground cumin

Two 6-inch white or whole
wheat pita breads

1/2 cup nonfat plain yogurt

1/4 cup finely chopped scallions
(both green and white
parts)

Dash of freshly ground black
pepper, or to taste

After roasting the peppers, position the oven rack about 6 inches from the broiler heating element. Pierce the eggplant several places with a fork; place it on a baking sheet. Turning once as it cooks, broil the eggplant for about 15 minutes, or until it is very tender when pierced with a fork. Set it aside to cool.

Move the oven rack to the center of the oven; preheat the oven to 350°F.

Whisk together the lemon juice, olive oil, garlic, 1/8 teaspoon of the salt, and pepper in a small bowl. Adjust the seasonings to taste.

When the eggplant has cooled, peel it and cut into 1-inch cubes. Toss the eggplant, cilantro, and lemon juice mixture in a medium bowl. Set aside.

Cut the peeled roasted red bell peppers lengthwise into 1/4-inch-wide strips. Set aside.

Combine the soybeans, cumin, and remaining 1/8 teaspoon salt in a small bowl.

Just before serving, wrap the pita breads in foil; place directly on the oven rack for about 5 minutes, or until softened. (Or put the unwrapped pitas in the microwave on high for about 45 seconds.) Use a serrated knife to cut each pita in half horizontally.

Place the 4 pita bread halves, rough sides up, on large salad plates. Evenly spread each pita round with the eggplant mixture; top with bell pepper strips and mounds of the bean mixture. Add a dollop of yogurt to each pita; sprinkle with the scallions and pepper.

Per serving: Cal 290/Pro 16.8g/Carb 32.2g/Fat 10.4g/Chol 0mg/Sod 266mg

ADVANCE PREPARATION The eggplant and bell peppers can be roasted early the day they are to be served; cover and refrigerate. The eggplant-cilantro and soybean-cumin mixtures can be combined several hours before serving; cover and refrigerate. Bring everything to room temperature and assemble just before serving.

tempeh-yam sandwiches

In the supermarket, be sure to select dark-skinned yams (rather than light-skinned sweet potatoes); their sweet orange flesh gives this unusual sandwich its identity.

Bring a small saucepan of water to a boil over high heat; add the yam. When the water returns to a boil, reduce the heat to medium. Cover and cook until the yam is tender, about 10 to 12 minutes; drain well. Mash the yam chunks in a small bowl. Put 3/4 cup of the mashed yam into a food processor; add the tofu. Process until the mixture is smooth; set aside. (The remaining yam, if any, can be discarded or eaten.)

Heat the oil in a medium nonstick skillet over medium-high heat. Add the tempeh strips and cook until lightly browned, about 4 to 5 minutes per side. Remove from the heat and set aside.

For each sandwich, spread one slice of bread with about 3 tablespoons of the yam-tofu mixture; top with 3 tempeh slices and 1/2 cup sprouts. Spread another slice of bread with 2 tablespoons guacamole; top with 2 tomato slices and sprinkle lightly with pepper. Put the sandwich halves together and slice diagonally.

Per serving: Cal 357/Pro 20.3/Carb 44.3/Fat 11g/Chol 0mg/Sod 388mg

ADVANCE PREPARATION Covered and refrigerated, the Tofu Guacamole will keep for up to 3 days. The yam can be cooked up to 1 day in advance; cover and refrigerate. Bring both to room temperature before preparing the sandwiches.

tip

Yams and sweet potatoes are actually not related to potatoes at all. The flesh of yams (sometimes called red sweet potatoes) is orange and quite sweet when cooked; sweet potatoes (sometimes called white sweet potatoes) have a lighter skin and yellow flesh. Store yams and sweet potatoes in a cool, dark, and dry place for up to 2 weeks; do not refrigerate.

makes 4 servings

Dash of salt

1 small yam, peeled and quartered (see Tip)

1/4 cup mashed silken firm tofu

1 tablespoon olive oil

8 ounces tempeh, cut into twelve 1/4-inch-thick slices

8 slices whole wheat bread

2 cups alfalfa sprouts

1/2 cup Tofu Guacamole (page 8)

Eight 1/4-inch-thick tomato slices

Dash of freshly ground black pepper

tempeh reubens

Here's a new twist on classic deli favorites. Serve the warm Tempeh Reuben sandwiches with Dijon Potato Salad (page 87) or Orange-Caraway Coleslaw (page 88) to complete the delicatessen theme.

makes 4 servings

1 tablespoon olive oil

8 ounces tempeh, halved both horizontally and vertically to form 4 pieces about 2^1/$_2$ inches long, 2 inches wide, and ^{1}/$_4$ inch thick

Four ^{1}/$_4$-inch-thick slices red onion, divided into rings

8 slices dark rye bread

4 teaspoons Dijon mustard

4 thin slices part-skim Swiss cheese (see Tip)

1 cup canned sauerkraut, drained

Four ^{3}/$_8$-inch-thick tomato slices (at room temperature)

Nonstick cooking spray

Heat the oil in a large nonstick skillet over medium-high heat. Add the tempeh and onion; turn the onion occasionally and cook the tempeh until lightly browned, about 4 to 5 minutes per side. Remove from the heat.

Spread the bread with the mustard. For each sandwich, top a slice of bread with 1 slice cheese, 1 slice tempeh and onion, ^{1}/$_4$ cup sauerkraut, and 1 tomato slice. Top each sandwich with another bread slice.

Coat the skillet with nonstick the cooking spray; heat over medium-high heat. Arrange the sandwiches in the skillet and heat until the cheese is melted and the bread is toasted, about 4 minutes per side.

Cut the sandwiches in half diagonally and serve warm.

Per serving: Cal 414/Pro 27.7g/Carb 44.9g/Fat 13.8g/Chol 19mg/Sod 783mg

VARIATION

❧ Stuff the sandwich filling ingredients into pita bread pockets; heat in a 350°F oven or in the microwave until the cheese melts.

tip

Firm, semifirm (including Swiss cheese), and semisoft cheeses should be wrapped airtight in plastic bags; store in the refrigerator cheese compartment (or warmest location) for up to several weeks. Mold may be cut away if it develops. Fresh and soft-ripened cheeses should be tightly wrapped. They will keep in the coldest part of the refrigerator for up to 2 weeks. Discard fresh or soft-ripened cheeses that become moldy. All cheeses taste best if brought to room temperature before serving.

curried tofu-carrot
sloppy joes

This recipe calls for tofu that has been frozen, thawed, and squeezed dry. If you prefer, substitute fresh silken extra-firm tofu (see Variation). I serve this mixture with a layer of thin tomato slices between toasted buns (preferably whole wheat).

Heat the oil in a large nonstick sauté pan over medium-high heat. Add the carrots, celery, onion, and garlic. Cook, stirring occasionally, until the vegetables are tender but not browned, about 5 minutes.

Meanwhile, combine the tomato paste and water in a small bowl; set aside.

Reduce the heat to medium and add the tofu, bread crumbs, and egg to the sauté pan. Stir constantly until the egg is cooked, about 3 minutes. Add the tomato paste mixture and the remaining ingredients; stir gently until heated through. Adjust the seasonings to taste.

Per serving: Cal 191/Pro 11.5g/Carb 19.3g/Fat 7.5g/Chol 53mg/Sod 265mg

ADVANCE PREPARATION This dish is best when prepared just before serving. Covered and refrigerated, leftovers will keep for up to 2 days.

VARIATIONS

❧ Substitute 1/4 cup cholesterol-free egg substitute for the egg.

❧ Substitute 1 1/2 cups mashed fresh silken extra-firm tofu (12 ounces) for the frozen tofu. Reduce the other ingredient quantities as follows: 1 shredded carrot, 2 tablespoons tomato paste, and 2 tablespoons water.

makes 4 servings

1 tablespoon safflower oil

2 carrots, finely shredded
(about 1 cup)

1 rib celery, diced

2 tablespoons finely chopped
onion

1 teaspoon minced garlic

1/4 cup tomato paste (see Tip,
page 4)

1/4 cup water

12 ounces silken extra-firm
tofu, frozen, thawed,
squeezed, and crumbled
(see page xxx)

1/2 cup dry bread crumbs
(see Tip, page 197)

1 large egg, lightly beaten

1 tablespoon minced fresh
flat-leaf parsley

1 teaspoon curry powder
(see Tip, page 46)

2 teaspoons minced fresh
thyme (or 1/2 teaspoon
dried)

1/2 teaspoon freshly ground
black pepper, or to taste

Dash of salt, or to taste

Burgers

veggie burgers

Serve these patties sandwiched between toasted buns with sliced tomatoes and frills of lettuce and, of course, ketchup.

makes 4 servings

1 cup texturized vegetable protein (TVP)

3/4 cup hot water

1 tablespoon olive oil

1/4 cup finely shredded carrot

1/4 cup minced green bell pepper

2 teaspoons minced garlic

2 large eggs

1/4 cup dry bread crumbs (see Tip, page 197)

2 tablespoons low-sodium soy sauce

1 tablespoon minced fresh flat-leaf parsley

1/2 teaspoon ground sage

1/2 teaspoon freshly ground black pepper

Nonstick cooking spray

Stir together the texturized vegetable protein and hot water in a medium bowl; allow to stand until the water is absorbed and the TVP is softened, about 5 minutes.

Meanwhile, heat the oil in a large nonstick sauté pan over medium-high heat. Add the carrot and pepper; cook, stirring occasionally, until tender, about 4 minutes. Add the garlic during the last minute. Remove from the heat.

Lightly beat the eggs in a medium bowl. Stir in the bread crumbs, soy sauce, parsley, sage, and pepper. Then stir in the softened TVP and the cooked vegetables. Form the mixture into 4 round patties, about 4 inches in diameter and 1/2 inch thick.

Coat a large nonstick skillet with the cooking spray; heat over medium-high heat. Cook the patties until lightly browned and cooked through, about 4 minutes on each side.

Per serving: Cal 182/Pro 16.5g/Carb 14.8g/Fat 6.3g/Chol 107mg/Sod 360mg

ADVANCE PREPARATION The burger mixture can be made a few hours in advance; shape into patties, then cover and refrigerate. If the patties are chilled, allow a little extra cooking time.

VARIATION

❯ Substitute 1/2 cup cholesterol-free egg substitute for the 2 eggs.

❯ Cook the patties on a stovetop grill pan or on an outdoor grill (see Tip, page 157).

spicy soybean patties

Cook these patties until they are crisp and golden on the outside, steamy and tender on the inside. Serve them with Riso–Sweet Bean Salad with Sun-Dried Tomato–Basil Vinaigrette (page 74). If time permits, rather than bottled salsa, top the soybean patties with warmed Roasted Sweet Red Pepper Dressing (page 92) or Ancho Chili Sauce (page 111).

Put the soybeans into a bowl; mash with a potato masher until they are slightly chunky. Stir in the egg, onion, flour, chili powder, and hot pepper sauce.

For each serving, scoop 1/3 cup of the mixture and flatten to form a patty about 4 inches in diameter and 1/2 inch thick.

Coat a large nonstick skillet with the cooking spray; heat over medium-high heat. Add the soybean patties; cook until lightly browned, about 4 minutes. Turn and cook until lightly browned and heated through, about 3 minutes.

Serve each soybean patty topped with 1 tablespoon salsa.

Per serving: Cal 149/Pro 12.1g/Carb 10.7g/Fat 6.4g/Chol 0mg/Sod 61mg

ADVANCE PREPARATION The soybean patty mixture can be prepared up to 1 day in advance; shape into patties, then cover and refrigerate. If the patties are chilled, allow a little extra cooking time.

VARIATION

↘ Substitute 1/4 cup cholesterol-free egg substitute for the egg.

↘ Cook the patties on a stovetop grill pan or on an outdoor grill (see Tip, page 157).

makes 4 servings

1 1/2 cups cooked soybeans (one 15-ounce can, drained and rinsed)

1 large egg, lightly beaten

1/4 cup finely chopped onion

1 tablespoon all-purpose unbleached or white flour

1 teaspoon chili powder

1/4 teaspoon hot pepper sauce (see Tip, page 185)

Nonstick cooking spray

1/4 cup bottled salsa

garnish *(optional)* ↗ sprigs of fresh cilantro

Wraps

tempeh-rice wraps with hoisin peanut sauce

Tortillas make the "envelopes." Tempeh, rice, and veggies form the contents. And robust peanut sauce creates the personality of these wraps. Vary the filling ingredients as you wish; here's the perfect use for odds and ends of vegetables and leftover cooked rice, whether it be brown, basmati, or wild rice.

makes 4 servings

3/4 cup Hoisin Peanut Sauce (at room temperature) (page 9)

1 cup warm cooked brown rice

1 tablespoon safflower oil

8 ounces tempeh, cut into 1/2-inch squares

1/2 medium red onion cut into 1/4-inch-wide strips (about 1/2 cup)

3 cups broccoli-coleslaw mix (julienned vegetables) (see headnote on page 146)

2 medium scallions, finely chopped

1 teaspoon minced garlic

Four 9-inch flour tortillas

garnish (optional) fresh cilantro or mint leaves

Prepare the peanut sauce; set aside to allow the flavors to blend. Meanwhile, cook or reheat the brown rice.

Heat the oil in a large nonstick sauté pan over medium-high heat. Add the tempeh and onion; cook, stirring occasionally, until the tempeh is lightly browned and the onion is crisp-tender, about 5 minutes. Add the broccoli-coleslaw mix, scallions, and garlic; cook, stirring occasionally, until the broccoli and onion are tender, about 5 minutes. Remove from the heat; cover and set aside.

Put the tortillas between 2 double layers of moistened paper towels; microwave until softened and warm, about 45 to 60 seconds. (Or wrap the tortillas in aluminum foil and heat in a 325°F oven for about 10 minutes.)

To assemble, spread the surface of each tortilla with about 3 tablespoons of the peanut sauce; spread 1/4 cup rice down the center to within 1 1/2 inches of the edges of the tortillas. Top the rice with about 1 cup of the cooked vegetables. Make envelope-style "wraps" by rolling up the bottoms of the tortillas and folding in opposite sides to overlap slightly and encase the filling. (If necessary, secure the overlapping edges with a toothpick.)

Per serving: Cal 437/Pro 22.1g/Carb 33.6g/Fat 14.9g/Chol 0mg/Sod 567mg

ADVANCE PREPARATION Covered and refrigerated, the peanut sauce will keep for up to 3 days. Since it thickens while standing, stir in water as needed. Cook the vegetables, cook or reheat the rice, and assemble the tortilla wraps just before serving.

VARIATIONS

❧ Substitute Spicy Peanut Sauce (page 115) for the Hoisin Peanut Sauce.

❧ Shred broccoli stalks in your food processor; substitute for the broccoli-coleslaw mix.

broccoli burritos

Broccoli is one of my favorite vegetables, so I was tempted to wrap it in a tortilla—one of my favorite ways of eating. To add a zesty topping to these vegetarian burritos, make Ancho Chili Sauce in advance; for speedier preparation, serve drizzled with your favorite "hot" bottled salsa. You can also add some shredded part-skim Monterey Jack cheese (see Tip) when assembling the burritos.

makes 8 burittos (4 servings)

1 cup texturized vegetable protein (TVP)

$3/4$ cup hot water

2 cups Ancho Chili Sauce (page 111)

1 tablespoon olive oil

2 cups small broccoli florets

$1/2$ cup finely chopped red bell pepper

$1/4$ cup finely chopped onion

$1/4$ cup finely chopped celery

$1/2$ teaspoon minced garlic

$1/2$ teaspoon freshly ground black pepper, or to taste

Dash of salt, or to taste

Eight 8-inch flour tortillas

$1/2$ cup nonfat sour cream

garnish *(optional)* sprigs of fresh cilantro, fresh orange wedges

Stir together the texturized vegetable protein and hot water in a medium bowl; allow to stand until the water is absorbed and the TVP is softened, about 5 minutes.

Reheat the Ancho Chili Sauce in a small covered saucepan over medium heat; stir occasionally. When heated through, remove from the heat, and set aside.

Meanwhile, heat the oil in a large nonstick skillet over medium-high heat. Add the broccoli, bell pepper, onion, celery, and garlic. Cook, stirring occasionally, until the broccoli is tender, about 5 minutes. Stir in the softened TVP, $1/2$ cup of the Ancho Chili Sauce, salt, and pepper. Remove from the heat. Adjust the seasonings to taste; cover and set aside.

Place the tortillas between 2 double layers of moistened paper towels; microwave until softened and warm, 45 to 60 seconds. (Or wrap the tortillas in aluminum foil and heat in a 325°F oven for about 10 minutes.)

For each burrito, spoon about $1/2$ cup of the TVP-broccoli mixture down the center of the tortilla; fold in the 2 uncovered edges of the tortilla to overlap over the filling. Place the burritos, seam sides down, on a plate. Microwave on high for about 1 minute to heat through. (Or heat in a 350°F oven for about 8 minutes, or until heated through.)

Place 2 burritos on each serving plate. Drizzle each serving with about $^1/3$ cup of the Ancho Chili Sauce; top with a dollop of sour cream. Serve immediately.

Per serving (2 burritos with Ancho Chili Sauce): Cal 460/Pro 24.6g/Carb 68.4g/Fat 9.8g/ Chol 0mg/ Sod 1,237mg

ADVANCE PREPARATION Covered and refrigerated, the Ancho Chili Sauce will keep for up to 3 days. Reheat the sauce, prepare the filling, and assemble the burritos just before serving.

VARIATION

❧ Substitute 2 cups frozen, thawed, squeezed, and crumbled silken extra-firm tofu for the TVP. You'll need to freeze two 12-ounce packages tofu (see page xxx).

tip

Monterey Jack cheese is available made from whole, partly skimmed, or skimmed cow's milk. Unaged Monterey Jack is a moist cheese that has good melting properties. Aged or dry Monterey Jack is yellower in color, firmer in texture, and sharper in flavor; because of its low moisture, it is used as a grating cheese.

rice paper spring rolls

The process for making Rice Paper Spring Rolls may sound complicated. But after one try, you'll have this simplified technique mastered. Serve three rolls per person with Spicy Peanut Sauce for dipping as an unusual light entrée. Or, for appetizer servings, slice the spring rolls in half and arrange them on a platter with a bowl of sauce nearby.

**makes 12 spring rolls
(4 servings)**

3/4 cup Spicy Peanut Sauce
(page 115)

2 ounces cellophane noodles
(see Tip, page 73)

1 carrot, cut into 24 strips
about 5 inches long by
1/4 inch thick

Twelve 9-inch round sheets of
rice paper (see Tip)

12 leaves tender, soft lettuce
(ribs removed)

1/2 cucumber, peeled and
cut into 24 strips about
5 inches long by 1/4 inch
thick

6 ounces silken extra-firm tofu,
cut into 24 strips about
1/4 inch wide

36 fresh mint leaves

special equipment

13 large sheets heavy-duty
paper towels

Prepare the Spicy Peanut Sauce. Set aside.

Bring a small pot of water to a boil over high heat; remove from the heat. Add the cellophane noodles and soak until they are softened and clear, about 8 to 10 minutes; drain well. Use kitchen shears to cut them into shorter lengths, about 4 inches. Set aside to cool.

Meanwhile, put the carrot strips into a small microwave-proof dish; add about 2 tablespoons water. Cover and microwave until tender, about 3 to 4 minutes; drain well. (Or cook the carrots in a stovetop steamer.)

To soften the rice paper, begin by holding a heavy-duty paper towel (or a thin kitchen towel) under hot running water. Squeeze out the excess moisture; lay the towel flat on the kitchen counter. Hold a sheet of rice paper under warm running water; wet both sides. Place the rice paper flat on top of the towel. Top with another layer of moist toweling, taking care to cover the edges of the rice paper; press gently. Repeat layers with 2 more sheets of rice paper and more warm moist toweling. Allow to stand until the rice paper is softened, about 5 minutes. (If the rice paper stands too long, it will become very soft and too fragile to handle.)

To assemble the first spring roll, remove the top layer of wet toweling and discard. Place 1 sheet of rice paper on a work surface.

1. The filling ingredients should be arranged in the center of the rice paper, allowing about 1^1/2 inches of rice paper on each side to remain uncovered.

   Place 1 lettuce leaf at the end of the rice paper closest to you, touching the edge of the rice paper. Starting at the end closest to you, on top of the lettuce, arrange a horizontal clump of noodles, about 3 inches by 1 inch. Above the noodles, moving toward the top of the rice paper, horizontally arrange 2 strips each of cucumber and tofu. Near the top of the rice paper, horizontally arrange 3 mint leaves.

2. Fold the 2 sides of the rice paper circle to the center until the edges just overlap.

3. Starting at the end closest to you, gently roll the paper and ingredients firmly, squeezing gently as you roll. (If, during the rolling process, the rice paper splits, simply roll another moistened sheet over the broken one.) Place the completed roll, seam edge down, on a serving plate. Cover with plastic wrap to prevent the roll from drying out.

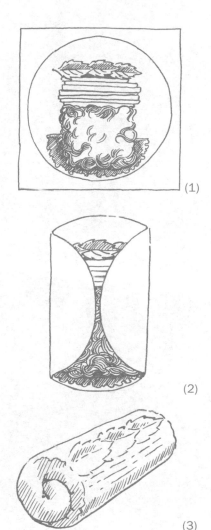

(1)

(2)

(3)

Remove the next layer of toweling and roll the next spring roll. Repeat the entire procedure with the remaining sheets of rice paper and filling ingredients.

To serve, pour the sauce into a small serving bowl. Eat the rolls with your fingers, dipping into the sauce as you go.

Per serving (3 spring rolls with 3 tablespoons sauce): Cal 272/Pro 8.7g/Carb 46.6g/ Fat 5.7g/Chol 0mg/Sod 1,124mg

ADVANCE PREPARATION Covered and refrigerated, the sauce will keep for up to 3 days; bring to room temperature for serving. The spring rolls are best when assembled just before serving. If necessary, wrap them individually in plastic wrap and refrigerate for up to 1 hour; allow to come to room temperature for serving.

VARIATIONS

❧ Add or substitute other raw vegetables cut into thin strips, such as mushrooms, bok choy, avocado, scallions, zucchini, or red bell pepper. If using firmer vegetables, such as thin strips of broccoli stalks or asparagus spears, microwave or steam until tender. (Take care not to overfill the spring rolls, or the rice paper is likely to split as you roll.)

❧ Substitute fresh cilantro, basil, or watercress for the mint.

tip

Rice paper, or rice sheet, is a flat, thin, opaque, brittle round sheet made from white rice, flour, salt, and water. It can be purchased in Asian markets in packages of various diameters and will keep indefinitely if stored flat and away from moisture. The edible paper is softened for use in spring rolls and for a variety of desserts.

Entrée Pies, Tartlets, and Pita and Tortilla Crusts

chili custard pie

This crustless pie is a good choice when you're after a flavor-ful dish but have little time for fussing. Serve it with warmed flour tortillas and a green salad topped with Creamy Avocado Dressing (page 86).

Preheat the oven to 325°F. Lightly coat a 9-inch square baking dish with the cooking spray.

Put the tofu and eggs into a food processor; process until smooth. Stir in the chili powder, oregano, cumin, and pepper.

Toss the tomato, chilies, and scallions in a medium bowl. Stir in the tofu-egg mixture.

Pour the mixture into the prepared baking dish. Top with the cheese and sprinkle with paprika. Bake for about 45 minutes, or until the filling tests done (see Tip). Allow to stand for about 5 minutes before cutting into wedges for serving.

Per serving: Cal 159/Pro 13.2g/Carb 3.7g/Fat 10.2g/Chol 223mg/Sod 701mg

ADVANCE PREPARATION Combine the ingredients early the day the dish is to be served. Pour into the prepared baking dish; cover and refrigerate. If chilled, allow about 5 minutes longer baking time. Leftovers reheat well in the microwave.

VARIATION

❧ Substitute 1 1/2 cups cholesterol-free egg substitute for the eggs.

tip

To test baked egg dishes for doneness, insert a knife in the center. The eggs are cooked through when the knife comes out clean. (Also see Huevos Rancheros, Tips, page 152.)

makes 6 servings

Nonstick cooking spray

1 1/2 cups mashed silken firm tofu (12 ounces)

6 large eggs

1 teaspoon chili powder

1 tablespoon minced fresh oregano (or 1 teaspoon dried)

1/2 teaspoon ground cumin

1/2 teaspoon freshly ground black pepper

1 large tomato, cut into 1/2-inch cubes (about 1 1/2 cups)

One 7-ounce can diced mild green chilies, drained

2 medium scallions, finely chopped

1/2 cup finely shredded cheddar cheese

Dash of paprika, or to taste

asparagus-mushroom quiche

**makes one 9-inch quiche
(8 servings)**

One unbaked 9-inch Whole
Wheat Pastry crust (page
182) (Note: recipe yield is
2 crusts)

For the quiche filling

1 tablespoon olive oil

$1^1/2$ cups asparagus in 2-inch
lengths (see Tips)

$1/4$ cup finely chopped red bell
pepper

2 cups sliced mushrooms

2 medium scallions, finely
chopped

1 teaspoon minced garlic

$1^1/2$ cups mashed silken firm
tofu (12 ounces)

3 large eggs

$1/2$ cup skim milk

$1/2$ cup freshly grated
Parmesan cheese

1 tablespoon minced fresh
flat-leaf parsley

1 teaspoon minced fresh basil
(or $1/4$ teaspoon dried)

1 teaspoon minced fresh
summer savory (or
$1/4$ teaspoon dried)

1 teaspoon minced fresh
tarragon (or $1/4$ teaspoon
dried)

This quiche is elegant enough for company lunch or brunch, yet it can easily become a casual Sunday supper. Use Whole Wheat Pastry or a commercially prepared frozen crust. When using either, it is important to partially prebake the crust before adding the quiche filling; this step ensures a flaky crust after the quiche is baked.

Preheat the oven to 375°F.

Use a fork to prick the bottom of the crust in 6 or 8 places with a fork. Bake in the preheated oven until the edges start to become firm, about 6 minutes. Set aside.

Heat the oil in a large nonstick skillet over medium-high heat. Add the asparagus and bell pepper. Cook, stirring constantly, until crisp-tender, about 4 minutes. Add the mushrooms, scallions, and garlic. Continue to cook, stirring constantly, until the asparagus and mushrooms are tender but not browned, about 2 minutes more. Use a slotted spoon to transfer the vegetables to the bottom of the partially baked crust. Set aside.

Put the tofu, eggs, and milk into a food processor. Process until the mixture is smooth and creamy. Stir in the remaining ingredients except the paprika.

Pour the tofu-egg mixture over the vegetables in the crust. Sprinkle with the paprika.

Bake for about 30 minutes, or until a knife inserted in the center comes out clean. Cool on a wire rack for about 5 minutes before slicing.

Per serving ($1/8$ quiche made with Whole Wheat Pastry): Cal 257/Pro 12.7g/Carb 16.8g/ Fat 15.4g/Chol 98mg/Sod 268mg

ADVANCE PREPARATION The crust, vegetables, and tofu-egg mixture can be prepared early the day the quiche is to be served; cover and refrigerate separately. Assemble and bake the quiche just before serving. If the vegetables and/or sauce are chilled, allow about 5 minutes longer baking time.

$1/4$ teaspoon dried thyme (or 1 teaspoon minced fresh)

Dash of ground white pepper

Dash of paprika

VARIATIONS

❧ Omit the crust; pour the filling into a lightly oiled pie plate and bake as directed.

Per serving: Cal 108/Pro 9.9g/Carb 5g/Fat 5.4g/Chol 85mg/Sod 165mg

❧ Substitute small broccoli florets for the asparagus.

❧ Substitute $3/4$ cup cholesterol-free egg substitute for the eggs.

tips

Asparagus is at its best in the early spring. Choose green spears with firm stalks; the tips should be tightly closed and have a lavender hue. Slender stalks will be more tender. Uniformity in size and shape is important for even cooking; if you can't find thin asparagus, halve or peel the thicker stalks.

To store, wrap asparagus in a plastic bag and store in the vegetable crisper; use within 2 to 3 days. Do not clean the asparagus until you are ready to cook it. If wilted, stand the stalks in a jar filled with 2 inches of very cold water. Cover with a plastic bag, seal, and refrigerate for 1 to 2 hours before cooking.

whole wheat pastry

makes two 9-inch crusts

1 cup whole wheat flour
  (see Tip)

1 cup all-purpose or
  unbleached white flour

3/4 cup margarine

1/4 cup finely chopped walnuts

1 teaspoon cider vinegar
  or white vinegar

2 to 3 tablespoons ice water

This versatile crust is equally appropriate whether used for entrées, such as the Asparagus-Mushroom Quiche (page 180) or Vegetable Tartlets (page 186), or for desserts, such as Tofu Pumpkin Pie (page 238). To add a hint of citrus flavor for desserts, substitute fresh orange juice for the vinegar. Using all whole wheat flour creates a heavy, dense crust, so it's best to use part whole wheat and part white flour; or substitute 2 cups whole wheat pastry flour (see Tip). This recipe cannot be halved; use 1 crust right away and store the other, or store both for use later (see Advance Preparation).

Put the flours and margarine into a food processor; use short bursts to process until the mixture is crumbly. Add the walnuts, vinegar, and 1 tablespoon of the ice water; process in a steady whirl until the dough forms a ball that does not separate. (While processing, add more water as needed.)

Divide the dough evenly into 2 balls; wrap in plastic wrap or seal in plastic bags. Refrigerate for at least 1 hour.

To roll, place 1 ball of dough between 2 sheets of waxed paper. Flatten with the palm of your hand; then use a rolling pin to roll out the crust. Work the ball, rolling from the center outward, to form a 12-inch round.

Insert the crust into a 9-inch pie plate; fold under the edges and press against the sides of the pie plate.

Repeat with the other ball of dough or store for use later (see Advance Preparation).

Per serving (1/8 unfilled crust): Cal 290/Pro 4.8g/Carb 23.5g/Fat 19.7g/Chol 0mg/ Sod 202mg

ADVANCE PREPARATION The balls of dough should be wrapped in plastic wrap or sealed in plastic bags; refrigerate for at least 1 hour or for up to 2 days before using. For longer storage, freeze the wrapped balls of dough for up to 2 months; thaw thoroughly in the refrigerator before using.

VARIATION

❧ Substitute chopped pecans or toasted sesame seeds for the walnuts, or omit the nuts.

tip

Whole wheat flour contains the wheat germ; therefore it has a higher fiber, nutritional, and fat content than white flours. To prevent rancidity, store it in a tightly closed bag or container in the refrigerator or freezer for up to 6 months.

soybean confetti pie with cornmeal crust

Don't be daunted by the long list of ingredients. They combine in a flash. Serve this hearty pie accompanied by Tomato Slices with Creamy Avocado Dressing (page 86).

makes 8 servings

For the Cornmeal Crust

Nonstick cooking spray

1 cup cornmeal

1/4 cup olive oil

1/4 cup vegetable stock (see page 34)

For the pie filling

1 tablespoon olive oil

1/2 cup finely chopped green bell pepper

1/2 cup finely chopped red bell pepper

1 rib celery, finely chopped

1/4 cup finely chopped onion

1 teaspoon minced garlic

1/4 cup vegetable stock (see page 34)

1 1/2 cups cooked soybeans (one 15-ounce can, drained and rinsed)

1 cup frozen corn, thawed

One 8-ounce can tomato sauce

2 teaspoons chili powder

1 tablespoon minced fresh oregano (or 1 teaspoon dried oregano)

1/2 teaspoon ground cumin

Preheat the oven to 350°F.

Lightly coat a 9-inch pie plate with the cooking spray.

Put the crust ingredients into a small bowl; mix thoroughly with a fork. Use the back of a spoon to press the mixture firmly and evenly onto the bottom and sides of the prepared pie plate; set aside.

Heat 1 tablespoon of the oil in a large nonstick skillet over medium-high heat. Add the bell peppers, celery, onion, and garlic. Cook, stirring occasionally, until the vegetables are crisp-tender, about 5 minutes. Remove from the heat. Stir in the remaining ingredients except the Monterey Jack and cheddar cheeses. Adjust the seasonings to taste. Set aside.

Toss the cheeses together in a small bowl. Sprinkle about 1/3 of the cheese mixture over the crust; pour in the pie filling and spread evenly.

Bake for 30 minutes, or until the filling tests nearly done (see Tip, page 179). Sprinkle with the remaining cheese mixture; bake about 10 minutes longer, or until the cheese is melted. Allow to stand for about 5 minutes before cutting into wedges for serving.

Per serving: Cal 285/Pro 12.3g/Carb 23.1/Fat 15.9g/Chol 12mg/Sod 263mg

ADVANCE PREPARATION The crust and filling can be made up to 1 day in advance. Press the crust into the pan; cover and refrigerate. Refrigerate the filling in a separate covered container. Bring the crust and filling to room temperature; assemble and bake the pie just before serving.

Cornmeal is made from dried corn kernels that have been ground. Most supermarket cornmeal will keep almost indefinitely in an airtight container in a cool, dry place. Water-ground or stone-ground cornmeal, available at health-food stores, retains some of the hull and germ of the corn. It is more nutritious but does not keep as long; store it in the refrigerator for up to 4 months.

Once opened, refrigerate hot pepper sauce to retain its flavor and color.

$1/2$ teaspoon freshly ground black pepper, or to taste

$1/4$ teaspoon hot pepper sauce, or to taste (see Tip)

$1/2$ cup finely shredded part-skim Monterey Jack cheese

$1/2$ cup finely shredded cheddar cheese

makes four 4¹/₂-inch tartlets

Unbaked dough for one 9-inch Whole Wheat Pastry crust (page 182) (Note: recipe yield is 2 crusts)

For the Herbed Tomato Sauce (makes 1 cup)

1 cup mashed silken firm tofu

3 tablespoons tomato paste (see Tip, page 4)

1 tablespoon minced fresh marjoram (or 1 teaspoon dried) (see Tip)

¹/₂ teaspoon freshly ground black pepper, or to taste

Pinch of red pepper flakes, or to taste

To complete the tartlets

1 tablespoon olive oil

1 cup finely chopped carrots

1 cup small cauliflower florets

2 cups sliced mushrooms

1 medium scallion, finely chopped

1 teaspoon minced garlic

1 cup frozen baby peas, thawed (see Tip, page 107)

Dash of freshly ground black pepper

¹/₄ cup freshly grated Parmesan cheese

garnish *(optional)* sprigs of fresh flat-leaf parsley

vegetable tartlets with herbed tomato sauce

Individual tart pans, called "tartlets," are available in most gourmet shops; my favorites have removable bottoms that make simple work of removing the baked tarts from the pans for serving. Be sure to prepare the Whole Wheat Pastry in advance to allow chilling time before rolling the dough and preparing this recipe.

Preheat the oven to 350°F.

Prepare the pastry; be sure the dough chills for at least 1 hour. Cut the ball of dough into 4 even-size pieces; form each piece into a ball. Place 1 ball of dough between 2 sheets of waxed paper. Flatten the ball with the palm of your hand; then use a rolling pin to roll out the crust. Work the ball, rolling from the center outward, to form a 6-inch round. Press the crust into a 4¹/₂-inch-diameter tartlet pan; fold under any excess crust at the edges and lightly press against the sides of the pan. Repeat for the remaining 3 tartlets.

Place the pastry-lined tartlet pans on a baking sheet. Use a fork to prick the bottom of each crust in 3 or 4 places; bake for about 10 minutes, or until the crusts become slightly firm but do not brown.

Put the sauce ingredients into a food processor; process until smooth. Adjust the seasonings to taste. Set aside.

Heat the oil in a large nonstick skillet over medium-high heat. Add the carrots and cauliflower; cook, stirring occasionally, until crisp-tender, about 4 minutes. Add the mushrooms, scallion, and garlic; continue to cook, stirring occasionally, until the mushrooms are tender, about 3 minutes. Remove the pan from the heat; stir in the peas and Herbed Tomato Sauce.

Spoon the vegetable-sauce mixture into the tartlet pans. Bake for about 20 minutes, or until the filling is heated through and the edges of the crusts are lightly browned. Sprinkle each tartlet with pepper and 1 tablespoon of the Parmesan cheese; bake for about 5 minutes, or until the cheese is melted.

Remove the tartlets from the baking sheet and cool on a wire rack for about 10 minutes. Loosen the edges of the crusts with the point of a knife. Remove the tartlets from the pans and transfer to serving plates; garnish and serve immediately.

Per serving: Cal 451/Pro 15.2g/Carb 38.9g/Fat 26.1g/Chol 5mg/Sod 415mg

ADVANCE PREPARATION The tartlet crusts can be rolled and prebaked in advance; cover and refrigerate for up to 1 day. Fill with the vegetable-sauce mixture and bake just before serving.

VARIATIONS

> Rather than rolling the crusts, use your fingers to press the pastry dough into the tartlet pans.

> Substitute for the carrots, cauliflower, or mushrooms or add other vegetables (up to 5 cups total) such as cut asparagus or small broccoli florets.

> Substitute cooked soybeans or sweet beans for the peas.

tips

Fresh herbs, which come from the leafy part of plants, contain more moisture and therefore are milder than dried herbs. When substituting, use 3 to 4 times more fresh herbs than dried herbs.

Marjoram, thyme, savory, bay leaf, rosemary, sage, and oregano are considered to be the "robust herbs," with tough leaves that are resistant to cold weather and to the heat of the sun—and to the heat of cooking. They are strong in aroma and hearty in flavor.

soybean pita pizzas

With crusts made from toasted pita bread rounds, these pizzas can be on the table quicker than the delivery man could have them at your door.

makes 4 servings

2 tablespoons olive oil

2 cups sliced mushrooms

2 medium scallions, finely chopped

1 teaspoon minced garlic

Two 6-inch white or whole wheat pita breads

1/4 cup tomato paste (see Tip, page 4)

1/4 cup drained and coarsely chopped oil-packed sun-dried tomatoes

16 fresh basil leaves (or 1/2 teaspoon dried)

1 cup cooked soybeans

2 plum tomatoes, each cut into 8 thin slices (see Tips)

1/4 teaspoon freshly ground black pepper, or to taste

2 tablespoons freshly grated Parmesan cheese

Adjust the oven broiler rack 4 to 5 inches from the heating element. Preheat the broiler.

Heat 1 tablespoon of the oil in a small nonstick skillet over medium-high heat. Add the mushrooms, scallions, and garlic; cook, stirring occasionally, until tender, about 4 minutes. Remove from the heat and set aside.

Slice each pita bread horizontally into 2 rounds. Place them, rough sides up, on a baking sheet. Lightly brush with the remaining 1 tablespoon of oil. Toast under the broiler until just lightly browned, about 2 minutes.

Spread 1 pita half with about 1 tablespoon of the tomato paste. Top with one-quarter of the mushroom-scallion mixture, 1 tablespoon of the sun-dried tomatoes, and 1/4 cup of the soybeans. Top with the basil leaves (or sprinkle with dried basil) and the plum tomato slices. Sprinkle with pepper and Parmesan cheese. Repeat with the remaining toasted pita halves.

Broil until the cheese is melted and the other ingredients are heated through, about 2 to 3 minutes. Watch closely.

Per serving: Cal 283/Pro 13.6g/Carb 30g/Fat 12.1g/Chol 2mg/Sod 227mg

ADVANCE PREPARATION The pita crusts can be toasted early on the day the pizzas are to be served; cover with foil and set aside at room temperature. Assemble the pizzas and broil just before serving.

VARIATIONS

❧ Substitute Roasted Red Pepper Hummus (page 17), Sun-Dried Tomato–Tofu Spread (page 4), or Roasted Sweet Red Pepper Dressing (page 92) for the tomato paste.

➤ Substitute for the mushrooms or add other vegetables (up to 1 cup total) such as chopped onion, shredded carrots, chopped celery, diced red or green bell peppers, or sliced zucchini.

➤ Substitute finely shredded Monterey Jack, cheddar, or soy cheese (see page xl) for the Parmesan.

tips

Because cool temperatures reduce the flavor of tomatoes and can make their texture mealy, do not store them in the refrigerator. On the counter at room temperature, tomatoes will continue to get redder, softer, juicier, and tastier; once they are fully ripened, use within 2 days. If you like, chill them for up to 1 hour just before serving.

To prevent tearing and bruising, use a knife with a serrated stainless-steel blade for slicing and cutting tomatoes.

tofu tostada

Although tofu is not a staple of Mexican cooking, here it absorbs those distinctive flavors. This light but hearty entrée needs nothing more than a green salad.

makes 4 servings

2 teaspoons olive oil

Four 6- or 7-inch flour tortillas (see Tip)

For the topping

One 8-ounce can tomato sauce

1 teaspoon chili powder, or to taste

1/2 teaspoon ground cumin

1/4 teaspoon freshly ground black pepper, or to taste

1/4 teaspoon hot pepper sauce, or to taste

1 tablespoon olive oil

1 medium zucchini, halved lengthwise and cut into 1/4-inch-thick slices

1 cup sliced mushrooms

1 medium carrot, coarsely shredded

1/4 cup coarsely chopped onion

1 teaspoon minced garlic

4 plum tomatoes, cut into 1/2-inch cubes (about 1 1/2 cups)

1 cup 1/2-inch cubes silken firm tofu

Adjust the oven rack to 4 to 5 inches from the broiling element; preheat the broiler.

Lightly brush both sides of each tortilla with olive oil, then prick the surfaces several places with a fork. Place the tortillas directly on the oven rack; broil until lightly browned, about 1 to 2 minutes on each side. Watch closely to ensure they don't burn. Transfer to a plate; set aside.

To prepare the topping, combine the tomato sauce, chili powder, cumin, pepper, and hot pepper sauce in a small bowl; set aside.

Heat the olive oil in a large nonstick skillet over medium heat. Add the zucchini, mushrooms, carrot, onion, and garlic. Cook, stirring occasionally, until the vegetables are tender, about 5 minutes. Gently stir in the tomato sauce mixture, tomatoes, and tofu. Cook until the tomatoes are softened and the tofu is heated through, about 5 minutes. Adjust the seasonings to taste.

As an optional garnish on the plates, make small mounds of alfalfa sprouts or shredded lettuce and top with orange slices. To serve, place the toasted tortillas on serving plates and top each with a mound of the topping; if desired, garnish with cheese.

Per serving: Cal 242/Pro 9.2g/Carb 29.6g/Fat 9.6g/Chol 0mg/Sod 372mg

ADVANCE PREPARATION The topping (minus the tofu) can be prepared and refrigerated up to 2 days in advance. Reheat and add the tofu, toast the tortillas, and assemble the tostadas just before serving.

VARIATIONS

❧ Omit the toasted tortillas; serve the warm topping in pita bread pockets.

❧ Substitute for the zucchini, mushrooms, or carrot or add other vegetables (up to 3 cups total) such as small broccoli florets or corn.

❧ With the tomatoes and tofu, add about $1/2$ cup cooked beans, such as black beans, kidney beans, soybeans, or garbanzo beans.

❧ With the tomatoes and tofu, add one 4-ounce can diced mild green chilies, drained.

❧ For a firmer texture, substitute pressed tofu (see page xxxii).

garnish *(optional)* on the tostada: freshly grated Parmesan cheese
on the plates: alfalfa sprouts or shredded lettuce, orange slices

tip

Tortillas are found on Mexican tables at nearly every meal. In most of Mexico, tortillas are usually made of corn; however, in the northern areas flour tortillas are favored. Corn and flour tortillas, both white and whole wheat, are found in most supermarkets, refrigerated or frozen. Fresh tortillas, available in some markets, are always preferable.

pepper-bean quesadillas

Accompanied by a green salad, these colorful quesadillas make a delightful light lunch, or cut them into small wedges to serve as an appetizer or soup accompaniment.

makes 4 servings

1 tablespoon olive oil

1 red bell pepper, finely chopped

1 yellow bell pepper, finely chopped

1 green bell pepper, finely chopped

1 teaspoon minced garlic

1 cup cooked soybeans

2 plum tomatoes, coarsely chopped (about 3/4 cup)

6 pitted black olives, thinly sliced

1 tablespoon red wine vinegar

1 tablespoon minced fresh oregano (or 1 teaspoon dried)

1/4 teaspoon freshly ground black pepper, or to taste

Eight 6- or 7-inch flour tortillas

1 cup finely shredded part-skim Monterey Jack cheese

Preheat the oven to 375°F.

Heat the oil in a large nonstick skillet over medium-high heat. Add the bell peppers and garlic; cook, stirring occasionally, until crisp-tender, about 4 minutes. Stir in the soybeans, tomatoes, olives, vinegar, fresh or dried oregano, and pepper. Continue to cook, stirring occasionally, until the bell peppers are tender, about 5 minutes. Adjust the seasoning to taste. Remove from the heat; set aside.

Place 4 tortillas on a baking sheet; sprinkle each with about 2 tablespoons of the cheese. Leaving a 1-inch border, spread one-quarter of the bell pepper mixture on each tortilla. Then sprinkle with the remaining cheese. Top each with another tortilla, pressing down gently to make the filling adhere.

Bake for about 8 to 10 minutes, or until the cheese is melted and the tortillas are softened and warm.

Cut each quesadilla into wedges before serving.

Per serving: Cal 427/Pro 20.1g/Carb 46.6g/Fat 17.8g/Chol 18mg/Sod 384mg

ADVANCE PREPARATION The bell pepper mixture can be cooked up to 1 day in advance; cover and refrigerate. Bring to room temperature, then assemble and bake the quesadillas just before serving.

VARIATION

❧ For part of the bell peppers, substitute other vegetables (up to 3 cups total) such as sliced onion or sliced mushrooms.

Stuffed Vegetables

stuffed acorn squash

Bake over extra stuffing separately in an oiled small casserole.

makes 4 servings

Preheat the oven to 400°F.

Lightly coat a baking sheet with the cooking spray.

Cut the squash in half lengthwise and remove the seeds and fibers; place, cut sides down, on the prepared baking sheet. Bake for about 30 minutes, or until the squash are easily pierced with a fork.

Meanwhile, put the tofu and orange juice into a food processor; process until the mixture is smooth. Set aside.

Also while the squash are baking, heat the oil in a medium nonstick skillet over medium-high heat. Add the apples and onion; cook, stirring occasionally, until the onion is translucent, about 5 minutes. Remove the pan from the heat. Stir in the tofu-juice mixture, raisins, and cinnamon.

When the squash are done, turn them upright. Make indentations with a fork across the cavities of the cut sides; drizzle with the maple syrup. Fill the cavities with the stuffing mixture and top with the walnuts (if using); cover with foil. Return to the oven for about 10 to 15 minutes, or until the stuffing is heated through.

Per serving: Cal 320/Pro 7g/Carb 60.5g/Fat 5.6g/Chol 0mg/Sod 46mg

ADVANCE PREPARATION The stuffing can be prepared early in the day; cover and refrigerate. Bake the squash and stuff them just before serving; allow 5 to 10 minutes longer to heat if the stuffing is chilled.

VARIATION

❧ Substitute dried cranberries for the raisins.

Nonstick cooking spray

2 medium acorn squash

For the stuffing

1 cup mashed silken firm tofu

2 tablespoons freshly squeezed orange juice (see Tip, page 241)

1 tablespoon olive oil

2 cups coarsely chopped apple (peeled or unpeeled)

1/2 cup finely chopped onion

1/4 cup raisins

1/4 teaspoon ground cinnamon

3 tablespoons pure maple syrup

garnish *(optional)* toasted chopped walnuts (see Tip, page 50)

bell peppers stuffed with herbed tofu and rice

makes 6 servings

2 tablespoons olive oil

1 carrot, diced

1/2 cup finely chopped onion

1 rib celery, diced

1 teaspoon minced garlic

1 1/2 cups mashed silken extra-firm tofu (12 ounces)

1 1/2 cups cooked brown rice

One 15-ounce can tomato sauce

3/4 cup freshly grated Parmesan cheese

1/4 cup chopped pecans

2 tablespoons low-sodium soy sauce

1 tablespoon minced fresh basil (or 1 teaspoon dried)

1 tablespoon minced fresh oregano (or 1 teaspoon dried)

1/2 teaspoon freshly ground black pepper

2 large eggs, lightly beaten

6 large green, red, or yellow bell peppers (see Tip)

1/4 cup toasted wheat germ

I call these peppers with pizzazz. For a stunning presentation, choose a variety of colors of peppers to stuff (see Tip) and arrange on a large platter. If your bell peppers are too small to accommodate all of the filling, bake the extra separately in an oiled small casserole dish until the mixture tests done (see Tip, page 179).

Preheat the oven to 350°F.

Heat a medium saucepan of water over medium heat.

Heat 1 tablespoon of the oil in a large nonstick skillet over medium-high heat. Add the carrot, onion, celery, and garlic; cook, stirring occasionally, until tender, about 5 minutes. Remove the pan from the heat and stir in the tofu, rice, tomato sauce, 1/2 cup of the Parmesan cheese, the pecans, soy sauce, dried basil and oregano (if using), and pepper. When the mixture is cool to the touch, stir in the eggs and the fresh basil and oregano (if using).

Remove the tops and centers from the bell peppers. Stand them upright in an 11- by 9-inch baking pan; if necessary, even off the bottoms so they will stand straight (avoid cutting holes). Spoon about 3/4 cup of the tofu-rice mixture into each bell pepper.

In a small bowl, combine the wheat germ, the remaining 1 tablespoon oil, and the remaining 1/4 cup cheese; sprinkle the mixture over the filling.

Pour the hot water around the peppers until about one-quarter of the way up the sides of the baking dish (see Tip, page 235). Bake for about 30 to 35 minutes, or until the peppers are tender when pierced with a fork. (Check occasionally during the baking period and add more water to the pan if necessary.)

Use a slotted spatula to transfer the peppers to a serving platter. Allow the peppers to stand for about 5 minutes before serving.

Per serving: Cal 310/Pro 16g/Carb 27.7g/Fat 15g/Chol 45mg/Sod 866mg

ADVANCE PREPARATION The stuffed peppers can be assembled early the day they are to be served; cover and refrigerate. Bake just before serving. If chilled, allow about 10 minutes longer baking time.

VARIATIONS

❯ Substitute $1/2$ cup cholesterol-free egg substitute for the eggs.

❯ For the mashed fresh tofu, substitute 12 ounces silken extra-firm tofu that has been frozen, thawed, squeezed, and crumbled (see page xxx); increase the brown rice to 2 cups.

tip

Bell peppers are most often sold in the mature green stage, fully developed but not ripe. Red bell peppers are vine-ripened green peppers, which are sweeter because they have ripened longer. Bell peppers are also available in gold, orange, and purple, all mildly flavored. Choose bell peppers that are plump, firm, and crisp, with no wrinkling or soft spots. Store in plastic bags in the refrigerator for up to a week. Extra bell peppers can be frozen without blanching: simply chop and freeze in small containers or zip-top bags. The thawed peppers will be limp but are fine to use in cooking.

zucchini with herbed tomato-soybean stuffing

Although the list of ingredients seems long, don't despair. Preparation for baking will take less than 15 minutes, I promise. Spoon any extra stuffing into an oiled casserole dish and bake along with the stuffed zucchini.

makes 6 servings

Nonstick cooking spray

6 medium zucchini

2 tablespoons olive oil

1 carrot, diced

1 rib celery, diced

1/4 cup finely chopped onion

1 teaspoon minced garlic

Dash of freshly ground black pepper, or to taste

1 1/2 cups cooked soybeans (one 15-ounce can, drained and rinsed)

One 6-ounce can tomato paste

1/2 cup dry bread crumbs (see Tip)

1/4 cup finely chopped walnuts

2 tablespoons minced fresh flat-leaf parsley

1 teaspoon minced fresh dill (or 1/2 teaspoon dried dill weed)

1 teaspoon minced fresh marjoram (or 1/2 teaspoon dried)

1 teaspoon minced fresh tarragon (or 1/2 teaspoon dried)

1 teaspoon minced fresh thyme (or 1/4 teaspoon dried)

Preheat the oven to 350°F.

Lightly coat a 13- by 9-inch baking pan with the cooking spray.

Bring a large saucepan or Dutch oven of water to a boil over high heat. When it comes to a boil, drop in the zucchini; cook until just tender when pierced with a fork, about 8 minutes. Drain and rinse with cool water; allow to cool until they can be handled.

Meanwhile, heat 1 tablespoon of the olive oil in a medium nonstick skillet over medium-high heat. Add the carrot, celery, and onion; cook, stirring occasionally, until tender but not browned, about 3 minutes. Add the garlic and cook for about 1 minute more. Remove from the heat.

Trim the stem ends and slice each zucchini in half lengthwise. Use a spoon to scoop out the zucchini flesh, leaving a 1/4-inch-thick shell. Put the flesh into a colander, press gently with the back of a large spoon, and allow to drain for a few minutes. Arrange the zucchini shells, scooped sides up, in the prepared baking pan and sprinkle lightly with pepper.

Meanwhile, in a medium bowl, stir together the soybeans, tomato paste, 1/4 cup of the bread crumbs, and the remaining ingredients except the Parmesan cheese. Stir in the drained zucchini flesh. Spoon about 1/4 cup of the soybean-zucchini mixture into each zucchini shell.

Combine the Parmesan cheese, the remaining 1/4 cup bread crumbs, and the remaining 1 tablespoon of the olive oil in a small bowl. Sprinkle over the stuffed zucchini.

Bake for about 25 minutes, or until the soybean stuffing is heated through and the cheese is melted. Use a spatula to transfer 2 stuffed zucchini halves to each serving plate.

Per serving: Cal 287/Pro 15.6g/Carb 23.2g/Fat 14.7g/Chol 7mg/Sod 322mg

ADVANCE PREPARATION Early in the day they are to be served, the zucchini can be cooked, stuffed, and assembled in the baking dish; cover and refrigerate. Bake just before serving. If chilled, allow about 10 minutes longer baking time.

tips

The best bread crumbs are homemade, and making dry bread crumbs is an ideal use for day-old bread, especially French baguettes. When using a loaf of whole wheat or white bread, begin by removing the crusts. If the bread is not dry, place a single layer of bread slices on a baking sheet and toast in a 200°F oven for about 10 to 15 minutes, or until the slices are thoroughly dried and lightly browned. After cooling, process them in your food processor until the bread crumbs are the desired consistency. Dry bread crumbs can also be purchased at the supermarket. Check the labeling; some bread crumbs are seasoned.

When stored in a tightly closed container (rather than in a box) in a dark, dry place, dried herbs will remain flavorful for about a year (it's a good idea to date the jar when you buy them). They should resemble the color they were when fresh and should not be dull and brownish green. To get the most out of your dried herbs, crumble them between your fingers as you add them to your recipes to release the aromatic compounds.

$1/2$ teaspoon freshly ground
    black pepper, or to taste

Dash of salt, or to taste

$1/2$ cup freshly grated
    Parmesan cheese

Baked Vegetable Dishes

spinach and leek ring

makes 6 servings

Nonstick cooking spray

2 tablespoons margarine

2 large leeks, halved length-
    wise and cut into $1/4$-inch-
    thick slices (see Tip)

Two 10-ounce packages frozen
    chopped spinach, thawed,
    drained, and squeezed dry
    (see Tip, page 207)

1 cup mashed silken firm tofu

3 large eggs

3 tablespoons freshly
    squeezed lemon juice

3 tablespoons low-sodium
    soy sauce

1 teaspoon ground nutmeg

$1/8$ teaspoon red pepper flakes

To serve, unmold this onto a serving platter; fill the center with Garlic Mashed Potatoes (page 200) or steamed carrot slices. To add a crispy element to the menu, serve with a green salad topped with Herbed Garlic Croutons (page 65) and warm, crusty bread.

Preheat the oven to 350°F.

Heat a medium saucepan of water over medium heat.

Lightly coat a 9-inch ring mold with the cooking spray. Place in a shallow baking pan.

Melt the margarine in a medium nonstick skillet over medium-high heat. Add the leeks; stir to coat with margarine. Reduce the heat to low; cover and cook until the leeks are softened, about 15 minutes.

Transfer the leeks to a food processor and add the remaining ingredients; process until smooth.

Pour the mixture into the prepared ring mold. Pour the hot water into the baking pan until it comes about halfway up the sides of the mold (see Tip, page 235). Bake for about 35 minutes, or until a knife inserted in the center of the spinach-leek mixture comes out clean.

Remove the mold from the water and cool on a wire rack for about 5 minutes. To unmold, gently loosen the edges of the spinach mixture with a knife; invert onto a serving plate.

Per serving: Cal 154/Pro 9.4g/Carb 11.9g/Fat 7.7g/Chol 107mg/Sod 420mg

VARIATIONS

❧ Substitute butter for the margarine.

❧ Substitute $3/4$ cup cholesterol-free egg substitute for the eggs.

❧ Bake the spinach-leek mixture in a lightly oiled $1^1/2$-quart casserole dish; increase the baking time to about 40 minutes, or until the mixture tests done (see Tip, page 179). Rather than unmolding, cut into squares for serving.

tip

Leeks, which look like giant scallions, are available year-round in most areas. Select those with crisp, bright green leaves and unblemished, thin white bulbs; leeks under $1^1/2$ inches in diameter will be the most tender and delicately flavored. Refrigerate them in a plastic bag for up to 5 days. Before using, trim the rootlets and leaf ends, slit the leeks from top to bottom, and wash thoroughly to remove the dirt and sand, which is often trapped between the leaf layers. Use both the white base and the tender portions of the green leaves; discard the tough dark green tops. The flavor is reminiscent of both garlic and onion, although both the taste and fragrance of leeks are milder.

garlic mashed potatoes

Serve this ultimate comfort food mounded in the center of the Spinach and Leek Ring (page 198) or as a side dish to accompany Tofu-Walnut Loaf (page 214) or Spicy Soybean Patties (page 171).

makes 4 servings

1/2 teaspoon salt

2 medium russet (baking) potatoes, peeled and cut into 2-inch-thick slices (about 1 1/2 pounds)

1/2 cup mashed silken firm tofu

1/4 cup soy milk, or as needed

1 tablespoon roasted garlic extra-virgin olive oil (see Tip)

1 tablespoon margarine

Dash of salt, or to taste

Dash of freshly ground black pepper, or to taste

garnish (optional) paprika, freshly grated Parmesan cheese

Bring a medium pot of salted water to a boil over high heat. Add the potato slices; when the water returns to a boil, reduce the heat to medium. Cover and cook until the potatoes are tender, about 15 to 18 minutes; drain well.

Meanwhile, put the tofu, soy milk, olive oil, margarine, and pepper into a food processor; process until the mixture is smooth and creamy.

Return the warm potatoes to the saucepan. Mash until chunky; pour in the tofu mixture. Whip with an electric hand mixer at medium speed until fluffy. (Add more soy milk, if necessary, to make the potatoes creamy.) Add salt and pepper to taste.

Per serving: Cal 94/Pro 2.6g/Carb 10g/Fat 4.9g/Chol 0mg/Sod 58mg

VARIATIONS

❧ Substitute skim milk for the soy milk.

❧ Substitute extra-virgin olive oil for the roasted garlic extra-virgin olive oil; peel 3 or 4 roasted garlic cloves and mash into the potatoes (see page 12 for instructions on roasting garlic).

❧ Substitute butter for the margarine.

tip

Garlic-infused or garlic-flavored olive oil is available in many supermarkets and gourmet shops. If you prefer, substitute extra-virgin olive oil and add minced fresh garlic or roasted garlic to taste.

yumm...

rosemary-parmesan potato bake *to*

To enhance the flavor and improve the texture of dried rosemary, crush the leaves between your fingers just before adding to the recipe. Rosemary has a bold taste, especially in dried form; use it sparingly.

Preheat the oven to 350°F. Lightly coat a 9-inch square baking dish with the cooking spray; set aside.

Bring a large pot of salted water to a boil over high heat. Meanwhile, scrub the potatoes; add to the pot. When the water returns to a boil, reduce the heat to medium; cover and cook until the potatoes are just tender, about 10 to 12 minutes (or about 20 to 25 minutes if the potatoes are large).

Heat the olive oil in a large nonstick skillet over medium heat. Add the shallots; cook, stirring occasionally, until tender but not browned, about 3 minutes. Remove the pan from the heat; set aside.

+shallot Put the tofu, cottage cheese, Parmesan cheese, and eggs into a food processor; process until smooth. Stir in the rosemary and pepper. Stir the tofu mixture into the skillet.

When the potatoes are done, drain well. When they are cool enough to handle, cut the potatoes into 1/2-inch-thick slices.

To assemble, arrange half of the potato slices in the baking dish. Spread evenly with half of the tofu mixture. Repeat the layers; sprinkle with the paprika.

Bake for about 30 minutes, or until the top is golden brown and the sauce is bubbly. Allow to stand for about 5 minutes before serving.

Per serving: Cal 252/Pro 16.6g/Carb 27g/Fat 8.6g/Chol 79mg/Sod 355mg

ADVANCE PREPARATION This dish is best when prepared just before serving. Covered and refrigerated, leftovers will keep for up to 2 days in the refrigerator; reheat in the microwave.

VARIATION

❧ Substitute 1/2 cup cholesterol-free egg substitute for the eggs.

makes 6 servings

Nonstick cooking spray

1/2 teaspoon salt

11/2 pounds medium new potatoes (about 12)

1 tablespoon olive oil

1/4 cup minced shallots

11/2 cups mashed silken firm tofu (12 ounces)

1 cup nonfat cottage cheese

1/2 cup freshly grated Parmesan cheese

2 large eggs

1 tablespoon minced fresh rosemary (or 1 teaspoon dried)

1/2 teaspoon freshly ground black pepper

Dash of paprika

herbed twice-baked potatoes

For evenings when I am dining alone, this is one my favorite entrées; the recipe can easily be reduced to serve one. I like to top my potato with a couple of tablespoons of Parmesan Cream (page 49) or Tofu Sour Cream (page 15) and accompany it with steamed broccoli florets and a green salad topped with sliced tomatoes.

makes 4 servings

4 large russet (baking) potatoes

1 teaspoon olive oil or roasted garlic extra-virgin olive oil (see Tip, page 200)

1 cup mashed silken firm tofu

1/2 cup freshly grated Parmesan cheese

2 tablespoons extra-virgin olive oil

2 teaspoons minced fresh basil (or 1/2 teaspoon dried)

1/2 teaspoon freshly ground black pepper, or to taste

Dash of salt, or to taste

garnish *(optional)* paprika, freshly ground black pepper

Preheat the oven to 400°F.

Scrub the potatoes, then rub about 1/4 teaspoon of the olive oil over the skin of each potato. Place the potatoes directly on the oven rack and bake until they are cooked through, about 1 hour. (To test for doneness, pierce the potatoes in the center with the point of a knife; when done, the insides will feel soft.)

Cut the potatoes in half lengthwise; leaving the skins intact, scoop out the pulp and transfer it to a medium bowl. Arrange the potato skins on a baking sheet, cut sides up.

Mash the potato pulp with a potato masher or fork; add the remaining ingredients and mash again. Adjust the seasonings to taste.

Fill the skins with the potato-tofu mixture; sprinkle with paprika and pepper. Return the potatoes to the oven until the stuffing is heated through and the cheese is melted, about 10 minutes.

Per serving: Cal 313/Pro 12.3g/Carb 35.6g/Fat 13.5g/Chol 10mg/Sod 294mg

VARIATIONS

For thick, crackly skin, do not oil the potatoes; bake them for 1 1/2 hours.

Substitute yams, red sweet potatoes (see Tip, page 167), for the russet potatoes; substitute 1/2 teaspoon ground sage for the basil.

caribbean squash and soybean casserole

The sweetness of squash, red peppers, and onions is complemented by the warmth of jalapeño pepper, ground coriander, and cumin. Leftovers are delicious reheated the next day in the microwave.

Preheat the oven to 350°F.

Lightly coat a baking sheet and a 2¹/₂-quart casserole dish with the cooking spray.

Cut the squash in half horizontally; do not remove the seeds. Place the halves, cut sides down, on the prepared baking sheet. Bake for about 30 minutes, or until tender when pierced with a fork.

Meanwhile, heat the oil in a large nonstick sauté pan over medium-high heat. Add the bell peppers and onion (rings separated); cook, stirring occasionally, until tender but not browned, about 7 minutes. Add the jalapeño pepper, garlic, coriander, cumin, and dry mustard; stir for about 1 minute. Remove the pan from the heat. Stir in the rice, sour cream, parsley, pepper, and salt. Adjust the seasonings to taste. Set aside.

When the squash halves are tender, set aside until cool enough to handle. Remove the seeds and discard; scoop out the pulp with a spoon.

Spread a layer of the vegetable-rice mixture in the prepared casserole dish. Top with a layer of the soybeans and a layer of the squash. Sprinkle with the Parmesan cheese.

Bake for about 25 minutes, or until the dish is bubbly and the cheese is melted.

Per serving: Cal 283/Pro 16.4g/Carb 32.6g/Fat 9.7g/Chol 7mg/Sod 283mg

ADVANCE PREPARATION This casserole can be assembled early on the day it is to be served; cover and refrigerate. Bake just before serving; if chilled, allow about 10 minutes longer baking time.

makes 6 servings

Nonstick cooking spray

1 large acorn squash

1 tablespoon safflower oil

2 red bell peppers, cut lengthwise into ¹/₂-inch-wide strips

1 large yellow onion, halved and cut into ¹/₂-inch-thick slices (about 1¹/₂ cups)

1 tablespoon minced jalapeño pepper, or to taste

2 teaspoons minced garlic

2 teaspoons ground coriander

2 teaspoons ground cumin (see Tip, page 239)

1 teaspoon dry mustard

1 cup cooked brown rice

1 cup nonfat sour cream

¹/₂ cup minced fresh flat-leaf parsley

¹/₄ teaspoon freshly ground black pepper, or to taste

Dash of salt, or to taste

1¹/₂ cups cooked soybeans (one 15-ounce can, drained and rinsed)

¹/₂ cup freshly grated Parmesan cheese

curried tofu en papillote

makes 4 servings

12 ounces silken firm tofu, cut into pieces 1-inch square by 1/2-inch thick (about 2 cups)

1 apple, cut into 1/2-inch cubes (see Tip, page 93)

1/4 cup currants (see Tip)

For the sauce

1/4 cup tomato paste (see Tip, page 4)

1/4 cup soy milk

1 tablespoon low-sodium soy sauce

2 teaspoons curry powder

1 teaspoon minced gingerroot

1/2 teaspoon freshly ground black pepper

special equipment

four 16-inch-long sheets of kitchen parchment (see Tip)

Preparing tofu with curry "en papillote," inside a wrapping of kitchen parchment paper, marries a savory blend of flavors with a sophisticated French-style presentation. Serve this dish accompanied by pasta or couscous, which can be prepared while the parchment packets are baking.

Preheat the oven to 425°F.

Toss the tofu, apple, and currants in a large bowl.

Stir together the sauce ingredients in a small bowl. Pour the sauce over the tofu-apple mixture and fold gently to combine.

Fold a parchment sheet in half and cut into the shape of a half circle. Open the circle; spoon one-quarter of the tofu-sauce mixture onto one half of the parchment. Close the parchment flap. Seal the parchment by starting at one end; fold the cut edges toward the packet contents, creating many small overlapping folds. Repeat the procedure with the remaining sheets.

Place the parchment packets on a baking sheet; bake for about 10 minutes.

To serve, transfer the packets to individual plates; let guests open them at the table to reveal the food and release the aromas.

Per serving: Cal 132/Pro 8.1g/Carb 18g/Fat 3.1g/Chol 0mg/Sod 205mg

ADVANCE PREPARATION The parchment packets can be made 1 hour in advance; place in a single layer on trays and refrigerate. (Do not exceed 1 hour, or the parchment will become soggy.) The chilled food requires about 2 minutes longer to bake.

VARIATIONS

❧ Substitute skim milk for the soy milk.

❧ Rather than using parchment packets, pour the curried tofu mixture into a lightly oiled shallow casserole dish; bake for about 20 minutes, or until heated through.

About one-quarter the size of raisins, currants are less sweet but have a stronger flavor. In the supermarket they are found with the raisins and other dried fruits.

Kitchen parchment is available in the plastic and aluminum wrap aisle in most supermarkets. When foods such as fish, chicken, vegetables, fruits—or tofu—are cooked in parchment packets, en papillote, *no added fat is necessary and nutrients are retained. Parchment also can be used to line baking pans and baking sheets as an oil-free method to prevent cakes, cookies, or broiled foods from sticking.*

Baked Pasta Dishes

tofu stuffed shells with tomato-basil sauce

These make a big hit at family gatherings, earning compliments from both adults and children. From my point of view, they're a perfect choice because they can be made ahead. Simply add a green salad and crusty bread to complete the menu.

makes 8 servings

Nonstick cooking spray

16 jumbo pasta shells

1 tablespoon olive oil

1/4 cup finely chopped onion

2 teaspoons minced garlic

One 10-ounce package frozen chopped spinach, thawed, drained, and squeezed dry (see Tip)

2 large eggs

1 1/2 cups mashed silken firm tofu (12 ounces)

1/2 cup freshly grated Parmesan cheese

One 29-ounce can tomato sauce

2 tablespoons minced fresh basil (or 1 teaspoon dried)

1/2 teaspoon freshly ground black pepper, or to taste

garnish *(optional)* freshly ground black pepper, freshly grated Parmesan cheese

Preheat the oven to 350°F.

Lightly coat a 13- by 9-inch baking pan with the cooking spray.

Bring a large pot of water to a boil over high heat; add the pasta shells. When the water returns to a boil, stir once to separate the shells. Reduce the heat to medium-high and cook until tender, about 12 minutes. Drain and rinse with cool water; drain again and set aside.

While the pasta is cooking, heat the oil in a small nonstick skillet over medium-high heat. Add the onion and garlic; cook, stirring occasionally, until tender but not browned, about 4 minutes. Stir in the spinach. Remove the pan from the heat and set aside.

Lightly beat the eggs in a small bowl. Stir in the tofu, 1/4 cup of the Parmesan cheese, and the spinach-onion mixture.

In another small bowl, combine the tomato sauce, fresh or dried basil, and pepper. Adjust the seasoning to taste.

Pour half of the tomato-basil sauce into the prepared baking pan; spread evenly.

Spoon the tofu-spinach mixture into the cooked shells, using about $1^1/2$ tablespoons per shell. Arrange the stuffed shells in the pan. Drizzle the remaining tomato-basil sauce over the shells; sprinkle with the remaining $1/4$ cup cheese.

Cover the pan with foil; bake for about 35 to 40 minutes. Remove the foil; continue to bake for about 10 minutes longer, or until the tomato-basil sauce is hot and bubbly and the top is lightly browned. Allow to stand for about 5 minutes before serving.

Per serving (2 shells): Cal 197/Pro 12.3g/Carb 22.3g/Fat 6.5g/Chol 58mg/Sod 775mg

ADVANCE PREPARATION The stuffed shells with sauce can be assembled up to 1 day in advance; cover and refrigerate. Bake just before serving; if chilled, allow about 10 minutes longer baking time.

VARIATIONS

❧ Substitute $1/2$ cup cholesterol-free egg substitute for the eggs.

❧ For the mashed fresh tofu, substitute 18 ounces silken extra-firm tofu that has been frozen, thawed, squeezed, and crumbled (see page xxx).

tip

Thaw frozen spinach before using. To remove the excess moisture, hold it over the sink and squeeze it with your hands. Then put the spinach on a double layer of paper toweling; bring up the edges of the towels and twist at the top until the liquid is removed from the spinach.

tofu-spinach lasagna

This is one of my favorites for serving a crowd because I can count on it to please vegetarians and nonvegetarians alike. Another bonus: It requires little last-minute attention.

makes 8 servings

Nonstick cooking spray

9 lasagna noodles

1 tablespoon olive oil

2 cups sliced mushrooms

2 carrots, coarsely grated

1/2 cup coarsely chopped green bell pepper

3/4 cup coarsely chopped onion

2 teaspoons minced garlic

One 29-ounce can tomato sauce (see Tip)

2 tablespoons minced fresh oregano (or 2 teaspoons dried)

2 tablespoons minced fresh basil (or 2 teaspoons dried)

1/2 teaspoon freshly ground black pepper, or to taste

1/2 teaspoon red pepper flakes, or to taste

Dash of salt, or to taste

1 1/2 cups mashed silken extra-firm tofu (12 ounces)

1 cup nonfat ricotta cheese

One 10-ounce package frozen chopped spinach, thawed, drained, and squeezed dry (see Tip, page 207)

1 cup freshly grated Parmesan cheese

1 cup shredded part-skim mozzarella cheese

Preheat the oven to 375°F.

Lightly coat a 13- by 9-inch baking pan with the cooking spray.

Bring a large pot of water to a boil over high heat; add the lasagna noodles. When the water returns to a boil, stir once to separate the noodles. Reduce the heat to medium-high and cook until *al dente*, about 12 to 15 minutes.

Meanwhile, heat the oil in a large nonstick sauté pan over medium-high heat. Add the mushrooms, carrots, bell pepper, onion, and garlic; cook, stirring occasionally, until the vegetables are tender, about 5 minutes. Remove the pan from the heat; stir in the tomato sauce, fresh or dried oregano and basil, pepper, red pepper flakes, and salt. Adjust the seasonings to taste. Set aside.

Put the tofu and ricotta cheese into a food processor; process until the mixture is smooth. Stir in the spinach and 1/2 cup of the Parmesan cheese. Set aside.

When the noodles are done, drain well; rinse with cool water and drain again.

To assemble the dish, spread about 1 cup of the tomato sauce mixture in the baking pan. Arrange 3 noodles lengthwise in a single layer; spread 1 cup of the tofu-spinach mixture over the noodles and sprinkle with 1/3 cup of the mozzarella cheese. Repeat the layers two more times; top the dish with the remaining 1 cup of the tomato sauce mixture.

Cover with aluminum foil and bake for 35 minutes. Uncover and sprinkle with the remaining 1/2 cup Parmesan cheese. Bake for about 10 minutes longer, or until the cheese is melted and the top is lightly browned. Allow to stand for about 5 minutes before serving.

Per serving: Cal 321/Pro 21.9g/Carb 37.3g/Fat 9.4g/Chol 23mg/Sod 1,035mg

ADVANCE PREPARATION This dish can be assembled up to 1 day before baking; cover and refrigerate. Bake just before serving. If possible, let stand at room temperature for about 15 minutes before baking; if chilled, allow about 10 minutes longer baking time.

VARIATION

❧ For the mashed fresh tofu, substitute 18 ounces silken extra-firm tofu that has been frozen, thawed, squeezed, and crumbled (see page xxx); stir into the ricotta cheese (do not purée) with the spinach and Parmesan cheese.

tip

Canned tomato purée is made from tomatoes that have been cooked and strained, resulting in a thick liquid. Canned tomato sauce has a slightly thinner consistency.

vegetarian pastitsio

Pastitsio is a popular baked Greek casserole dish that traditionally contains ground beef or lamb and a béchamel sauce seasoned with cinnamon. Here, the meat is replaced with soybeans, and the sauce is made from a mixture of nonfat cottage cheese, feta cheese, and egg. This makes a good choice for entertaining, since the casserole can be assembled in advance; it also can be doubled to serve a crowd.

makes 6 servings

Nonstick cooking spray

8 ounces linguine (see Tip)

2 tablespoons olive oil

1/2 cup finely chopped onion

1 medium eggplant, peeled and cut into 1/2-inch cubes (about 4 cups) (see Tip, page 157)

1 teaspoon minced garlic

1 1/2 tablespoons minced fresh oregano (or 1 1/2 teaspoons dried)

1/2 teaspoon freshly ground black pepper

1/4 teaspoon ground cinnamon

3 medium tomatoes, cut into 1/2-inch cubes (about 3 cups)

1 1/2 cups cooked soybeans (one 15-ounce can, drained and rinsed)

One 8-ounce can tomato sauce

1 cup nonfat cottage cheese

1/2 cup crumbled mild feta cheese

1 large egg

garnish *(optional)* freshly ground black pepper, freshly grated Parmesan cheese

Preheat the oven to 400°F.

Lightly coat a 9-inch square glass baking dish with the cooking spray.

Bring a large pot of water to a boil over high heat; add the linguine. When the water returns to a boil, stir once to separate the linguine. Reduce the heat to medium-high and cook until barely *al dente*, about 8 minutes.

While the linguine is cooking, heat the oil in a large nonstick sauté pan over medium-high heat. Add the onion; cook, stirring constantly, until soft, about 3 minutes. Reduce the heat to medium-low; stir in the eggplant, garlic, fresh or dried oregano, pepper, and cinnamon. Cover and cook, stirring occasionally, until the eggplant is softened, about 5 minutes. Add the tomatoes, soybeans, and tomato sauce; cook, stirring occasionally, until the tomatoes are softened, about 5 minutes. Remove from the heat.

Put the cottage cheese, feta cheese, and egg into a food processor; process until the mixture is smooth and creamy. Set aside.

When the pasta is done, drain well. Spread half of the noodles in the prepared baking pan. Cover with about half of the eggplant mixture; repeat the layers. Pour the cottage cheese mixture over all; poke several places with a knife to allow the sauce to run through the layers.

Cover with aluminum foil and bake for about 40 minutes. Remove the cover and bake for about 10 minutes longer, or until the casserole is heated through and the top is lightly browned and puffed. Allow to stand for about 5 minutes before serving.

Per serving: Cal 309/Pro 20g/Carb 25.1g/Fat 14.3g/Chol 66mg/Sod 598mg

ADVANCE PREPARATION This dish can be assembled early on the day it is to be served; cover and refrigerate. If chilled, allow about 10 minutes longer baking time.

VARIATION

❧ Substitute $1/4$ cup cholesterol-free egg substitute for the egg.

Tip

When cooking pasta, be sure to use a large pot that is deeper than it is wide; this allows the pasta to move freely as it cooks and prevents sticking. Keep the heat high so the water will return to a boil after the pasta is added. Stir the pasta just once; reduce the heat to medium-high and begin timing, being certain to keep the water at a rapid boil throughout the cooking period. Cooking time will depend on the shape and thickness of the pasta. Perfectly cooked pasta should be al dente—firm but not hard, and evenly cooked, so it offers some resistance to the teeth yet is cooked through. Drain the pasta just as soon as it is done; there is no need to rinse pasta unless you must cool it quickly.

Loaves and Accompanying Sauces

vegetable-soybean loaf

To serve the most discriminating vegetarians on your guest list, top the servings of this loaf with Tomato–Red Pepper Sauce (page 217) or Cremini Mushroom Sauce (page 216); either can be prepared while the loaf is baking. Accompany the dish with steamed asparagus spears and warm crusty bread.

makes 6 servings

Nonstick cooking spray

1 tablespoon olive oil

2 cups finely shredded carrots

2 cups finely chopped broccoli (both stems and florets)

1/2 cup diced red bell pepper

3 medium scallions, finely chopped (see Tip)

1 rib celery, diced

1 teaspoon minced garlic

1 1/2 cups cooked soybeans (one 15-ounce can, drained and rinsed)

2 large eggs

2 plum tomatoes, cut into 1/2-inch cubes (about 3/4 cup)

1/4 cup dry bread crumbs (see Tip, page 197)

2 teaspoons minced fresh basil (or 1/2 teaspoon dried)

2 teaspoons minced fresh marjoram (or 1/2 teaspoon dried)

1/2 teaspoon freshly ground black pepper

1/4 teaspoon salt

Dash of paprika (see Tip)

Preheat the oven to 375°F.

Lightly coat a 9 × 5 × 3-inch loaf pan with the cooking spray.

Heat the oil in a large nonstick sauté pan over medium-high heat. Add the carrots, broccoli, bell pepper, scallions, and celery. Cook, stirring occasionally, until the vegetables are tender but not browned, about 4 minutes. Add the garlic during the last minute. Remove the pan from the heat; set aside.

Put the soybeans and eggs into a food processor. Process until the mixture is smooth, then stir into the sauté pan. Stir in the remaining ingredients except the paprika.

Press the vegetable-soybean mixture into the prepared loaf pan; sprinkle with paprika.

Bake for about 40 minutes, or until the top is lightly browned and a knife inserted in the center comes out clean. Allow to stand for about 5 minutes before serving. Serve the slices topped with your choice of sauce.

Per serving: Cal 187/Pro 12.1g/Carb 15.4g/Fat 8.6g/Chol 71mg/Sod 169mg

ADVANCE PREPARATION The loaf mixture can be prepared and pressed into the pan early on the day it is to be served; cover and refrigerate. Bake just before serving. If chilled, allow about 10 minutes longer baking time.

VARIATIONS

❧ Substitute $1/2$ cup cholesterol-free egg substitute for the eggs.

❧ Substitute toasted wheat germ for the dry bread crumbs.

tips

Scallions, also called green onions or spring onions, are delicately flavored members of the onion family. They come from the thinnings of immature onion bulbs as well as certain kinds of onions that produce long, thin stems. The leaves should be bright green and firm; the white bulbs should be firm, unblemished, and free of soil. Both parts can be used in recipes calling for scallions. The size varies from very slender to large and thick; as a rule, the more slender the bottoms, the sweeter the flavor. Store for up to a week, wrapped in a plastic bag, in the vegetable crisper section of the refrigerator.

Paprika is a powder made by grinding aromatic sweet red pepper pods. The flavor can range from mild to pungent and hot, and the color from red-orange to deep red. Most paprika comes from Spain, South America, California, or Hungary; the Hungarian variety is considered by many to be the best. Hungarian paprika comes in three levels of hotness: mild (also called "sweet"), hot, and exceptionally hot. To preserve the color and flavor, store paprika in a cool, dark place for no longer than 6 months.

tofu-walnut loaf

To make your entrée complete, top slices of this loaf with Cremini Mushroom Sauce (recipe follows) or Tomato–Red Pepper Sauce (page 217). Serve it with Garlic Mashed Potatoes (page 200) and steamed broccoli florets to add color and texture to the meal.

makes 6 servings

Nonstick cooking spray

1 tablespoon olive oil

2 cups finely chopped mushrooms

1/2 cup finely chopped celery

1/2 cup finely chopped onion

1 teaspoon minced garlic

1 1/2 cups mashed silken firm tofu (12 ounces)

1/2 cup cooked brown or white rice

1/4 cup toasted wheat germ

2 large eggs, lightly beaten

1/2 cup finely chopped walnuts (see Tip)

2 tablespoons freshly grated Parmesan cheese

1 tablespoon low-sodium soy sauce

1/2 teaspoon ground sage

1/2 teaspoon freshly ground black pepper (see Tip)

One 6-ounce can tomato paste

1/4 cup water

Preheat the oven to 375°F.

Lightly coat a 9-inch square baking pan with the cooking spray.

Heat the oil in a large nonstick sauté pan over medium-high heat. Add the mushrooms, celery, onion, and garlic. Cook, stirring occasionally, until tender but not browned, about 5 minutes. Remove the pan from the heat. Stir in the remaining ingredients except the tomato paste and water. Gently press the mixture into the prepared baking pan.

Combine the tomato paste and water in a small bowl; spread over the Tofu-Walnut Loaf.

Bake for about 40 minutes, or until a knife inserted in the center comes out clean. Allow to stand for about 5 minutes before serving. Serve the slices topped with your choice of sauce.

Per serving: Cal 235/Pro 13.2g/Carb 16.5g/Fat 12.9g/Chol 73mg/Sod 253mg

ADVANCE PREPARATION The loaf mixture can be prepared and pressed into the pan early on the day it is to be served; cover and refrigerate. Top with the tomato paste and bake just before serving. If chilled, allow about 10 minutes longer baking time.

VARIATION

➤ Substitute 1/2 cup cholesterol-free egg substitute for the eggs.

tips

There are two kinds of walnuts. Black walnuts are stronger in flavor than English (or Persian) walnuts. (Either can be used in this recipe.) Shelled walnuts should be tightly covered and refrigerated for up to 6 months or frozen for up to a year.

Berries of the pepper vine are used to produce both black pepper and white pepper. For black pepper, green berries are picked and sun-dried, turning black and shrinking in the process. For white pepper, the berries are allowed to ripen on the vine; they are picked and soaked in water to remove the outer coating, leaving the inner gray-white kernel. The inner kernels are sun-dried to produce white pepper. White pepper is slightly less spicy than black pepper. It is often used in Asian recipes and in light-colored sauces where dark specks of black pepper would stand out.

cremini mushroom sauce

makes 1 1/2 cups

1 tablespoon olive oil

2 cups sliced cremini mushrooms (see Tip, page 3)

1/4 cup minced shallots

2 tablespoons margarine

2 tablespoons all-purpose white or unbleached flour

1 1/2 cups soy milk

1 tablespoon low-sodium soy sauce

1/4 teaspoon white ground pepper, or to taste

For elegant vegetarian dining, serve this extraordinary sauce atop Tofu-Walnut Loaf (page 214) or Vegetable-Soybean Loaf (page 212), or it can stand alone served over rice, couscous, or egg noodles. If necessary, ordinary white mushrooms can be substituted for the cremini mushrooms.

Heat the oil in a small nonstick skillet over medium-high heat. Add the mushrooms and shallots; cook, stirring occasionally, until tender but not browned, about 4 minutes. Remove the pan from the heat; set aside.

Make a roux: Melt the margarine in a medium nonstick saucepan over medium heat. Add the flour and stir constantly until the mixture is smooth and bubbly. Gradually add the soy milk, whisking constantly until the sauce is smooth and thickened, about 3 to 4 minutes (see Tip).

Reduce the heat to low; stir in the cooked mushrooms, soy sauce, and white pepper. Adjust the seasoning to taste.

Per 1/4 cup: Cal 110/Pro 3.7g/Carb 7.8g/Fat 7.1g/Chol 0mg/Sod 165mg

ADVANCE PREPARATION Covered and refrigerated, this sauce will keep for up to 2 days. Stir as you warm it over low heat.

VARIATIONS

❧ Substitute butter for the margarine.

❧ Substitute skim milk for the soy milk.

tip

A roux is a mixture of flour and fat that is slowly cooked over low heat and then used to thicken sauces or soups.

tomato-red pepper sauce V

This sauce is as colorful as it is flavorful. Spoon it over slices of Vegetable-Soybean Loaf (page 212) or Tofu-Walnut Loaf (page 214). Or double the recipe and serve the sauce over pasta such as spaghetti or penne.

Heat the oil in a small nonstick saucepan over medium-high heat. Add the bell pepper; cook, stirring constantly, until tender but not browned, about 4 minutes. Add the garlic during the last minute. Reduce the heat to medium; add the remaining ingredients. Stir until the sauce is heated through. Adjust the seasonings to taste.

Per 1/4 cup: Cal 90/Pro 2.5g/Carb 12.4g/Fat 3.4g/Chol 0mg/Sod 264mg

ADVANCE PREPARATION Covered and refrigerated, this sauce will keep for up to 2 days.

tip

Red pepper flakes, also called crushed red pepper, are the seeds and flakes of fiery hot peppers; a small amount goes a long way! Refrigerate to preserve the color and flavor.

makes 1 cup

1 tablespoon olive oil

1/4 cup diced red bell pepper

1 teaspoon minced garlic

One 8-ounce can tomato sauce

1/4 cup drained and finely chopped oil-packed sun-dried tomatoes

2 tablespoons minced fresh basil (or 2 teaspoons dried)

1/4 teaspoon freshly ground black pepper, or to taste

Pinch of red pepper flakes, or to taste (see Tip)

Entrées for Brunch

tofu-nut pancakes

Here's a light but filling breakfast to begin the day, or prepare these nutty pancakes for a quick lunch or dinner. Serve them with maple syrup or fruit sauce, such as Honey-Raspberry Sauce (page 258), or yogurt and fresh fruit.

**makes 12 pancakes
(4 servings)**

1 cup mashed silken firm tofu

1/2 cup nonfat cottage cheese

3 large eggs

1/4 cup whole wheat flour

1/2 cup soy milk, or as needed

2 tablespoons finely chopped
    almonds

1/4 cup toasted wheat germ

1/2 teaspoon baking soda

Dash of ground nutmeg

Nonstick cooking spray

3 teaspoons poppyseeds

Put the tofu, cottage cheese, eggs, flour, soy milk, almonds, wheat germ, baking soda, and nutmeg into a food processor; process until smooth. Check the consistency of the batter and add more soy milk if it is too thick. (The amount needed may vary, depending on the amount of liquid in the tofu and cottage cheese.)

Coat a large nonstick skillet with the cooking spray; heat over medium-high heat. For each pancake, spoon a scant 1/4 cup of batter into a 4-inch round. Cook the pancakes until bubbles rise and begin to break, about 2 minutes. Sprinkle each pancake with about 1/4 teaspoon poppyseeds; turn with a spatula and cook the other side until the pancakes are lightly browned and cooked through, about 1 minute. Serve immediately.

Per serving (3 pancakes): Cal 234/Pro 18.4g/Carb 15.5g/Fat 10.9g/Chol 161mg/Sod 298mg

ADVANCE PREPARATION The batter can be made up to 1 day in advance; cover and refrigerate. Stir and check the consistency before pouring it onto the skillet. If the batter is chilled, the pancakes will take slightly longer to cook.

VARIATIONS

❧ Substitute skim milk for the soy milk.

❧ Substitute 3/4 cup cholesterol-free egg substitute for the eggs.

❧ To reduce the fat and calories, omit the almonds and poppy seeds.

noodle pudding

Here is a slimmed-down version of Grandma Rose's Noodle Kugel, a friend's treasured family recipe. For brunch, serve this warm or at room temperature; it's good with fresh fruit and an assortment of your favorite muffins.

makes 6 servings

Nonstick cooking spray

4 cups medium egg noodles
   (see Tip, page 113)

1 cup mashed silken firm tofu

1 cup nonfat cottage cheese

3 large eggs

$1/2$ cup sugar

$1/3$ cup soy milk

1 teaspoon pure vanilla extract

$1/8$ teaspoon ground cinnamon

Preheat the oven to 350°F.

Lightly coat a 9-inch square glass baking dish with the cooking spray.

Bring a large pot of water to a boil over high heat; add the noodles. When the water returns to a boil, stir once to separate the noodles. Reduce the heat to medium-high and cook until tender, about 5 to 7 minutes.

Put the remaining ingredients into a food processor; process until smooth.

When the noodles are done, drain well. Return them to the pan; stir in the tofu mixture. Pour into the prepared baking dish.

Bake for about 30 minutes, or until the top is lightly browned and a knife inserted in the center comes out clean. Allow to stand for about 5 minutes before serving.

Per serving: Cal 255/Pro 14.9g/Carb 37.9g/Fat 4.9g/Chol 132mg/Sod 206mg

ADVANCE PREPARATION This dish can be prepared early on the day it is to be served. After it cools, cover and refrigerate. Bring to room temperature for serving; do not reheat.

VARIATION

❯ When adding the tofu mixture to the cooked noodles, also stir in one well-drained 8-ounce can crushed pineapple.

Desserts

Puréed Desserts

Chocolate-Maple Tofu Pudding

Gingered Banana Parfaits

Lemon Mousse

Tofu Tiramisu

Mocha Mousse

Tofu-Ricotta–Topped Peach
Halves

Strawberry-Banana Smoothie

Frozen Strawberry-Banana
Dessert

Baked Desserts

Spiced Pumpkin Bread Pudding

Cranberry-Rice Pudding

Pear Clafouti

Caramel Custard

Cream Puffs

Pies

Tofu Pumpkin Pie

Tofu Key Lime Pie

Pineapple-Orange Tofu-Ricotta
Cheesecake

Chocolate Mousse Pie

Low-Fat Graham Cracker Crust

Cookie Crust

Cooked Desserts

Pineapple Tapioca Pudding

Vanilla Poached Pears with
Orange-Honey Sauce

Tofu Cream-Filled Crêpes with
Strawberry Purée

Wheat Germ Crêpes

Dessert Toppings

Vanilla Tofu Cream

Tofu Whipped Cream

Honey-Raspberry Sauce

*T*here's no question about it: desserts are comfort food. Their flavors, textures, and aromas evoke happy memories. Unfortunately, many of our favorite mealtime finales are calorie and fat laden. The good news is that light desserts can be truly delectable, and in addition to being low in fat, they can provide a way to incorporate the nutritional advantages of soy in your diet. For vegans many of these dreamy desserts are also dairy-free.

Developing the recipes for this chapter was the most fun of any in this book. The custardlike texture of silken firm tofu inspired me; it became particularly useful when I desired a creamy, rich texture. Its rich "mouth feel" makes it seem as if the desserts contain fat.

Since the puréed desserts require no cooking, another plus is that they can be prepared in a flash in your food processor. Just be certain to push down the mixture from the sides of the work bowl to achieve a consistently smooth texture (do this in several batches if using a blender), and plan ahead to refrigerate these desserts for an hour or so before serving to allow the flavors to blend. Admittedly, glossy, rich-tasting puddings like Chocolate-Maple Tofu Pudding (page 223) and Mocha Mousse (page 227) are quite different from the puddings Mom used to make—but they are great.

Some of the puréed mixtures also make delectable pie fillings, such as Tofu Key Lime Pie (page 240) and Pineapple-Orange Tofu-Ricotta Cheesecake (page 242). And even classic baked desserts like pumpkin pie, bread pudding, and rice pudding can be redefined with the addition of tofu (see pages 231, 232, and 238).

Comfort food aside, you don't have to abandon elegant desserts when eating healthfully. Tofu desserts such as Caramel Custard (page 234), Tofu Cream-Filled Crêpes (page 252), Vanilla Poached Pears with Orange-Honey Sauce (page 250)—and even Tofu Tiramisu (page 226)—will dazzle your guests. And then there are the Gingered Banana Parfaits (page 224)—definitely my favorite of all!

In this chapter you will also find diverse cooked and baked desserts, including Pineapple Tapioca Pudding (page 248) and Caramel Custard (page 234). To transform simple desserts into something really special, try the dessert toppings like Vanilla Tofu Cream (page 256), Tofu Whipped Cream (page 257), and Honey-Raspberry Sauce (page 258).

Much of the pleasure of desserts is visual, so go all-out for presentation. Serve them in just the right dish, and add a pretty garnish as the final touch.

The nutritional benefits alone will inspire you to serve these desserts often. Just as much a selling point: They look appealing—they taste delicious—and they are guaranteed to tempt all dessert lovers of all ages.

Puréed Desserts

chocolate-maple tofu pudding

Serve this glossy, rich-tasting pudding in small individual dessert cups topped with Tofu Whipped Cream (page 257) or fresh fruit. For variety, double the pudding quantities and pour into a 9-inch crust (pages 246 or 247) or atop a layer of crumbled graham crackers or chocolate wafer cookies (about 3/4 cup).

Put all the ingredients into a food processor; process until very smooth and creamy.

Transfer the mixture to a medium bowl or to individual dessert cups. Cover and refrigerate for at least 1 hour before serving.

Per serving: Cal 140/Pro 6.6g/Carb 22.2g/Fat 2.8g/Chol 0mg/Sod 58mg

ADVANCE PREPARATION Covered and refrigerated, this pudding will keep for up to 2 days.

VARIATIONS

❧ When puréeing, add 1 tablespoon smooth peanut butter.

❧ Freeze the mixture and serve as a frozen dessert (peanut butter is necessary to prevent the mixture from becoming icy).

tip

For the best flavor and quality, buy "pure maple syrup," not "maple-flavored syrup," which is stretched with corn syrup. Even less desirable is "pancake syrup," which rarely contains any maple syrup at all. Pure syrup is maple tree sap that has been boiled until much of the water has evaporated; it takes approximately 35 gallons of maple sap to produce 1 gallon of maple syrup. Once opened, maple syrup should be refrigerated. If crystals develop, place the syrup container in a pan of hot water until they disappear.

makes 4 servings

1 1/2 cups mashed silken firm tofu (12 ounces)

1/3 cup pure maple syrup (see Tip)

1/3 cup unsweetened cocoa powder

1 teaspoon pure vanilla extract

Dash of ground cinnamon, or to taste (see Tip, page 227)

garnish *(optional)* ❧ whole fresh strawberries or raspberries

gingered banana parfaits

makes 4 servings

10 chocolate wafer cookies

1 1/2 cups mashed silken firm tofu (12 ounces)

1/4 cup nonfat ricotta cheese

1/3 cup sugar

1 large ripe banana

1 tablespoon freshly squeezed lemon juice

1 tablespoon minced crystallized ginger (see Tip)

This impressive light dessert is surprisingly quick to prepare. Simply layer the packaged chocolate wafers with the uncooked puréed mixture—I like to use parfait glasses. This is my favorite tofu dessert, which I often serve after Asian-inspired entrées.

Put the cookies into a zip-top plastic bag; use a rolling pin to crush them into coarse crumbs.

Put the remaining ingredients into a food processor; process until smooth and creamy.

Spoon 1/4 cup of the tofu-banana mixture into the bottom of 4 clear stemmed glasses; sprinkle each with 1 tablespoon of the cookie crumbs. Repeat the layers.

Cover each glass with plastic wrap and refrigerate for at least 1 hour or up to 3 hours before serving.

Per serving: Cal 231/Pro 8.7g/Carb 38.5g/Fat 4.7g/Chol 5mg/Sod 162mg

ADVANCE PREPARATION This dessert is best when prepared no more than a few hours before serving; if refrigerated for longer than 3 hours, the color darkens.

VARIATIONS

❧ Substitute cottage cheese for the ricotta cheese.

❧ Slice a firm but ripe banana; dip the slices into fresh lemon juice. Add the slices as a layer when assembling the parfaits, or add them as a topping just before serving.

tip

Crystallized (or candied) ginger has been cooked in a sugar syrup and coated with coarse sugar. This sweet ginger is generally used as a confection or added to desserts.

lemon mousse

The taste of lemon is often appealing after a highly flavored meal. Almond butter adds richness to this dessert in addition to a hint of roasted almond.

Put all the ingredients into a food processor; process until smooth. Refrigerate in a covered container for at least 1 hour before serving.

Per serving: Cal 198/Pro 7.1g/Carb 27.2g/Fat 6.8g/Chol 0mg/Sod 33mg

ADVANCE PREPARATION Covered and refrigerated, this mousse will keep for up to 2 days.

tip

Liquid extracts are concentrated flavorings that can be used to add flavor to foods without altering either the volume or the consistency. Stored in a tightly closed container in a cool, dark place, they will keep indefinitely. Pure extracts are always preferable to those containing artificial flavorings.

makes 4 servings

1 1/2 cups mashed silken firm tofu (12 ounces)

1/3 cup honey

2 tablespoons smooth almond butter

1 tablespoon lemon zest (see Tip, pages 6–7)

1 teaspoon pure vanilla extract (see Tip)

1 teaspoon pure lemon extract (see Tip)

garnish *(optional)* thin lemon slices, toasted almond slices (see Tip, page 50)

tofu tiramisu

Tiramisu is an Italian dessert composed of ladyfingers or sponge cake dipped in a mixture of coffee and Marsala wine, then layered with mascarpone. Popular restaurant versions contain whipped cream and eggs, which I have eliminated here and replaced with tofu. Espresso made from freshly ground beans is best, but instant espresso powder will do.

makes 6 servings

3/4 cup prepared strong espresso coffee

1/2 cup sweet Marsala wine (see Tip, page 105)

1 cup mashed silken firm tofu

1/2 cup mascarpone (see Tip)

1/2 cup sugar

1 teaspoon orange zest (see Tip, pages 6–7)

12 ladyfingers

1 teaspoon bittersweet cocoa powder

Combine the espresso and wine in a shallow bowl. Set aside. Put the tofu, mascarpone, sugar, and 2 tablespoons of the espresso-wine mixture into a food processor; process until smooth. Stir in the orange zest.

Dip the ladyfingers, one at a time, in the espresso-wine mixture; immerse the ladyfingers long enough to be moistened but not saturated. As they are dipped, place half of the ladyfingers in a single layer in the bottom of a 1-quart serving dish.

Cover the ladyfingers with half of the tofu-mascarpone mixture. Repeat with another layer of ladyfingers and mascarpone.

Cover the dish with plastic wrap and refrigerate for at least 2 or for up to 8 hours. Just before serving, sprinkle the top with cocoa powder sifted through a fine wire mesh strainer.

Per serving: Cal 226/Pro 5.3g/Carb 27.4g/Fat 10.6g/Chol 49mg/Sod 127mg

ADVANCE PREPARATION This dessert is best when prepared the day it is to be served. Cover and refrigerate for at least 2 hours or for up to 8 hours before serving.

tip

Mascarpone is a rich Italian cream cheese.

mocha mousse

Mocha is a marriage of chocolate and coffee—a union of two of my favorite flavors. Because this low-fat nondairy mousse seems decidedly rich, serve small portions in individual dessert cups.

Put all the ingredients into a food processor; process until very smooth and creamy.

Spoon about $1/3$ cup of the mixture into 6 small, individual dessert cups. Cover and refrigerate for at least 1 hour before serving.

Per serving: Cal 133/Pro 7.3g/Carb 19.2g/Fat 3g/Chol 0mg/Sod 35mg

ADVANCE PREPARATION Covered and refrigerated, this mousse will keep for up to 2 days.

VARIATION

❧ Substitute 1 tablespoon instant espresso powder for the instant coffee granules.

tips

Store cocoa powder, a nondairy product, in a cool, dark place for up to 2 years. In recipes, do not substitute cocoa mixes or instant cocoa, which are sweetened and usually contain milk powder.

Dutch-process cocoa powder offers superior flavor; it has been treated with alkali, which helps neutralize cocoa's natural acidity.

Cinnamon comes from the inner bark of a tropical evergreen tree. It is dried and sold as cinnamon sticks, and it is also ground into a powder. The flavor is pungent and slightly bittersweet.

makes 6 servings

$2 1/2$ cups mashed silken firm tofu (about 20 ounces)

$1/2$ cup sugar

$1/3$ cup unsweetened cocoa powder (see Tips)

2 tablespoons freeze-dried instant coffee granules

1 teaspoon orange zest (see Tip, pages 0–7)

$1/2$ teaspoon ground cinnamon (see Tip)

garnish *(optional)* orange zest (see Tip, pages 6–7)

tofu-ricotta-topped peach halves

makes 6 servings

For the Tofu-Ricotta Topping

1/2 cup mashed extra-firm tofu

1/2 cup nonfat ricotta cheese

2 tablespoons freshly
squeezed orange juice

2 tablespoons honey

1/4 teaspoon almond extract

2 tablespoons slivered
almonds

2 tablespoons semisweet
chocolate chips

2 tablespoons currants

1 teaspoon grated orange rind
(see Tip, pages 6–7)

To complete the recipe

3 ripe fresh peaches, peeled,
halved, and pitted
(see Tip)

garnish (optional) sweetened
cocoa powder

Here's the perfect dessert to follow an Italian entrée. In the winter, substitute fresh pear halves for the peaches. For an elegant presentation, serve the ricotta-topped fruit on a bed of Honey-Raspberry Sauce (page 258). Or refrigerate the tofu-ricotta mixture to firm it up, then stuff it into 6 cannoli shells. These hand-rolled Italian pastry shells are available in packages in many gourmet shops and in some supermarkets; better yet, some Italian delis sell the shells freshly made.

Put the tofu, ricotta cheese, orange juice, honey, and almond extract into a food processor; process until smooth. Stir in the almonds, chocolate chips, currants, and orange rind. Refrigerate in a covered container for at least 1 hour before serving.

To serve, place the peach halves, cut sides up, on dessert plates; top each with about 1/3 cup of the tofu-ricotta mixture.

Per serving: Cal 184/Pro 6.4g/Carb 28.6g/Fat 4.9g/Chol 5mg/Sod 54mg

ADVANCE PREPARATION Covered and refrigerated, the filling will keep for up to 3 days. Assemble with the peaches just before serving. For the cannoli shell variation, the shells can be filled up to 3 hours before serving; cover and refrigerate.

tip

To peel a peach, immerse it in boiling water for 1 minute. Then drop the peach into cold water. Remove the peel with firm downward pulls.

strawberry-banana smoothie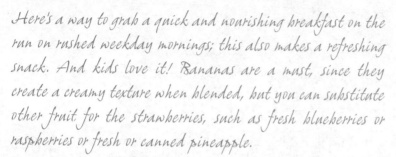

Here's a way to grab a quick and nourishing breakfast on the run on rushed weekday mornings; this also makes a refreshing snack. And kids love it! Bananas are a must, since they create a creamy texture when blended, but you can substitute other fruit for the strawberries, such as fresh blueberries or raspberries or fresh or canned pineapple.

Put all the ingredients into a blender; blend until smooth. Serve immediately.

Per serving (2 cups): Cal 296/Pro 12.1g/Carb 50.5g/Fat 5.1g/Chol 0mg/Sod 108mg

ADVANCE PREPARATION This smoothie is best when prepared just before serving. Leftovers can be covered and refrigerated; serve later the same day.

VARIATIONS

❧ Blend in 2 tablespoons soy protein powder.

❧ Blend in 1 tablespoon honey or sugar, or to taste.

❧ For a slushy consistency, use 3/4 cup soy milk and blend the mixture with 1 cup ice cubes (about 10).

❧ For a thick, malt-consistency drink, use frozen fruit in place of the fresh fruit. Peel and freeze a ripe banana; add to the drink while still frozen—or use frozen strawberries.

tip

Keep bananas at room temperature until ripe. Once ripened, bananas can be stored in the refrigerator for 3 or 4 days. The skin will darken when refrigerated, but the edible portion will remain unchanged.

makes 1 serving

1 cup cold soy milk

1 cup sliced strawberries (see Tip, page 253)

1 ripe banana, cut into 1-inch-thick chunks (see Tip)

1/4 teaspoon pure vanilla extract

garnish *(optional)* sprig of fresh mint

frozen strawberry-banana dessert

Plan ahead to freeze a ripe banana before preparing this luscious frozen dessert. Frozen bananas create a thick, creamy texture when blended.

makes 4 servings

1 cup mashed silken firm tofu

1 cup frozen unsweetened
   strawberries

1 frozen banana, cut into
   1-inch pieces

1/4 cup freshly squeezed
   orange juice

2 tablespoons honey,
   or to taste

1/4 teaspoon pure vanilla
   extract

garnish *(optional)* sprigs of
fresh mint (see Tip)

Put all the ingredients into a food processor; process until the mixture is thick and smooth. Adjust sweetness to taste. Serve immediately.

Per serving: Cal 120/Pro 4.7g/Carb 20.9g/Fat 2g/Chol 0mg/Sod 22mg

ADVANCE PREPARATION At least 1 day prior to making this dessert, remove the banana's peel, wrap it in plastic wrap, and freeze. The dessert should be served icy cold immediately after preparing; do not freeze. Leftovers can be covered, refrigerated, and served up to 1 day later as a beverage (the mixture thins as the banana and strawberries thaw).

tip

Of the many varieties of mint, spearmint is the most commonly used in cooking. Fresh mint is available in the produce section of most markets, and if you have a sunny spot outdoors, mint is among the easiest herbs to grow.

Baked Desserts

spiced pumpkin
bread pudding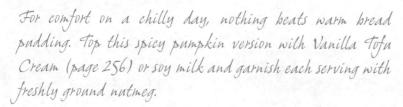

For comfort on a chilly day, nothing beats warm bread pudding. Top this spicy pumpkin version with Vanilla Tofu Cream (page 256) or soy milk and garnish each serving with freshly ground nutmeg.

Preheat the oven to 350°F. Lightly coat a 1 1/2-quart baking dish with cooking spray; set aside.

Put all the ingredients except the bread cubes into a food processor; process until smooth.

Put half of the bread cubes into the prepared baking dish. Cover with half of the tofu-pumpkin mixture. Repeat the layers.

Bake for about 1 hour, or until the top is firm and a knife inserted in the center comes out nearly clean. Allow to stand for about 10 minutes before serving.

Serve warm in dessert bowls with the topping of your choice.

Per serving: Cal 227/Pro 9.1g/Carb 40.5g/Fat 3.2g/Chol 36mg/Sod 79mg

ADVANCE PREPARATION This pudding is best when served warm from the oven. Covered and refrigerated, it will keep for up to 2 days. Serve chilled or at room temperature; do not reheat.

VARIATIONS

❧ Substitute skim milk for the soy milk.

❧ Substitute 1/4 cup cholesterol-free egg substitute for the egg.

❧ Substitute raisin bread or whole wheat bread for the sourdough white bread.

makes 6 servings

Nonstick cooking spray

1 cup mashed silken firm tofu

2/3 cup canned pumpkin

1/3 cup sugar

1/2 cup soy milk

1 large egg

1 teaspoon pure vanilla extract

1 teaspoon ground cinnamon

1/2 teaspoon ground ginger

1/4 teaspoon ground nutmeg
   (see Tip, page 256)

1/8 teaspoon salt

4 cups day-old sourdough white
   bread in 1/2-inch cubes

cranberry-rice pudding

Leftover rice shines again as dessert with this variation on the custard theme. For a special treat, spoon the warm pudding into bowls and top with Vanilla Tofu Cream (page 256) or soy milk.

makes 6 servings

Nonstick cooking spray

1 cup soy milk

1 cup mashed silken firm tofu

2 large eggs

1/4 cup lightly packed light brown sugar

2 teaspoons pure vanilla extract

1 teaspoon grated orange rind (see Tip, pages 6–7)

1/2 teaspoon ground nutmeg

1/4 teaspoon salt

2 cups cooked brown or basmati rice

1/3 cup dried cranberries (see Tip)

Preheat the oven to 300°F.

Lightly coat a 1 1/2-quart baking dish with cooking spray.

Pour the soy milk and tofu into a food processor; process until smooth. Add the eggs, brown sugar, vanilla, orange rind, nutmeg, and salt; process until well combined.

Toss the rice and dried cranberries in a medium bowl. Stir in the soy milk mixture. Pour the pudding mixture into the prepared baking dish.

Bake for about 1 hour 10 minutes, or until a knife inserted in the center comes out clean and the pudding is lightly browned on top.

Per serving: Cal 202/Pro 8.1g/Carb 33g/Fat 4.2g/Chol 71mg/Sod 147mg

ADVANCE PREPARATION Covered and refrigerated, this pudding will keep for up to 2 days. Serve chilled or allow to come to room temperature.

VARIATIONS

❧ Substitute skim milk for the soy milk.

❧ Substitute 1/2 cup cholesterol-free egg substitute for the 2 eggs.

❧ Substitute raisins for the dried cranberries.

tip

Dried and sweetened cranberries are commonly available in the dried fruits section of supermarkets. They are delicious as a snack, colorful as an ingredient or garnish, and can be used as an alternative to raisins.

pear clafouti

Clafouti is a country-French dessert made by topping a layer of fresh fruit with batter and then baking it. As a winter dessert, this is high on my list of favorites served warm with Vanilla Tofu Cream (page 256) or vanilla frozen yogurt. When summer provides raspberries, blueberries, rhubarb, and peaches, substitute these fresh fruits.

makes 8 servings

Nonstick cooking spray

3 large ripe pears (at room temperature), peeled, cored, and sliced in half lengthwise

1 cup soy milk

3 large eggs

1/2 cup all-purpose white or unbleached flour

1/3 cup sugar

1/2 teaspoon baking powder

1/4 teaspoon salt

1 teaspoon lemon zest (see Tip, pages 6–7)

Preheat the oven to 425°F.

Lightly coat a 10-inch tart pan with cooking spray.

Place the pear halves, flat sides down, on a cutting board; cut each crosswise into 1/8-inch-thick slices. Arrange a row of overlapping slices inside the edge of the tart pan; arrange another circular row in the center.

Pour the soy milk and eggs into a food processor; process until smooth. Add the flour, sugar, baking powder, and salt. Process until smooth, about 15 seconds; scrape down the sides of the bowl as necessary (the mixture will be runny). Stir in the lemon zest.

Pour this batter over the pears and spread evenly.

Bake for 15 minutes, then reduce the oven temperature to 350°F. Continue baking for about 30 minutes, or until the clafouti is lightly browned and a knife inserted in the center comes out clean.

Cool on a wire rack until warm or room temperature.

Per serving: Cal 144/Pro 4.6g/Carb 25.3g/Fat 2.7g/Chol 80mg/Sod 124mg

ADVANCE PREPARATION This dessert can be prepared early on the day it is to be served. After it has cooled, cover and keep at room temperature.

VARIATION

↘ Substitute 3/4 cup cholesterol-free egg substitute for the eggs.

caramel custard

makes 6 servings

Nonstick cooking spray

3/4 cup sugar

1 1/2 cups soy milk

1/2 cup mashed silken firm tofu

3 large eggs

1 teaspoon orange zest
(see Tip, pages 6–7)

1/2 teaspoon pure vanilla
extract

This traditional—and most elegant—French custard is baked in a caramel-coated mold; the addition of tofu adds to the creamy (and surprisingly rich) texture. Bake the dessert in advance to serve later at room temperature or chilled.

Preheat the oven to 325°F.

Heat a medium saucepan of water over medium heat.

Lightly coat six 1/2-cup custard cups with the cooking spray. Place them in a large shallow baking pan.

Put 1/2 cup of the sugar in a heavy-bottomed skillet over medium heat. Caramelize the sugar by stirring until it melts and is golden colored, about 10 minutes. Immediately (and quickly) pour about 1 tablespoon of the melted sugar into each custard cup. Tilt the cups as you pour; the sugar will harden as it cools.

Pour the soy milk and tofu into a food processor; process until smooth.

Lightly whisk the eggs in a medium mixing bowl; whisk in the remaining 1/4 cup of sugar, the orange zest, and the vanilla. Whisk in the soy milk mixture.

Pour into the prepared custard cups. Pour hot water into the baking pan until it comes about halfway up the sides of the custard cups (see Tip). Bake for about 1 hour, or until a knife inserted in the center of the custard comes out clean.

Remove the custard cups from the water and cool on a wire rack for about 1 hour.

When ready to serve, gently loosen the edges of the custard with a knife. Place a dessert plate upside down on top of a custard cup and invert the custard onto the plate. Drizzle any remaining syrup over the custard. Repeat for each serving.

Per serving: Cal 178/Pro 7g/Carb 28.2g/Fat 4.1g/Chol 107mg/Sod 65mg

ADVANCE PREPARATION This custard is best when prepared the day it is to be served. To serve chilled, after the custard has cooled, cover with plastic wrap and refrigerate for about 2 hours. If necessary, refrigerate the covered custard cups for up to 2 days. Unmold the custard just before serving chilled or at room temperature.

VARIATIONS

❧ Substitute skim milk for the soy milk.

❧ Substitute 3/4 cup cholesterol-free egg substitute for the eggs.

❧ Rather than baking in individual custard cups, use a $1^1/2$-quart baking dish. Pour all the caramelized sugar into it and swirl quickly to coat the bottom; top with all of the custard mixture. Use the *bain marie* method (see Tip) and bake for about 1 hour, or until a knife inserted in the center of the custard comes out clean.

tip

*The cooking technique of using a water bath (*bain marie *in French) consists of placing a dish containing food in a large shallow pan of warm water. This method will allow delicate custards, sauces, and mousses to cook without breaking or curdling because the food is not in direct contact with the heat source. A water bath can also be used on top of the stove to keep cooked foods warm.*

cream puffs

makes 6 servings

1/4 cup margarine

1/2 cup boiling water

1/4 teaspoon salt

1/2 cup all-purpose white or
unbleached flour (see Tip)

2 large eggs (at room
temperature)

Few creations in the world of gourmet cooking qualify both as elegant and as easy to fix as cream puffs. Fill these no-fail puffs with your choice of Chocolate Mousse Pie Filling (page 244), Chocolate-Maple Tofu Pudding (page 223), Mocha Mousse (page 227), or Lemon Mousse (page 225).

Preheat the oven to 400°F.

Line a baking sheet with foil.

Put the margarine, water, and salt into a medium nonstick saucepan. Bring the liquid to a rolling boil over high heat. (Watch closely; do not allow the water to evaporate.)

Remove the pan from the heat. (At this point, reduce the temperature to medium if using an electric stove.) Immediately add the flour all at once and stir vigorously with a wooden spoon. Return the pan to the heat and continue to cook over medium heat, stirring constantly, only until the mixture leaves the sides of the pan and forms a ball that does not separate. Remove from the heat and cool slightly, about 3 to 5 minutes.

Add the eggs, one at a time, beating vigorously with a wooden spoon after the addition of each, until the mixture is smooth and no longer "slippery."

Drop large rounded tablespoons of dough onto the prepared baking sheet (space them at least 2 inches apart).

Bake for 20 minutes, then reduce the heat to 350°F and bake for 20 minutes more. The cream puffs are done when golden brown with rigid sides.

Use a spatula to transfer the puffs to a wire rack. With a sharp knife, make a small slit in the side of each puff; allow to cool.

Once the puffs have cooled, gently slice them horizontally with a sharp knife to remove the tops; use a small knife to remove any strings of uncooked dough from the inside.

Just before serving, spoon $1/4$ to $1/3$ cup of the filling of your choice into the bottom of each puff; replace the cream puff tops.

Per cream puff (without filling): Cal 129/Pro 3.2g/Carb 8.2g/Fat 9.3g/Chol 71mg/Sod 199mg

ADVANCE PREPARATION The cream puffs can be baked early on the day they are to be served. Store, uncovered, at room temperature. It is best to serve the puffs soon after baking on humid days because the moist air will make them lose their crisp exterior and become soggy. If necessary to recrisp the puffs, place them on a baking sheet in a 400°F oven until crisp but not overbrowned. The filling can be made in advance, covered, and refrigerated; fill the cream puffs just before serving.

VARIATION

❧ Substitute butter for the margarine.

tip

All-purpose flour comes in two basic forms, bleached and unbleached; they can be used interchangeably. Store white flours at room temperature for up to 6 months.

Pies

tofu pumpkin pie

For me, nothing says "autumn" like pumpkin pie. The way it perfumes my kitchen is a preview of its perfectly mingled spices. As a finishing touch, top each serving with a dollop of Tofu Whipped Cream (page 257) or Vanilla Tofu Cream (page 256).

makes one 9-inch pie (8 servings)

For the crust

One unbaked 9-inch Whole Wheat Pastry crust (page 182) (Note: Recipe yield is 2 crusts)

For the pie filling

1 1/2 cups mashed silken firm tofu (12 ounces)

One 15-ounce can pumpkin

3/4 cup honey

1 large egg

1 teaspoon pure vanilla extract (see Tip)

2 teaspoons ground cinnamon (see Tip)

1/2 teaspoon ground nutmeg (see Tips)

1/2 teaspoon allspice (see Tip)

1/2 teaspoon ground ginger

Preheat the oven to 400°F.

Line the pie plate with the crust; do not bake.

Put the tofu, pumpkin, honey, egg, and vanilla into a food processor; process until the mixture is smooth and creamy. Add the remaining ingredients; process just long enough to blend.

Pour the filling into the unbaked crust.

Bake for about 50 minutes, or until a knife inserted in the center comes out nearly clean. (The filling will still be somewhat soft, but it will firm up as the pie cools.)

Allow the pie to cool on a wire rack; serve at room temperature.

Per serving (1/8 pie made with Whole Wheat Pastry): Cal 307/Pro 6.8g/Carb 43.5g/ Fat 11.8g/ Chol 27mg/Sod 125mg

ADVANCE PREPARATION The crust can be prepared in advance (see page 183). This pie is best when prepared the day it is to be served. Leftovers can be covered and refrigerated for up to 2 days.

VARIATIONS

➤ Use a commercially prepared frozen pie crust (available made with either white or whole wheat flour); pour the filling mixture into the frozen crust and bake as described.

❧ Omit the crust; pour the pie filling into a lightly oiled 9-inch pie plate and bake as described.

❧ Substitute $1/4$ cup cholesterol-free egg substitute or 2 egg whites for the egg.

tips

Buy pure vanilla extract rather than "imitation vanilla," made entirely from artificial flavorings that leave a bitter aftertaste. "Vanilla flavoring," which is a blend of pure and imitation vanillas, also lacks quality and flavor.

Spices, such as cinnamon, nutmeg, allspice, and cumin, are aromatic seasonings obtained from the seeds, flowers, stems, bark, and roots of various plants. Many are sold in both whole and ground forms. After grinding, spices quickly lose their aroma and flavor, so buy them in small quantities. Whole spices can be ground as needed. Store whole spices in airtight containers in a cool, dark place for up to 6 months.

Freshly grated or ground nutmeg is much more aromatic and flavorful than preground nutmeg. Whole nutmeg will keep its flavor for years stored in a tightly closed jar in your spice cabinet. Many types of nutmeg graters and grinders are available in gourmet shops.

tofu key lime pie

**makes one 9-inch pie
(8 servings)**

For the crust

One 9-inch Low-Fat Graham
Cracker Crust (page 246)

For the Key Lime Pie filling

1 1/2 cups mashed silken
firm tofu (12 ounces)

1 cup nonfat ricotta cheese

One 14-ounce can sweetened
condensed skim milk

1/2 cup freshly squeezed Key
lime juice (juice from about
8 Key limes)

1 envelope (1 tablespoon)
unflavored gelatin

garnish *(optional)* thin lime
slices

Key lime pie originated in the Florida Keys, where the small, yellowish Key limes are grown. Some supermarkets and specialty produce markets around the country stock them. If necessary, regular limes will work quite nicely in this creamy-tart dessert, and bottled Key lime juice will do in a pinch. For a striking presentation, drizzle servings with Honey-Raspberry Sauce (page 258) and garnish with thin lime slices.

Prepare the crust; set aside on a wire rack to cool.

Put the tofu, ricotta cheese, and condensed milk into a food processor; process until the mixture is smooth and creamy.

Pour the lime juice into a small saucepan and stir in the gelatin; allow to stand for about 3 to 5 minutes to soften the gelatin. Stir the mixture over low heat until the gelatin is dissolved, about 2 minutes. Stir in the tofu-ricotta cheese mixture.

Pour the filling into the completely cooled crust. Refrigerate until the filling is firm, about 2 to 3 hours, before serving.

Per serving (1/8 pie): Cal 281/Pro12.4g/Carb 44.5g/Fat 5.8g/Chol 13mg/Sod 124mg

ADVANCE PREPARATION This pie is best when prepared the day it is to be served. Leftovers can be covered and refrigerated for up to 2 days.

VARIATION

❧ Substitute Cookie Crust (page 247) for the Low-Fat Graham Cracker Crust.

❧ Rather than a crust, spread a layer of 3/4 cup crushed chocolate wafer cookies or graham crackers in the bottom of the pie plate.

Freshly squeezed citrus juice is always the most flavorful. Frozen pure juice is also acceptable. Avoid the chemical-laden and artificial-tasting reconstituted lemon and lime juices that come in bottles and plastic "lemons" and "limes."

When selecting citrus fruits for juicing, those that have a fine-textured skin and are heavy for their size are best. To squeeze more juice from citrus fruits, first bring them to room temperature, or microwave chilled fruit (pierce the fruit with a fork or knife first) for 30 seconds on high. Then roll the fruit around on a hard surface, pressing hard with the palm of your hand for a minute, to break the inner membranes. If you need only a small amount of juice, save the fruit for future use by making a deep X-shaped incision into the fruit with a paring knife. Squeeze out the juice you need, then store the fruit in a sealed plastic bag in the refrigerator.

pineapple-orange tofu-ricotta cheesecake

This do-ahead dessert is a tried-and-true crowd pleaser. For variety, substitute orange juice concentrate or pineapple juice concentrate for the mixed concentrate. For a colorful presentation, top servings with Honey-Raspberry Sauce (page 258) and fresh fruit.

makes one 9-inch pie (8 servings)

For the crust
One 9-inch Low-Fat Graham Cracker Crust (page 246)

For the cheesecake filling
1 1/2 cups mashed silken firm tofu (12 ounces)

1 cup nonfat ricotta cheese

2 tablespoons honey

1 1/2 cups pineapple-orange juice concentrate, thawed (not diluted)

1 envelope (1 tablespoon) unflavored gelatin (see Tip)

garnish *(optional)* sprigs of fresh mint, strawberries

Prepare the crust (when pressing the crust mixture into the pan, reserve about 2 tablespoons for sprinkling over the top of the pie filling as a garnish). Set aside on a wire rack to cool.

Put the tofu, ricotta cheese, and honey in a food processor; process until smooth and creamy. Set aside.

Pour the juice concentrate into a small saucepan and stir in the gelatin; allow to stand for about 3 to 5 minutes to soften the gelatin. Stir the mixture over low heat until the gelatin is dissolved, about 2 minutes. Stir in the tofu-ricotta cheese mixture.

Pour the cheesecake filling into the completely cooled crust. Sprinkle with the reserved crust mixture.

Refrigerate until the filling is firm, about 3 hours, before serving.

Per serving (1/8 pie made with Graham Cracker Crust): Cal 229/Pro 8.1g/Carb 41.6g/Fat 3.4g/Chol 5mg/Sod 119mg

ADVANCE PREPARATION This cheesecake is best when prepared the day it is to be served. Leftovers can be covered and refrigerated for up to 2 days, although the crust may become soggy.

VARIATION

Substitute Cookie Crust (page 247) for the Low-Fat Graham Cracker Crust.

↘ Rather than a crust, spread a layer of 3/4 cup crushed chocolate wafer cookies or graham crackers in the bottom of the pie plate.

tip

Unsweetened granulated gelatin can be used solidify a liquid by adding about 1 tablespoon of gelatin per 2 cups of liquid; more will result in a rubbery texture. Begin by stirring the gelatin into a cool liquid; allow it to stand for 3 to 5 minutes to soften and swell the gelatin granules. Then stir the mixture over low heat to dissolve the gelatin; be careful—if the mixture boils, the gelatin will lose its thickening abilities. Generally, allow a few hours for chilling to set the gelatin mixture and ready the dish for serving.

chocolate mousse pie

Chocolate lovers, watch out! This pie is exquisitely smooth. For Chocolate-Mint Mousse Pie, add ¹/8 teaspoon peppermint extract to the pie filling mixture when puréeing it.

makes one 9-inch pie (8 servings)

For the crust

One 9-inch Low-Fat Graham Cracker Crust (page 246)

For the pie filling

8 ounces semisweet baking chocolate (see Tips)

2 tablespoons honey

2¹/2 cups mashed silken firm tofu

garnish *(optional)* Tofu Whipped Cream (page 257), finely chopped pecans or almonds

Prepare the crust; set aside on a wire rack to cool.

Put the chocolate into a microwave-proof measuring cup; microwave at 50 percent power until melted, about 2 to 3 minutes. (Or put the chocolate in a small nonstick saucepan over low heat; stir constantly until melted.) Stir in the honey.

Put the tofu into a food processor. Add the chocolate-honey mixture; process until the mixture is completely smooth.

Pour the filling into the completely cooled crust. Refrigerate until firm, about 1 hour, before serving.

Per serving (¹/8 pie made with Graham Cracker Crust): Cal 265/Pro 7.5g/Carb 35.9g/ Fat 10.2g/Chol 0mg/Sod 114mg

ADVANCE PREPARATION This pie is best when prepared the day it is to be served; cover and refrigerate. Leftovers will keep for up to 2 days.

VARIATIONS

❧ Substitute Cookie Crust (page 247) for the Low-Fat Graham Cracker Crust.

❧ Rather than a crust, spread a layer of ³/4 cup crushed chocolate wafer cookies or graham crackers in the bottom of the pie plate.

❧ Omit the crust; chill and serve the chocolate mousse pie filling in individual dessert cups.

❧ Substitute 8 ounces semisweet chocolate chips for the baking chocolate.

Store chocolate, tightly wrapped, in a cool (60°to 70°F) dry place, where it will keep for years. If chocolate partially melts at warmer temperatures, it will develop streaks and blotches. If stored in a damp place, chocolate may form sugar crystals on the surface. In both cases the chocolate can still be used.

Cocoa powder and unsweetened baking chocolate are nondairy products; semisweet baking chocolate and semisweet chocolate chips contain milk solids.

low-fat graham cracker crust

makes one 9-inch crust

Nonstick cooking spray

2 tablespoons sugar

1 tablespoon margarine, melted

1 large egg white

1¼ cups graham cracker crumbs (about 11 crackers)

Incorporating an egg white allows you to use less margarine in this nontraditional crumb crust.

Preheat the oven to 325°F.

Lightly coat a 9-inch pie plate with cooking spray.

Put the sugar, margarine, and egg white into a food processor; process until the margarine is evenly distributed. Add the graham cracker crumbs and process again, using an on-off motion, until the mixture is crumbly.

Use the back of a spoon to press the mixture firmly and evenly onto the bottom and sides of a 9-inch plate.

Bake until the crust is lightly browned and slightly firm, about 15 minutes. Cool completely on a wire rack before filling.

Per serving (¹/8 unfilled crust): Cal 63/Pro 1.1g/Carb 9.9g/Fat 2.1g/Chol 0mg/ Sod 69mg

ADVANCE PREPARATION This crust is best when prepared the day it is to be filled and served.

VARIATIONS

❧ Substitute 2 tablespoons cholesterol-free egg substitute for the egg white.

❧ Add a dash of ground cinnamon.

❧ For a traditional graham cracker crust, omit the egg white and use 6 tablespoons melted margarine.

Per serving (¹/8 unfilled crust): Cal 126/Pro 0.8g/Carb 10g/Fat 9.2g/Chol 0mg/Sod 144mg

cookie crust

This crunchy cookielike dessert crust, made from ingredients you are likely to have on hand, is an alternative to the Low-Fat Graham Cracker Crust for Chocolate Mousse Pie (page 244), Pineapple-Orange Tofu-Ricotta Cheesecake (page 242), and Tofu Key Lime Pie (page 240). If you wish, when pressing the crust into the pan, reserve about 1/4 cup of the crumbly mixture to sprinkle over the top of the pie.

makes one 9-inch crust

1/4 cup margarine

1/3 cup sugar

1 large egg yolk

1 cup whole wheat flour

Preheat the oven to 400°F.

Put the margarine into a food processor; process until creamy. Add the sugar and egg yolk; process until evenly incorporated. Add the flour; process until the mixture is crumbly.

Use the back of a spoon to press the mixture firmly and evenly onto the bottom and sides of a 9-inch pie plate.

Bake for about 12 minutes, or until the crust is lightly browned on the edges and slightly firmed. (The crust will become firmer as it cools.) Cool completely on a wire rack before filling.

Per serving (1/8 unfilled crust): Cal 145/Pro 2.5g/Carb 19g/Fat 6.6g/Chol 27mg/Sod 68mg

ADVANCE PREPARATION This crust is best when prepared the day it is to be used.

VARIATIONS

❯ Substitute butter for the margarine.

❯ Substitute 2 tablespoons cholesterol-free egg substitute for the egg yolk.

❯ Add 1/4 cup chopped nuts, such as walnuts or pecans, when incorporating the flour.

Cooked Desserts

pineapple tapioca pudding

makes 8 servings

1/2 cup small pearl tapioca
    (see Tip)

3 cups skim milk

1/4 teaspoon salt

1/2 cup sugar

2 large eggs

1 cup mashed silken firm tofu

1/4 cup pineapple juice
    concentrate, thawed
    (not diluted)

1 teaspoon pure vanilla extract

garnish *(optional)* pineapple
chunks

I have fond childhood memories of tapioca pudding, but Mom never made it with tofu! Instant (or quick-cooking) tapioca has a fairly smooth texture when cooked; I prefer small pearl tapioca, which makes a pudding with more texture yet still is quick to prepare.

Combine the tapioca, milk, and salt in a medium nonstick saucepan. Cook over medium-high heat, stirring constantly, until the mixture comes to a boil. Reduce the heat to low and cook for 5 minutes, stirring constantly. Remove from the heat; stir in the sugar.

Lightly beat the eggs in a medium bowl. Stir a few spoonfuls of the hot tapioca mixture into the eggs, then stir the eggs into the saucepan. Bring to a boil over medium heat, stirring constantly and scraping the sides frequently. Reduce the heat to low; cook, stirring constantly, until the pudding thickens, about 3 minutes. Remove from the heat and cool for about 15 minutes. (The tapioca pudding will continue to thicken as it cools.)

Meanwhile, put the tofu, juice concentrate, and vanilla into a food processor; process until the mixture is smooth and creamy. Fold into the cooled pudding.

Pour the pudding into a medium bowl or individual dessert cups. Serve warm or at room temperature, or cover and refrigerate.

Per serving: Cal 223/Pro 9.1g/Carb 39.8g/Fat 3g/Chol 73mg/Sod 187mg

ADVANCE PREPARATION Covered and refrigerated, this pudding will keep for up to 3 days.

VARIATIONS

❧ Substitute soy milk for the skim milk (some brands will make the completed pudding a butterscotch color).

❧ Substitute $1/2$ cup cholesterol-free egg substitute for the eggs.

tip

Tapioca comes from the root of the cassava plant. It is available in a variety of forms including granules, flakes, pellets (called pearl tapioca), and flour. Pearl tapioca, used for pudding, is available in regular or instant forms. (Large pearl tapioca must be soaked for several hours before it can be used. Small pearl tapioca and instant, or quick-cooking, tapioca cook in about 5 minutes.) If stored in a cool, dark place, all types of tapioca will keep indefinitely.

vanilla poached pears with orange-honey sauce

makes 4 servings

For the pears

2 tablespoons pure vanilla extract

2 tablespoons honey

4 pears (at room temperature), peeled and cored (see Tip)

For the Orange-Honey Sauce

1/2 cup mashed silken firm tofu

3 tablespoons freshly squeezed orange juice

2 tablespoons honey

1/4 teaspoon pure vanilla extract

1/4 teaspoon grated orange rind (see Tip, pages 6–7)

garnish (optional) shaved semisweet chocolate or sweetened cocoa powder, fresh mint leaves

Poached pears are pretty and delicious on their own, but dress them up and they're truly memorable. This sweetened tofu sauce and a garnish of chocolate will do the trick. As a variation, in place of the Orange-Honey Sauce, top the pears with Vanilla Tofu Cream (page 256).

Fill a Dutch oven or large saucepan halfway with water; bring to a boil over high heat. Stir in the vanilla and honey, then add the pears. When the water returns to a boil, reduce the heat to medium-high; cook the pears until fork-tender but not soft, about 10 minutes. Use a slotted spoon to gently transfer them to a plate. Discard the poaching liquid.

While the pears are cooking, prepare the sauce. Combine the tofu, orange juice, honey, and vanilla in a food processor; process until the mixture is smooth and creamy. Stir in the orange rind.

To serve, stand each pear upright in a dessert bowl. Drizzle with the Orange-Honey Sauce and garnish.

Per serving: Cal 169/Pro 2.8g/Carb 36g/Fat 1.5g/Chol 0mg/Sod 11mg

ADVANCE PREPARATION To serve warm, poach the pears and serve immediately. To serve chilled, poach the pears in advance; allow to cool, then cover and refrigerate for 4 to 6 hours. The sauce can be made up to 1 day in advance; cover and refrigerate. Serve the pears and sauce chilled or bring to room temperature.

Buy pears when they are firm but not rock hard; pears develop a finer flavor and smoother texture when ripened off the tree. Ripen them on your kitchen counter in a paper bag; this may require 2 to 7 days. Once ripe, they will keep for 3 to 5 days in the refrigerator. Most pears do not show ripeness with a color change because they ripen from the inside out; the best indicator of ripeness is the stem ends yielding slightly to pressure. Somewhat underripe pears are best for cooking and baking. It is not always necessary to peel pears before using, but if they are peeled, they should be dipped in acidulated water (water with a small amount of lemon, lime, or orange juice added) to prevent the flesh from browning.

tofu cream-filled crêpes with strawberry purée

With Wheat Germ Crêpes made in advance, this light and not-too-sweet dessert can be ready to eat in less than 5 minutes. Keep this idea in mind for brunch or a quick snack— or for last-minute entertaining.

makes 4 servings

For the crêpes
8 Wheat Germ Crêpes
  (page 254)

For the Tofu Cream Filling
1 cup mashed silken firm tofu

1 cup nonfat ricotta cheese

3 tablespoons honey

1 tablespoon freshly squeezed
  orange juice

1 teaspoon grated orange rind
  (see Tip, pages 6–7)

Dash of ground cinnamon

For the Strawberry Purée
2 cups sliced strawberries
  (see Tip)

1 tablespoon freshly squeezed
  orange juice

1 tablespoon honey, or to taste

Dash of ground nutmeg

garnish (optional) strawberry
fans (see Tips), toasted sliced
almonds (see Tip, page 50),
sprigs of fresh mint

If made in advance, remove the crêpes from the refrigerator or freezer; bring to room temperature.

Put all the filling ingredients into a food processor; process until smooth and creamy.

To prepare the strawberry purée, put all the ingredients into a food processor; process until smooth.

To assemble the crêpes, place a crêpe, "less cooked" side up, on a cutting board. Spread about 2 tablespoons of the filling mixture on the center third; fold over the sides of the crêpe to cover the filling, overlapping the edges at the center. Place the crêpe on a dessert plate, seam side down. Repeat with the remaining crêpes, allowing 2 crêpes per serving.

Drizzle the Strawberry Purée in a horizontal stripe across the crêpes, garnish, and serve immediately.

Per serving (2 crêpes with filling and sauce): Cal 272/Pro 15.5g/Carb 42g/Fat 4.7g/Chol 82mg/Sod 129mg

ADVANCE PREPARATION Prepare the crêpes in advance and freeze or refrigerate following the recipe instructions. The Tofu Cream Filling and Strawberry Purée can be prepared early on the day they are to be served; cover and refrigerate. Assemble the crêpes just before serving.

VARIATIONS

❧ Along with the Tofu Cream Filling, roll fruit (such as chopped peaches, chopped kiwi, or blueberries) into the crêpes.

❧ Substitute Honey-Raspberry Sauce (page 258) for the Strawberry Purée.

tips

Do not wash strawberries or remove their caps until ready to use. Strawberries do not ripen after they are picked; store them in a moisture-proof container in the refrigerator for 2 to 3 days.

To make a strawberry fan, choose a firm red, ripe strawberry. Place the berry, hull down, on a cutting board. Make parallel cuts in the berry from the bottom nearly to the leaves, taking care not to slice all the way through. (The number of cuts will depend on the size of the berry; for the best effect, make the slices thin.) Grasp the strawberry gently and twist so that the slices fan out. The hull can be left intact or removed and replaced with a sprig of fresh mint.

wheat germ crêpes

makes about 12 crêpes

1 cup skim milk

2 large eggs

1/2 cup all-purpose white or unbleached flour

1/4 cup toasted wheat germ (see Tip, page 25)

1/2 teaspoon olive oil

Nonstick cooking spray

Crêpes can become wrappers for a wide variety of foods; this versatility inspires recipes for both entrées and desserts. Traditionally, crêpes are made from white flour, but my version also includes toasted wheat germ, which lends a nutty flavor and pleasing texture.

If you're a beginner at making crêpes, the procedure may appear to be lengthy, but it is really quite simple. Don't be discouraged: my experience is that the first crêpe rarely is usable. It serves the purpose of absorbing the excess oil from the pan and serves as a test for finding the best stove temperature setting.

Put the milk, eggs, flour, wheat germ, and olive oil into the bowl of a food processor; process for 30 seconds. Scrape the sides of the container; process for an additional 30 seconds. Pour the batter into a bowl; cover and refrigerate for 1 to 2 hours. The thin batter will thicken as it stands (see Tip).

When you are ready to prepare the crêpes, spread a clean lightweight kitchen towel on your counter. Lightly coat a crêpe pan with cooking spray. Heat the pan over medium to medium-high heat until hot but not smoking. (The pan should be hot enough so the crêpe batter begins to cook immediately when it hits the pan; the stove temperature may need adjusting during the procedure.)

Remove the pan from the heat. Use a 1/4 cup measuring cup or small ladle to pour a scant 1/4 cup of batter into the middle of the pan (this quantity is ideal for a standard 7-inch crêpe pan—adjust if your pan size differs). Quickly rotate the pan with a turn of the wrist so that the batter covers the bottom in a thin film (with too much batter, the crêpe will be thick; with too little, it will have holes). Tilt the pan to pour the excess batter back into the bowl. Return the pan to the heat and cook the crêpe until it is lightly browned and still pliable, about 30 seconds.

When the edges of the crêpe begin to darken and pull away from the pan, lift the crêpe with a spatula, flip, and lightly brown the other side for about 30 seconds (this side is usually lighter and spotty brown; it is the side on which the filling will be placed). Remove the crêpe from the pan, turning it out onto the towel to cool. (If you prefer, cook only 1 side of the crêpe; remove it from the pan after the first side is cooked. Cool on the towel, cooked side down.)

Repeat the procedure with the remaining batter. For the best results, whisk or stir the batter before making each crêpe. The pan will need to be oiled for only every third or fourth crêpe, possibly less, depending upon your pan.

To serve, spread the filling of your choice in the center third (of the less cooked or uncooked side) of each crêpe and roll the two edges toward the center to cover the filling. Place the crêpes, seam sides down, on serving plates.

One crêpe: Cal 49/Pro 2.9g/Carb 6.2g/Fat 1.4g/Chol 36mg/Sod 21mg

ADVANCE PREPARATION After making the crêpes, allow them to cool. For storing, stack them between sheets of waxed paper to prevent sticking. The crêpes will keep for 1 day in a tightly closed plastic bag in the refrigerator. Bring to room temperature before using. For longer storage, wrap the stack of crêpes and waxed paper in aluminum foil and freeze for up to 2 months. To thaw, separate the desired number of crêpes from the wrapping; let stand at room temperature for 10 to 15 minutes, or thaw in the microwave for about 15 seconds.

VARIATION

- Substitute 1/2 cup cholesterol-free egg substitute for the eggs.

tip

Refrigerating crêpe batter allows the flour particles to swell and soften, so that the crêpes will be light in texture and smoother.

Dessert Toppings

vanilla tofu cream

Use this nondairy alternative to whipped cream as a topping for Tofu Pumpkin Pie (page 238), Spiced Pumpkin Bread Pudding (page 231), and Mocha Mousse (page 227). Or drizzle it over Vanilla Poached Pears (page 250).

makes 1¹/2 cups

1 cup mashed silken firm tofu

¹/4 cup honey

1 tablespoon freshly squeezed lemon juice

1 tablespoon pure vanilla extract

Dash of salt

¹/2 cup soy milk

1 tablespoon arrowroot powder (see Tip)

Put the tofu, honey, lemon juice, vanilla, and salt into a food processor; process until smooth and creamy. Set aside.

In a medium saucepan, stir together the soy milk and arrow-root until smooth; cook over medium heat, stirring constantly, until the liquid thickens, about 3 minutes.

Add the soy milk mixture to the food processor; process until the mixture is smooth.

Refrigerate in a covered container for at least 1 hour before serving.

Per tablespoon: Cal 23/Pro 0.9g/Carb 3.9g/Fat 0.4g/Chol 0mg/Sod 11mg

ADVANCE PREPARATION Covered and refrigerated, this topping will keep for up to 3 days.

tip

Arrowroot is the ground root of a tropical tuber. Used as a thickener for puddings, sauces, and other cooked foods, it is tasteless and becomes clear when cooked. Mix it with a cold liquid before adding to hot mixtures. In recipes calling for cornstarch, arrowroot can be substituted measure for measure. The appearance of arrowroot-thickened sauces is slightly glossier than those made with cornstarch.

tofu whipped cream

This nondairy topping, with its hint of peanut flavor, adds the perfect finishing touch for Tofu Pumpkin Pie (page 238) or Chocolate-Maple Tofu Pudding (page 223).

(page 238)

Put all the ingredients into a food processor; process until smooth and creamy.

Refrigerate in a covered container for at least 1 hour before serving.

Per tablespoon: Cal 25/Pro 1.5g/Carb 1.5g/Fat 1.4g/Chol 0mg/Sod 15mg

ADVANCE PREPARATION Covered and refrigerated, this topping will keep for up to 3 days.

makes 1 cup

1 cup mashed silken firm tofu

2 tablespoons smooth peanut butter

2 teaspoons honey (see Tip, page 258)

1/2 teaspoon pure vanilla extract

honey-raspberry sauce v

Because I like having it on hand, I often double the recipe for this delectable nonfat fruit sauce, which can be used warm, at room temperature, or chilled. Drizzle it over Tofu Cream-Filled Crêpes (page 252) or Tofu-Ricotta-Topped Peach Halves (page 228), or spread it on a dessert plate to serve under slices of Pineapple-Orange Tofu-Ricotta Cheesecake (page 242). To add elegance to a simple dessert, use it as a topping for frozen yogurt, ice cream, or fresh fruit. For break-fast or brunch, serve it with Tofu-Nut Pancakes (page 218).

makes 1 cup

One 10-ounce package lightly sweetened frozen raspberries, thawed

2 tablespoons honey (see Tip)

1/4 cup cold water

1 tablespoon cornstarch

Stir together the raspberries with their sauce and honey in a small nonstick saucepan. Cook over low heat, stirring constantly, until the mixture is just about to boil. Remove from the heat.

Stir together the water and cornstarch in a small bowl until smooth. Add to the raspberry-honey mixture. Cook over low heat, stirring constantly, until the mixture is thickened, smooth, and clear, about 5 minutes.

Pour the mixture into a coarse strainer over a bowl; stir with a wooden spoon and press the sauce through the strainer to catch the seeds. Discard the seeds.

Per 1/4 cup: Cal 119/Pro 0.5g/Carb 28.9g/Fat 0.1g/Chol 0mg/Sod 2mg

ADVANCE PREPARATION Covered and refrigerated, this sauce will keep for up to 4 days. Since it thickens while standing, stir in water as needed.

tip

Store honey at room temperature. If it crystallizes, stand the opened jar in hot water for 10 to 15 minutes to dissolve the crystals; or micro-wave the opened jar of honey for about 15 to 30 seconds, depending on the amount.

Appendix

RECIPES LISTED BY SOY FOOD CATEGORIES

Whole Soybeans

Appetizers

Roasted Red Pepper Hummus
Spinach-Bean Dip
Soybean-Salsa Dip
Soybean Hummus
Roasted Soybeans
Stuffed Mushrooms

Soups

Soybean Gazpacho
Spicy Soybean Soup
Potage Mentonnaise
Soybean Chili
Tuscan Soybean Soup

Salads

Soybean Tabbouleh
Pepper-Bean Pasta Salad with Italian Dressing
Two-Bean Salad in Walnut Vinaigrette
Warm Soybean and Sweet Red Pepper Salad
    with Basil-Sherry Vinaigrette

Entrées

Soybeans Bourguignonne
Soybean-Mushroom Risotto
Rotini with Parsley-Nut Pesto
Bell Pepper–Soybean Toss with Pasta

Romaine Spring Rolls with
    Five-Spice Soybeans
Huevos Rancheros
Roasted Vegetable Pitas
Bruschetta
Spicy Soybean Patties
Vegetable Tartlets with
    Herbed Tomato Sauce
    (variation)
Soybean Confetti Pie with
    Cornmeal Crust
Pepper-Bean Quesadillas
Soybean Pita Pizzas
Zucchini with Herbed
    Tomato-Soybean
    Stuffing
Caribbean Squash and
    Soybean Casserole
Vegetarian Pastitsio
Vegetable-Soybean Loaf

Sweet Beans

Appetizers

Sweet Bean–Corn Salsa

Salads

Riso–Sweet Bean Salad with
    Sun-Dried
    Tomato–Basil
    Vinaigrette
Marinated French Herb Bean
    Salad
Sweet Beans and Corn in
    Sesame-Soy Dressing
Tortilla-Salsa Salad with
    Roasted Sweet
    Red Pepper Dressing

Entrées

Vegetable Tartlets with
    Herbed Tomato Sauce
    (variation)
Sweet Bean Stir-Fry with
    Hoisin-Orange Sauce

Tofu

Appetizers

Mushroom-Almond Spread
Sun-Dried Tomato–Tofu
    Spread
Tofu-Chèvre Spread
Tofu-Basil Pesto
Tofu Guacamole
Hoisin Peanut Sauce
Parmesan-Peppercorn Dip
Peanut Chili Dip
Roasted Garlic-Tofu
    Spread
Tofu Baba Ghanoush
Green Goddess Dip
Tofu Sour Cream
Fruit Dip
Batter-Dipped Tofu with
    Ginger Sauce
California Rolls

Soups

Roasted Red Bell
    Pepper Soup
Beet Soup
Curried Sweet Potato Soup
Creamy Tomato-Basil Soup
Creamy Acorn Squash Soup
Chinese Noodle Soup

Salads

Chinese Tofu Salad
    with Sesame-Ginger
    Dressing
Lemon Caesar Salad
Romaine Lettuce Salad with
    Blue Cheese Dressing
Tofu Pesto-Rice Salad
Couscous Salad with
    Lemon-Cinnamon
    Vinaigrette
Thai Noodle Salad with
    Tofu Teriyaki
Greek Tofu Salad
Tofu–Chèvre-Stuffed Roasted
    Red Bell Peppers
    with Shallot and Caper
    Dressing
Tomato Slices with Creamy
    Avocado Dressing
Dijon Potato Salad
Orange-Caraway Coleslaw
Tofu "Egg Salad"
Tortilla-Salsa Salad with
    Roasted Sweet Red
    Pepper Dressing
Maple-Walnut Apple Salad

Entrées and Accompaniments

Tofu and Portobello
    Mushrooms Marsala
Tofu with Chinese
    Tahini Sauce
Tofu and Vegetable Curry
Tofu-Mushroom Stroganoff
Tofu and Fruit in Mango
    Chutney Sauce

Tofu Newburg
Vegetable Medley with
    Hoisin Peanut Sauce
Vegetable Stir-Fry with
    Ginger Sauce
Spicy Cashew Stir-Fry
Sweet-and-Sour Tofu
Tofu Fried Rice
Penne with Cremini
    Mushrooms and
    Tomato-Tofu Pesto
Spicy Asian Peanut Pasta
Mostaccioli and Plum
    Tomatoes with Tofu-
    Basil Pesto
Penne Rigate with Parmesan-
    Peppercorn Sauce
Curried Acorn Squash Ragout
Mu Shu Tofu
Garden Frittata
Scrambled Tofu
Tofu Tacos
Grilled Tofu-Vegetable Towers
    with Parmesan
    Vinaigrette
Tofu Teriyaki
Curried Tofu-Carrot Sloppy
    Joes (variation)
Tempeh-Rice Wraps with
    Hoisin Peanut Sauce
Rice Paper Spring Rolls
Vegetable Tartlets with
    Herbed Tomato Sauce
Asparagus-Mushroom Quiche
Chili Custard Pie
Tofu Tostada
Soybean Pita Pizzas
    (variation)

Bell Peppers Stuffed
    with Herbed Tofu
    and Rice
Stuffed Acorn Squash
Spinach and Leek Ring
Garlic Mashed Potatoes
Curried Tofu en Papillote
Rosemary-Parmesan
    Potato Bake
Herbed Twice-Baked
    Potatoes
Tofu Stuffed Shells with
    Tomato-Basil Sauce
Tofu-Spinach Lasagna
Tofu-Walnut Loaf
Tofu-Nut Pancakes
Noodle Pudding

Desserts

Chocolate-Maple Tofu
    Pudding
Gingered Banana Parfaits
Lemon Mousse
Tofu Tiramisu
Mocha Mousse
Tofu-Ricotta-Topped
    Peach Halves
Frozen Strawberry-Banana
    Dessert
Tofu Pumpkin Pie
Tofu Key Lime Pie
Pineapple-Orange
    Tofu-Ricotta
    Cheesecake
Chocolate Mousse Pie
Pineapple Tapioca Pudding
Vanilla Poached Pears with
    Orange-Honey Sauce

Tofu Cream-Filled Crêpes
    with Strawberry Purée
Spiced Pumpkin Bread
    Pudding
Caramel Custard
Cranberry-Rice Pudding
Vanilla Tofu Cream
Tofu Whipped Cream

Frozen and Thawed Tofu

Entrées

Cabbage and Noodles with
    Tofu
Scrambled Tofu (variation)
Tofu Teriyaki (variation)
Sherried Tofu Steaks
Sherried Tofu–Roasted
    Eggplant Sandwiches
Curried Tofu-Carrot
    Sloppy Joes
Broccoli Burritos (variation)
Bell Peppers Stuffed with
    Herbed Tofu and Rice
Tofu Stuffed Shells with
    Tomato-Basil Sauce
    (variation)
Tofu-Spinach Lasagna
Scrambled Tofu (variation)
Bell Peppers Stuffed with
    Herbed Tofu and Rice
    (variation)
Tofu Stuffed Shells with
    Tomato-Basil Sauce
    (variation)
Tofu-Spinach Lasagna
    (variation)

Pressed Tofu

Appetizer

Batter-Dipped Tofu with
Ginger Sauce (variation)

Salad

Thai Noodle Salad with Tofu
Teriyaki (variation)

Entrées

Tofu and Portobello
Mushrooms Marsala
(variation)
Tofu with Chinese Tahini
Sauce (variation)
Tofu and Vegetable Curry
(variation)
Vegetable Stir-Fry with
Ginger Sauce (variation)
Spicy Cashew Stir-Fry (varia-
tion)
Grilled Tofu-Vegetable
Towers with Parmesan
Vinaigrette (variation)
Tofu Teriyaki (variation)

Sherried Tofu Steaks
(variation)
Sherried Tofu–Roasted
Eggplant Sandwiches
(variation)
Tofu Tostada (variation)

Tempeh

Salads

Wild Rice and Apricot Salad
with Marinated Tempeh
Tempeh–Green Bean Salad
with Creamy Peanut-
Chutney Dressing
Tempeh Stir-Fry Salad with
Gingered Plum
Vinaigrette

Entrées

Tofu and Portobello
Mushrooms Marsala
(variation)
Tempeh Strips and Broccoli
with Ancho Chili
Sauce

Tempeh with Spicy
Peanut Sauce
Tempeh with Black
Bean–Tomato Sauce
Tempeh Paella
Italian Tempeh, Vegetable,
and Rice Skillet
Udon Noodles with Tempeh
and Hijiki
Spaghetti with Tempeh in
Mexican Chili Sauce
Tempeh Reuben
Tempeh-Yam Sandwiches
Tempeh-Rice Wraps with
Hoisin Peanut Sauce

Texturized Vegetable Protein (TVP)

Soup

Soybean Chili (variation)

Entrées

Chili-Rice Skillet
Veggie Burgers
Broccoli Burritos

Soy Milk

Soups

Chilled Fresh Tomato Bisque
Curried Corn and Pepper
  Chowder
Fresh Pea Soup
Carrot-Cashew Soup

Entrées and
Accompaniments

Garlic Mashed Potatoes
Tofu Newburg
Cremini Mushroom Sauce

Desserts

Strawberry-Banana Smoothie
Pineapple Tapioca Pudding
  (variation)
Spiced Pumpkin Bread
  Pudding
Caramel Custard
Cranberry-Rice Pudding
Pear Clafouti
Vanilla Tofu Cream

Index

Acorn squash
    ragout, curried, 145
    soup, creamy, 46
    stuffed, 193
Advance preparation, xlvi–xlvii
Allergies, xli
Ancho Chili Sauce, 111
Appetite, color and, 145
Appetizers, 1–31
    Baked Tortilla Chips, 22
    Batter-Dipped Tofu with
      Ginger Sauce, 24–25
    California Rolls, 28–30
    Fruit Dip, 14
    Ginger Sauce, 26
    Green Goddess Dip, 16
    Hoisin Peanut Sauce, 9
    Mushroom-Almond Spread, 3
    Parmesan-Peppercorn Dip, 10
    Peanut Chili Dip, 11
    Pita Crisps, 21
    Roasted Garlic-Tofu Spread, 12
    Roasted Red Pepper Hummus, 17
    Roasted Soybeans, 31
    Soybean Hummus, 20
    Soybean-Salsa Dip, 19
    Spinach-Bean Dip, 18
    Stuffed Mushrooms, 27
    Sun-Dried Tomato–Tofu Spread, 4
    Sweet Bean–Corn Salsa, 23
    Tofu Baba Ghanoush, 13
    Tofu-Basil Pesto, 6
    Tofu-Chèvre Spread, 5
    Tofu Guacamole, 8
    Tofu Sour Cream, 15
Apples, choosing, 93
Apple-walnut salad with maple dressing, 93
Apricots, dried, 67
Arborio rice, 131
Arrowroot, 256
Arugula, 95
Asparagus, 181
Asparagus-Mushroom Quiche, 180–81
Avocado dressing, creamy, 86
Avocados, 8

Baba ghanoush, tofu, 13
Bain marie, 235
Baked desserts
    Caramel Custard, 234–35
    Cranberry-Rice Pudding, 232
    Cream Puffs, 236–37

Pear Clafouti, 233
Spiced Pumpkin Bread Pudding, 231
Baked pasta dishes
Tofu-Spinach Lasagna, 208–9
Tofu Stuffed Shells with Tomato-Basil
Sauce, 206–7
Vegetarian Pastitsio, 210–11
Baked Tortilla Chips, 22
Baked vegetable dishes
Caribbean Squash and Soybean
Casserole, 203
Curried Tofu en Papillote, 204
Garlic Mashed Potatoes, 200
Herbed Twice-Baked Potatoes, 202
Rosemary-Parmesan Potato Bake, 201
Spinach and Leek Ring, 198–99
Baking sheets, selecting, 22
Balsamic vinegar, 18
-Garlic Vinaigrette, 82
Vinaigrette, 94–95
Banana
parfaits, gingered, 224
storing, 229
-strawberry, frozen dessert, 230
-strawberry, smoothie, 229
Basil pesto with tofu, 6
Basmati rice, 114
Batter-Dipped Tofu with Ginger Sauce, 24–25
Bean curd. See Tofu
Bean salad in walnut vinaigrette, 77
Beano, xxvii
Beet Soup, 37
Bell peppers, 195
dressing, 92
roasting, 92
soup, 36
soybean toss with pasta, 142–43
stuffed with herbed tofu and rice, 194–95
tofu-chèvre stuffed, 84
Black beans, 118
Black Bean–Tomato Sauce, 118
Blanching, 63
Blue Cheese Dressing, 61
Bok choy, 123
Bone density, soy and, xviii–xix
Bread
crumbs, 197
pudding, spiced pumpkin, 231
selecting, 65
slicing, 163
Broccoli, 128
burritos, 174–75
-tempeh with ancho chili sauce, 110
Brunches
Noodle Pudding, 219
Tofu-Nut Pancakes, 218

Bruschetta, 163
Bulgur wheat, 68
Burgers
Spicy Soybean Patties, 171
Veggie Burgers, 170
Burritos, broccoli, 174–75

Cabbage, 139
Cabbage and Noodles with Tofu, 144
Caesar salad with lemon, 64
California Rolls, 28–30
Cancer, soy and, xv–xvii
Canned soybeans, xxiii
Capers, 85
Caramel Custard, 234–35
Caraway seeds, 88
Caribbean Squash and Soybean Casserole, 203
Carrot-Cashew Soup, 56
Carrots, 56
Carver, George Washington, xxii
Cashews, 126
Celery seeds, 93
Cellophane noodles, 73
Cheese
creamy, 4
storing, 168
Cheesecake, pineapple-orange tofu-ricotta,
232–43
Chili, 54–55
custard pie, 179
dried, 111
paste, 9
peppers, 137
powder, 11
-rice skillet, 132
Chilled soup
Beet Soup, 37
Chilled Fresh Tomato Bisque, 40
Roasted Red Bell Pepper Soup, 36
Soybean Gazpacho, 38
Chinese
cabbage, 63
five-spice powder, 149
Noodle Soup, 52–53
plum sauce, 97
Tahini Sauce, 103
tofu, xxx
Tofu Salad with Sesame-Ginger Dressing,
62–63
Wheat-Flour Noodles with Sesame-Pepper
Dressing, 162
Chives, 36
Chocolate
Maple Tofu Pudding, 223
Mousse Pie, 244
storing, 245

Cholesterol, soy and, xvii–xviii
Chunky soups
Carrot-Cashew Soup, 56
Chinese Noodle Soup, 52–53
Potage Mentonnaise, 51
Soybean Chili, 54–55
Tuscan Soybean Soup, 57
Chutney, 83
Cilantro, 45
Cinnamon, 227
Citrus fruits and juice, 241
Clafouti, pear, 233
Cocoa powder, 227, 245
Coconut milk, 107
Coleslaw, orange-caraway, 88
Color, appetite and, 145
Complete Book of Dressings, The (Mitchell), 59
Cookie Crust, 247
Corn, 42
pepper chowder with, curried, 42
white shoepeg, 23
Cornmeal, 185
Cornstarch, 26
Couscous, 71
Couscous Salad with Lemon-Cinnamon
Vinaigrette, 70
Cranberries, 232
Cranberry-Rice Pudding, 232
Cream Puffs, 236–37
Creamy
Acorn Squash Soup, 46
Avocado Dressing, 86
Dijon Dressing, 87
Peanut-Chutney Dressing, 83
Tomato-Basil Soup, 48
Cremini Mushroom Sauce, 216
Crêpes, 252–55
Croutons, herbed-garlic, 65
Crystallized ginger, 224
Cumin, 40
Currants, 205
Curried
Acorn Squash Ragout, 145
Corn and Pepper Chowder, 42
Sweet Potato Soup, 50
Tofu-Carrot Sloppy Joes, 169–70
Tofu en Papillote, 204
vegetable with tofu, 106–7
Curry powder, 46
Custard, caramel, 234–35

Dairy analogs, xl–xli
Desserts, 220–58
Caramel Custard, 234–35
Chocolate-Maple Tofu Pudding, 223
Chocolate Mousse Pie, 244

Desserts *(cont.)*
  Cookie Crust, 247
  Cranberry-Rice Pudding, 232
  Cream Puffs, 236–37
  Frozen Strawberry-Banana
    Dessert, 230
  Gingered Banana Parfaits, 224
  Honey-Raspberry Sauce, 258
  Lemon Mousse, 225
  Low-Fat Graham Cracker Crust, 246
  Mocha Mousse, 227
  Pear Clafouti, 233
  Pineapple-Orange Tofu-Ricotta
    Cheesecake, 242–43
  Pineapple Tapioca Pudding, 248–49
  Spiced Pumpkin Bread Pudding, 231
  Strawberry-Banana Smoothie, 229
  Tofu Cream-Filled Crêpes with Strawberry
    Purée, 252–53
  Tofu Key Lime Pie, 240
  Tofu Pumpkin Pie, 238–39
  Tofu-Ricotta–Topped Peach Halves, 228
  Tofu Tiramisu, 226
  Tofu Whipped Cream, 257
  Vanilla Poached Pears with Orange-Honey
    Sauce, 250
  Vanilla Tofu Cream, 256
  Wheat Germ Crêpes, 254–55
Diabetes, soy and, xix–xx
Diet for a Small Planet (Lappé), xiv
Dijon mustard, 89
Dijon Potato Salad, 87
Dips. *See* Spreads and dips
Dressing
  Balsamic-Garlic Vinaigrette, 82
  Balsamic Vinaigrette, 94–95
  Blue Cheese, 61
  Creamy Avocado, 86
  Creamy Dijon, 87
  Creamy Peanut-Chutney, 83
  French Herb, 77
  Gingered Plum Vinaigrette, 96
  Italian, 76
  Lemon-Cinnamon Vinaigrette, 70
  Lemon-Mint, 68
  Maple Dressing, 93
  Orange-Caraway Dressing, 88
  Parmesan, 64
  Parmesan Vinaigrette, 156
  Peanut-Ginger Dressing, 72–73
  Roasted Sweet Red Pepper, 92
  Sesame-Ginger, 62–63
  Sesame-Orange Vinaigrette, 66–67
  Sesame-Pepper, 162
  Sesame-Soy, 80
  Shallot and Caper, 84

Sun-Dried Tomato–Basil Vinaigrette,
  74–75
  Walnut Vinaigrette, 77
Dried
  beans, cooking procedure for, xxiv–xxvi
  tomatoes, 132

Edamame (sweet beans), xxvi–xxvi
Egg dishes, testing for doneness, 179
Egg noodles, 113
Eggplant, 157
  baba ghanoush, 13
  tofu sandwiches, sherried, 164–65
Eggs
  handling, 153
  hard cooking, 64
  Garden Frittata, 150–51
  Huevos Rancheros, 152–53
Entrées, 98–219
  baked pasta dishes, 206–11
  baked vegetable dishes, 198–205
  brunch, 218–19
  burgers, 170–72
  loaves with sauces, 212–17
  pies, tartlets & pita and tortilla crusts,
    179–92
  rice dishes, 127–32
  sandwiches, 163–69
  soy with sauces, 103–19
  stir-fries, 120–26
  stovetop dishes, 145–62
  stovetop pasta dishes, 133–44
  stuffed vegetables, 193–97
  wraps, 172–78
Epazote, xxvii
Estrogens, soy and, xv–xvi, xix

Feta cheese, 91
Firm tofu, xxx
Five-spice powder, 149
Flatulence, beans and, xxvii
Flour, 237
Freezing tofu, xxix–xxx, xxxii
French Herb Dressing, 77
Fresh Pea Soup, 41
Fried rice with tofu, 129
Frittata, garden-style, 150–51
Frozen Strawberry-Banana
  Dessert, 230
Fruit
  dip, 14
  mango chutney sauce with
    tofu, 114
  salad, maple-walnut apple, 93
Fusilli, 138
Fusion cooking, x

Garden Frittata, 150–51
Garlic, 38–39
  Mashed Potatoes, 200
  roasting, 12
  Tofu Spread, 12
Garnishes, xlvi
Gas (flatulence), beans and, xxvii
Gazpacho, 38
Gelatin, 243
Ginger, 161
  crystallized, 224
  pickled, 30
  sauce, 26
Gingered
  Banana Parfaits, 224
  Plum Vinaigrette, 96
Goldin, Dr. Barry, xix
Grapes, buying and storing, 14
Greek Tofu Salad, 82
Green Goddess Dip, 16
Grill pans, 157
Grilled Tofu-Vegetable Towers with Parmesan
  Vinaigrette, 156–57
Guacamole, tofu, 8

Health benefits of soy, xiv–xxi
Heart disease, soy and, xvii–xviii
Herbed
  Garlic Croutons, 65
  Tomato Sauce, 186
  Twice-Baked Potatoes, 202
Herbs, xlv
  de Provence, 78
  fresh vs. dried, 187
  storage of, 20
Hijiki, 135
Hoisin, 147
  Orange Sauce, 122
  Peanut Sauce, 9
Honey-Raspberry Sauce, 258
Hot pepper sauce, 185
Huevos Rancheros, 152–53
Hummus
  roasted red pepper, 17
  soybean, 20
Hydrogenation, xxxvii

Icons, xlviii
Iron, soy and, xxxiii
Isolated soy protein (ISP), xxxix–xl
Italian
  Dressing, 76
  Tempeh, Vegetable and Rice Skillet, 128

Jalapeños, 137
Japanese tofu, xxxi

Kale, 57
Key lime pie with tofu, 240
Kitchen equipment, xlix

Lacto-ovo vegetarians, xlviii
Lacto vegetarians, xlviii
Lappé, Frances Moore, xiv
Lasagna, 208–9
Leeks, 199
Lemon
    Caesar Salad, 64
    Cinnamon Vinaigrette, 70
    Mint Dressing, 68
    Mousse, 225
Lettuce, washing, 61
Liquid extracts, 225
"Lite" tofu, xxxi
Loaves
    tofu-walnut, 214
    vegetable soybean, 212–13
Loriva Supreme Foods, 77
Low-Fat Graham Cracker Crust, 246

Mango chutney sauce with fruit
    and tofu, 114
Maple
    Dressing, 93
    Walnut Apple Salad, 93
Marinade
    sesame-soy, 66
    Teriyaki, 160
Marinated salads
    Greek Tofu Salad, 82
    Marinated French Herb Bean Salad, 78
    Sweet Beans and Corn in Sesame-Soy
        Dressing, 80
    Two-Bean Salad in Walnut
        Vinaigrette, 77
Marinating tofu, xxxii–xxxiii
Marsala Sauce, 104–5
Mascarpone, 226
Measurements, xliv–xlvi
Meat analogs, xl–xli
Menopause, soy and, xix
Messina, Dr. Mark, xvii
Mexican Chili Sauce, 136
Microwave cooking, 79
Mint, 230
Miso, xxxix
Mocha Mousse, 227
Monterrey Jack cheese, 175
Morel mushrooms, 113
Mori-Nu tofu, xxix
Mostaccioli and Plum Tomatoes with
    Tofu-Basil Pesto, 139
Mu Shu Tofu, 146–47

Mushrooms, 3
    almond spread, 3
    morel, 113
    oyster-type, 53
    portobello and tofu with Marsala sauce,
        104–5
    storing, 151
    stuffed, 27
    tofu stroganoff, 112–13

Newburg sauce, tofu with, 116
Noodle
    pudding, 219
    soup, Chinese-style, 52–53
Nori, 30
Nutmeg, 239
Nutritional analysis, xlvii
Nuts, toasting, 50

Oil, xlv–xlvi
    garlic-infused, 200
    spray, 31
Okara, xxxviii
Olive oil, garlic-infused, 200
Olives, 82
Onions, 55, 143
Orange
    Caraway Coleslaw, 88
    Honey Sauce, 250
Orzo, 75
Osteoporosis, soy and, xviii–xix
Ovo vegetarians, xlix
Oyster mushrooms, 53

Paella with tempeh, 127
Pancakes, tofu-nut, 218
Paprika, 213
Parchment paper, 205
Parmesan
    cheese, 141
    Cream, 49
    Dressing, 64
    Peppercorn Dip, 10
    Vinaigrette, 156
Parsley, 16
    mincing, 116
    Nut Pesto, 141
Pasta, cooking, 211
Pasta dishes, baked, 206–11
    Tofu-Spinach Lasagna, 208–9
    Tofu Stuffed Shells with Tomato-Basil
        Sauce, 206–7
    Vegetarian Pastitsio, 210–11
Pasta dishes, stovetop, 133–44
    Bell Pepper–Soybean Toss with Pasta,
        142–43

Cabbage and Noodles with Tofu, 144
Mostaccioli and Plum Tomatoes with
    Tofu-Basil Pesto, 139
Penne with Cremini Mushrooms and
    Tomato-Tofu Pesto, 133
Penne Rigate with Parmesan-Peppercorn
    Sauce, 140
Rotini with Parsley-Nut Pesto, 141
Spaghetti with Tempeh in Mexican Chili
    Sauce, 136–37
Spicy Asian Peanut Pasta, 138
Udon Noodles with Tempeh and Hijiki,
    134–35
Pastitsio, vegetarian, 208–9
Pea soup, 41
Peach
    halves topped with tofu and ricotta, 228
    peeling, 228
Peanut
    butter, 115
    chili dip, 11
    chutney dressing, creamy, 83
    ginger dressing, 72–73
    oil, 149
    sauce, hoisin-style, 9
    sauce, spicy, 115
Pears, 251
    clafouti, 233
    poached with orange-honey sauce, 250
Peas, frozen, 107
Penne
    with Cremini Mushrooms and Tomato-
        Tofu Pesto, 133
    Rigate with Parmesan-Peppercorn
        Sauce, 140
Pepper
    Bean Pasta Salad with Italian
        Dressing, 76
    Bean Quesadillas, 192
Peppercorns, 10, 215
Peppers. See Bell peppers; Peppercorns
Pesto
    parsely-nut, 141
    tofu-basil, 6
    tomato-tofu, 133
Pies, tartlets & pita and tortilla crusts, 179–92
    Asparagus-Mushroom Quiche, 180–81
    Chili Custard, 179
    Chocolate Mousse Pie, 244
    Cookie Crust, 247
    Low-Fat Graham Cracker Crust, 246
    Pineapple-Orange Tofu-Ricotta
        Cheesecake, 242–43
    Soybean Confetti Pie with Cornmeal
        Crust, 184
    Tofu Key Lime Pie, 240

Pies, tartlets & pita and tortilla crusts (cont.)
  Tofu Pumpkin Pie, 238–39
  Whole Wheat Pastry (crust), 182–83
Pine nuts, 75
Pineapple
  Orange Tofu-Ricotta Cheesecake, 242–43
  Tapioca Pudding, 248–49
Pita
  crisps, 21
  pizzas, soybean, 188–89
  with roasted vegetables, 166
Pizzas, soybean pita, 188–89
Plum tomatoes, 163
Portobello mushrooms, 105
Potage Mentonnaise, 51
Potatoes
  baked with rosemary and parmesan, 201
  mashed with garlic, 200
  new, 87
  salad, Dijon-style, 87
  twice baked with herbs, 202
Pressed tofu, xxxi–xxxii
Protein, soy and, xiii–xiv
Pumpkin
  bread pudding, spiced, 231
  pie with tofu, 238–39
Puréed desserts
  Chocolate-Maple Tofu Pudding, 223
  Frozen Strawberry-Banana Dessert, 230
  Gingered Banana Parfaits, 224
  Lemon Mousse, 225
  Mocha Mousse, 227
  Parmesan Cream, 49
  Strawberry-Banana Smoothie, 229
  Tofu-Ricotta–Topped Peach Halves, 228
  Tofu Tiramisu, 226
Puréed soups
  Creamy Acorn Squash, 46
  Creamy Tomato-Basil, 48
  Curried Corn and Pepper Chowder, 42
  Curried Sweet Potato, 50
  Fresh Pea, 41
  Spicy Soybean, 44

Quesadillas, pepper-bean, 192
Quiche, asparagus-mushroom, 180–81

Raisins, 56
Recipe tips, xliv–xlvi
Red pepper flakes, 217
Reducing stocks and sauces, 109
Reuben sandwiches with tempeh, 168
Rice
  arborio-style, 131
  basmati-style, 114
  Chili-Rice Skillet, 132

Italian Tempeh, Vegetable and Rice
  Skillet, 128
  pudding with cranberries, 232
  Rice Paper Spring Rolls, 176–78
  Soybean-Mushroom Risotto, 130–31
  Tempeh Paella, 127
  Tofu Fried Rice, 129
  vinegar, 15
Rigate, 139
Riso–Sweet Bean Salad with Sun-Dried
  Tomato-Basil Vinaigrette, 74–75
Risotto, soybean-mushroom, 130–31
Roasted
  Garlic-Tofu Spread, 12
  peanut oil, 149
  Red Bell Pepper Soup, 36
  Red Pepper Hummus, 17
  Soybeans, 31
  soynuts, xxxix
  Sweet Red Pepper Dressing, 92
  Vegetable Pitas, 166
Romaine
  Lettuce Salad with Blue Cheese Dressing, 61
  Spring Rolls with Five-Spice Soybeans,
    148–49
Rosemary-Parmesan Potato Bake, 201
Rotini with Parsley-Nut Pesto, 141
Roux, 216

Saffron, 127
Salad, 58–97
  Chinese Tofu Salad with Sesame-Ginger
    Dressing, 62–63
  Couscous Salad with Lemon-Cinnamon
    Vinaigrette, 70
  Dijon Potato, 87
  Greek Tofu, 82
  Lemon Caesar, 64
  Maple-Walnut Apple, 93
  Marinated French Herb Bean, 78
  Orange-Caraway Coleslaw, 88
  Pepper-Bean Pasta Salad with Italian
    Dressing, 76
  Riso–Sweet Bean Salad with Sun-Dried
    Tomato-Basil Vinaigrette, 74–75
  Romaine Lettuce Salad with Blue Cheese
    Dressing, 61
  Soybean Tabbouleh, 68
  Sweet Beans and Corn in Sesame-Soy
    Dressing, 80
  Tempeh–Green Bean Salad with Creamy
    Peanut-Chutney Dressing, 83
  Tempeh Stir-Fry Salad with Gingered Plum
    Vinaigrette, 96
  Thai Noodle Salad with Tofu Teriyaki,
    72–73

Tofu "Egg Salad," 89
  Tofu-Chèvre–Stuffed Roasted Red Bell
    Peppers, 84
  Tofu-Pesto Rice, 69
  Tomato Slices with Creamy Avocado
    Dressing, 86
  Tortilla-Salsa with Roasted Sweet Red
    Pepper Dressing, 90–91
  Two-Bean Salad in Walnut Vinaigrette, 77
  Warm Soybean and Sweet Red Pepper with
    Basil-Sherry Vinaigrette, 94–95
  Wild Rice and Apricot with Marinated
    Tempeh, 66–67
Salad dressing. See Dressing
Salsa
  Soybean-Salsa Dip, 19
  Sweet Bean–Corn, 23
Salt, xlv
Sandwiches, 163–69
  Bruschetta, 163
  Curried Tofu-Carrot Sloppy Joes, 169–70
  Roasted Vegetable Pitas, 166
  Sherried Tofu–Roasted Eggplant
    Sandwiches, 164–65
  Tempeh Reubens, 168
  Tempeh-Yam Sandwiches, 167
Sauces
  Ancho Chili, 111
  Black Bean–Tomato, 118
  Chinese Tahini, 103
  Cremini Mushroom, 216
  Herbed Tomato, 186
  Hoisin-Orange, 122
  Honey-Raspberry, 258
  Marsala, 104–5
  Mexican Chili, 136
  Newburg, 116
  Orange-Honey, 250
  Parsley-Nut Pesto, 141
  reducing, 109
  Spicy, 126
  Spicy Peanut, 115
  Sweet-and-Sour, 124
  Tomato–Red Pepper, 217
Scallions, 121, 213
Scrambled Tofu, 154
Serving information, xlviii
Sesame
  Ginger Dressing, 62–63
  oil, 81
  Orange Vinaigrette, 66–67
  Pepper Dressing, 162
  seeds, 124–25
  Soy Dressing, 80
  Soy Marinade, 66
Shallot and Caper Dressing, 84–85

Sherried Tofu
    Roasted Eggplant Sandwiches, 164–65
    Steaks, 158–59
Sherry, 159
Shoepeg corn, white, 23
Shredding, 97
Silken tofu, xxxi
Simple Soybean and Your Health, The
    (Messina), xvii
Slicing bread, 163
Sloppy Joes, curried tofu-carrot, 169–70
Smoothie, strawberry-banana, 229
Soba noodles, 135
Soft tofu, xxxi
Soups, 32–57
    Beet Soup, 37
    Carrot-Cashew Soup, 56
    Chilled Fresh Tomato Bisque, 40
    Chinese Noodle Soup, 52–53
    Creamy Acorn Squash Soup, 46
    Creamy Tomato-Basil Soup, 48
    Curried Corn and Pepper Chowder, 42
    Curried Sweet Potato Soup, 50
    Fresh Pea Soup, 41
    Parmesan Cream, 49
    Potage Mentonnaise, 51
    Roasted Red Bell Pepper Soup, 36
    Soybean Chili, 54–55
    Soybean Gazpacho, 38
    Spicy Soybean Soup, 44
    Tuscan Soybean Soup, 57
Sour cream, 19
Sour cream substitute, 15
Soy
    flour, xxxvi
    food ingredients, xxii–xlii
    milk, xxxiv–xxxvi
    milk recipes, 263
    oil, xxxvii
    sauce, xxxvii–xxxviii, 81
Soybeans, xxii–xxvi
    Bourguignonne, 108–9
    Chili, 54–55
    Confetti Pie with Cornmeal Crust, 184
    Gazpacho, 38
    Hummus, 20
    Mushroom Risotto, 130–31
    Pita Pizzas, 188–89
    Salsa Dip, 19
    Soynuts, xxxix
    sprouts, xxxviii
    Tabbouleh, 68
    See Appendix for complete list of recipes
Soybean spreads and dips
    Roasted Red Pepper Hummus, 17
    Soybean Hummus, 20

Soybean-Salsa Dip, 19
Spinach-Bean Dip, 18
Spaghetti with Tempeh in Mexican Chili
    Sauce, 136–37
Spiced Pumpkin Bread Pudding, 231
Spices, 239
Spicy
    Asian Peanut Pasta, 138
    Cashew Stir-Fry, 126
    Peanut Sauce, 115
    Sauce, 126
    Soybean Patties, 171
    Soybean Soup, 44
Spinach, 165, 207
    Bean Dip, 18
    Leek Ring, 198–99
Spray oil, 31
Spreads and dips
    Fruit Dip, 14
    Green Goddess Dip, 16
    Hoisin Peanut Sauce, 9
    Mushroom-Almond Spread, 3
    Parmesan-Peppercorn Dip, 10
    Peanut Chili Dip, 11
    Roasted Garlic-Tofu Spread, 12
    Roasted Red Pepper Hummus, 17
    Soybean Hummus, 20
    Soybean-Salsa Dip, 19
    Spinach-Bean Dip, 18
    Sun-Dried Tomato–Tofu Spread, 4
    Tofu Baba Ghanoush, 13
    Tofu-Basil Pesto, 6
    Tofu-Chèvre Spread, 5
    Tofu Guacamole, 8
    Tofu Sour Cream, 15
Spring rolls
    with five-spice soybeans, 148–49
    rice paper, 176–78
Squash, 46
    and soybean casserole, Caribbean-style, 203
Stir-fries, 120–26
    salad with gingered plum vinaigrette, 96
    Spicy Cashew Stir-Fry, 126
    Sweet Bean Stir-Fry with Hoisin-Orange
        Sauce, 122–23
    Sweet-and-Sour Tofu, 124
    Vegetable Stir-Fry with Ginger Sauce, 120–21
Stocking refrigerator and pantry, xlii–xliv
Stocks, reducing, 109
Stovetop dishes, 145–62
    Chinese Wheat-Flour Noodles with
        Sesame-Pepper Dressing, 162
    Curried Acorn Squash Ragout, 145
    Garden Frittata, 150–51
    Grilled Tofu-Vegetable Towers with
        Parmesan Vinaigrette, 156–57

Huevos Rancheros, 152–53
Mu Shu Tofu, 146–47
Romaine Spring Rolls with Five-Spice
    Soybeans, 148–49
Scrambled Tofu, 154
Sherried Tofu Steaks, 158–59
Tofu Tacos, 155
Tofu Teriyaki, 160–61
Stovetop grill pans, 157
Stovetop pasta dishes, 133–44
    Bell Pepper–Soybean Toss with Pasta,
        142–43
    Cabbage and Noodles with Tofu, 144
    Mostaccioli and Plum Tomatoes with
        Tofu-Basil Pesto, 139
    Penne with Cremini Mushrooms and
        Tomato-Tofu Pesto, 133
    Penne Rigate with Parmesan-Peppercorn
        Sauce, 140
    Rotini with Parsley-Nut Pesto, 141
    Spaghetti with Tempeh in Mexican Chili
        Sauce, 136–37
    Spicy Asian Peanut Pasta, 138
    Udon Noodles with Tempeh and Hijiki,
        134–35
Strawberries, 253
    banana frozen dessert, 230
    banana smoothie, 229
Stroganoff, tofu-mushroom 112–13
Stuffed shells, 206–7
Stuffed vegetables, 27, 193–97
Substitutions, xlvii
Sudare, 30
Sun-dried tomatoes, 132
    basil vinaigrette, 74–75
    tofu spread, 4
Sushi California Rolls, 27–30
Sweet beans (edamame), xxvi–xxvii
    Corn Salsa, 23
    Corn in Sesame-Soy Dressing, 80
    Stir-Fry with Hoisin-Orange Sauce, 122–23
    See Appendix for complete list of sweet
        bean recipes
Sweet potatoes, 167
    soup, curried, 50
Sweet-and-Sour
    Sauce, 124
    Tofu, 124

Tabbouleh, 68
Tacos, tofu, 155
Tahini, 13
Tamari, xxxvii
Tapioca, 249
Tartlets, vegetable with herbed tomato sauce,
    186–87

Tempeh, xxxiii–xxxiv
  Green Bean Salad with Creamy Peanut-
    Chutney Dressing, 83
  Paella, 127
  Reubens, 168
  Rice Wraps with Hoisin Peanut Sauce,
    172–73
  Stir-Fry Salad with Gingered Plum
    Vinaigrette, 96
  Strips and Broccoli with Ancho Chili
    Sauce, 110
  with Black Bean-Tomato Sauce, 118
  with Spicy Peanut Sauce, 115
  Yam Sandwiches, 167
  See Appendix for complete list of tempeh
    recipes
Teriyaki Marinade, 160
Texturized vegetable protein (TVP), xxxiv, 262
Thai Noodle Salad with Tofu Teriyaki, 72–73
Thyme, 116
Tiramisu, 226
Tofu, xxvii–xxxiii
  Baba Ghanoush, 13
  Basil Pesto, 6
  Chèvre Spread, 5
  Chèvre-Stuffed Roasted Red Bell Peppers
    with Shallot and Caper Dressing, 84
  Cream-Filled Crêpes with Strawberry
    Purée, 252–53
  "Egg Salad," 89
  Fried Rice, 129
  Fruit in Mango Chutney Sauce, 114
  Guacamole, 8
  Key Lime Pie, 240
  Mushroom Stroganoff, 112–13
  Newburg, 116
  Nut Pancakes, 218
  Pesto-Rice Salad, 69
  Portobello Mushrooms Marsala, 104–5
  Ricotta-Topped Peach Halves, 228
  Sour Cream, 15
  Spinach Lasagna, 208–9
  Stuffed Shells with Tomato-Basil Sauce,
    206–7
  Tacos, 155
  Teriyaki, 160–61
  Tiramisu, 226
  See Appendix for complete listing of tofu
    recipes

Tofu spreads and dips
  Fruit Dip, 14
  Green Goddess Dip, 16
  Hoisin Peanut Sauce, 9
  Mushroom-Almond Spread, 3
  Parmesan-Peppercorn Dip, 10
  Peanut Chili Dip, 11
  Roasted Garlic-Tofu Spread, 12
  Sun-Dried Tomato–Tofu Spread, 4
  Tofu Baba Ghanoush, 13
  Tofu-Basil Pesto, 6
  Tofu-Chèvre Spread, 5
  Tofu Guacamole, 8
  Tofu Sour Cream, 15
Tomato
  basil soup, creamy, 48
  bisque, chilled, 40
  canned, 118
  cooking, 48
  dried, 132
  paste, 4
  peeling and seeding, 45
  plum, 163
  purée, 209
  Red Pepper Sauce, 217
  sauce, herbed, 186
  Slices with Creamy Avocado
    Dressing, 86
  storing and cutting, 189
  Tofu Pesto, 133
Tortillas, 191
  chips, baked, 22
  Salsa Salad with Roasted Sweet Red Pepper
    Dressing, 90–91
Tostada, tofu, 190–91
Tuscan Soybean Soup, 57
Two-Bean Salad in Walnut Vinaigrette, 77

Udon Noodles with Tempeh and Hijiki,
  134–35
United Soybean Board, xli

Vanilla
  extract, 239
  Poached Pears with Orange-Honey
    Sauce, 250
  Tofu Cream, 256
Variations, xlvii
Vegans, xlviii

Vegetable
  curry with tofu, 106–7
  dishes, baked, 198–205
  Medley with Hoisin Peanut Sauce, 117
  Soybean Loaf, 212–13
  Stir-Fry with Ginger Sauce, 120–21
  stuffed, 193–97
  Tartlets with Herbed Tomato Sauce, 186–87
Vegetarian categories, xlviii–xlix
Vegetarian Pastitsio, 210–11
Veggie Burgers, 170
Vinegar
  balsamic, 18
  white rice, 15
  wine, 86

Walnut Loaf, 214
Walnuts, 215
  apple salad with maple dressing, 93
  loaf with tofu, 214
  oil, 77
  Vinaigrette, 77
Warm Soybean and Sweet Red Pepper Salad
  with Basil-Sherry Vinaigrette, 94–95
Wasabi, 30
Water bath technique, 235
Westbrae Natural Canned Organic Soy
  Beans, xxiii
Wheat germ, 25
Wheat Germ Crêpes, 254–55
Whipped cream, tofu, 257
White rice vinegar, 15
White shoepeg corn, 23
Whole Wheat Pastry, 182–83
Wild Rice and Apricot Salad with Marinated
  Tempeh, 66–67
Wine vinegar, 86
Wraps, 172–78
  Broccoli Burritos, 174–75
  Rice Paper Spring Rolls, 176–78
  Tempeh-Rice Wraps with Hoisin Peanut
    Sauce, 172–73

Yam-tempeh sandwiches, 167
Yogurt, 49

Zesting, 6–7
Zucchini with Herbed Tomato-Soybean
  Stuffing, 196–97